RICHARD SANDOVAL'S NEW LATIN FLAVORS

RICHARD SANDOVAL'S NEW LATIN FLAVORS

Hot Dishes, Cool Drinks

•

RICHARD SANDOVAL

PHOTOGRAPHS BY PENNY DE LOS SANTOS

STEWART, TABORI & CHANG
NEW YORK

DISCARD

Published in 2014 by Stewart, Tabori & Chang

An imprint of ABRAMS

Text copyright © 2014 Richard Sandoval

Photographs copyright © 2014 Penny De Los Santos

Library of Congress Control Number: 2014930942

ISBN: 978-1-61769-124-9

EDITOR: Leslie Stoker
DESIGNER: Laura Palese
PRODUCTION MANAGER: Tina Cameron

The text of this book was composed in Brandon Printed, Brandon Grotesque, League Gothic, Benton Sans, Benton Gothic Compressed, and Benton Gothic Condensed.

Printed and bound in the United States

10 9 8 7 6 5 4 3 2 1

Stewart, Tabori & Chang books are available at special discounts when purchased in quantity for premiums and promotions as well as fundraising or educational use. Special editions can also be created to specification. For details, contact specialsales@abramsbooks.com or the address below.

THE ART OF BOOKS SINCE 1949

115 West 18th Street
New York, NY 10011
www.abramsbooks.com

CONTENTS

INTRODUCTION

*I spend my life entertaining people
with Latin food and drink.*

I OPERATE RESTAURANTS ALL OVER THE WORLD, and while they all share the exciting, palate-tingling cuisine and heady spirits of Latin America, they are also mostly distinct from each other. However, they all have one big common element: People go to them to have a good time. In *New Latin Flavors*, I will show you how to entertain *your* guests the same way that I entertain *my* guests.

Over my entire career, I have used bold flavors to create food that makes the diner sit up and take notice. In this book, you will learn about new tastes, such as unusual chilies and Japanese-influenced Peruvian cuisine. You'll find my versions of some favorite Mexican dishes, and together we'll travel throughout the world of Latin-inspired cuisine. From Mexico to Spain, and many places in between, this book pays homage to wherever Spanish is spoken and delicious food is cooked.

The value of being a good host was impressed upon me at an early age. My parents divorced when I was quite young, and my father's parents in Acapulco, Mexico, helped bring me up. My grandfather Felipe was a banker, and he hosted a lot of corporate parties, exquisitely run by my grandmother Maruca. I remember how she would carefully orchestrate every detail. I can still see her attending to the lush flower arrangements, tasting the food prepared by the cooks in the kitchen, and making sure that the table was perfectly set with silver and crystal. Back then, Mexico was fairly isolated, and there wasn't a lot of imported food. However, my grandparents were able to mail-order special French cheeses to share with their guests. At one gathering, the cheese was Gruyère, and the guests oohed and ahhhed over its nutty flavor as they slowly nibbled their way through the precious chunk. Similarly, opening a bottle of fine wine was more than a prelude to drinking—it was an event.

These days, my entertaining is much more casual, but my early love of sharing food, drink, and good times with friends and family remains an important part of my life. I use "the lesson of the French cheese" at my parties now—serve interesting food and the entire party is elevated. The food doesn't have to be fancy, but intriguing flavors will spark lively conversation as your guests are exposed to new tastes.

Of course, food is just one element of a party. Without the right drinks to fuel the feast, you may as well not send the invitations. In a world where flavorless vodka is still at the top of the list of Americans' favorite liquors, I am on a mission to popularize the much tastier spirits of Latin America—Mexican tequila and mezcal, Peruvian (or Chilean) *pisco*, Brazilian *cachaça* (even though Brazil speaks Portuguese, it shares many flavors with the Latin kitchen), and Caribbean rum, as well as some beer, wine, and nonalcoholic cocktails.

Offer your guests an interesting alternative from their usual drink, and the unexpected change will be another way to bring excitement to the party. I share cocktail recipes not only for new libations but also for the classics, because some of the old favorites are incredible when they are properly prepared. For example, I'll show you how to make a margarita with homemade sweet-and-sour mix, and you will never use the store-bought stuff again.

Even though I serve many of these dishes at my restaurants, they were reconceived and simplified for the home cook and tested in a home kitchen. In addition to recipes for dinner parties, I also suggest ideas for weeknight suppers, weekend brunches, and leisurely lunches—all with Latin soul. I have provided make-ahead instructions, too. And there is a complete ingredients glossary (see pages 12–27) to help you become familiar with the new flavors that I am encouraging you to enjoy.

New Latin Flavors is really about having a good time. This journey began in my grandmother's kitchen, and now I bring my cooking to yours.

¡BUEN PROVECHO! / ¡SALUD! / RICHARD SANDOVAL

1

THE LATIN KITCHEN

TIPS

AND

TRICKS

Professional cooks use a battery of tricks to make their work easier. You can do the same at home with these tips.

SERVE EXCITING FOOD & DRINK

My cooking is influenced by the cuisines of Spanish-speaking countries around the world. Even though I was born in Mexico and cooking with chilies is literally second nature to me, I also enjoy playing with the flavors of Peru's Japanese Nikkei culture, so I cook with Asian ingredients, too. I love sharing new culinary discoveries with my friends. Intriguing cooking does not happen without interesting ingredients, so if you are not familiar with some of these groceries, please expand your culinary horizons . . . and then sit back and wait for the compliments.

DO YOUR HOMEWORK

Read the recipe a couple of times to be sure that you understand the instructions and their sequence. Every good cook knows the concept of layering flavors and textures to build a cohesive culinary masterpiece. At a glance, you may think that a recipe looks complicated or beyond your skill set. Read it again, and you are likely to find that the recipe really isn't that hard, but just made up of various components, many of which are made ahead and assembled right before serving. After all, that is how many restaurants work. I don't make salsa a couple of minutes before I serve it, or the food would never get out onto the tables.

PLAN AHEAD

Especially when you are making a dish for the first time, use *mise en place*, the classic chef's technique of preparing every necessary component before you begin cooking. This way you won't be digging through a cupboard looking for a key ingredient at a crucial point in the recipe.

MAKE AHEAD

Look for the components that can be made ahead. I've provided make-ahead instructions whenever possible. Please . . . use them!

SUBSTITUTE AS NEEDED

As a restaurateur with operations on both coasts and in between, I travel all over the country. I have been pleased to see how formerly unusual (and delicious) ingredients can now be purchased at supermarkets, as new immigrants bring their cooking to America. That being said—don't be afraid of making a substitution. I have provided substitution suggestions for unusual ingredients, but everything in this book is readily available at Latin and Asian markets and most supermarkets. To order online, check the Resources on page 221.

DON'T SPREAD YOURSELF TOO THIN

Balance your menu with easy and slightly challenging recipes. A complicated menu is a recipe for disaster. A great selection of cheese is always a welcome appetizer, and a simple variety of fresh, ripe fruit is a satisfying dessert, especially when the choices include papaya, mango, and other fragrant and juicy tropical treats. Simplifying these two courses means that you can spend a bit more energy on the remaining dishes. Conversely, spend the time making a showstopping appetizer or dessert, and then do an easy grilled main course. That's how I entertain at my house.

THE
LATIN
PANTRY

Here is a listing of basic ingredients that can be stored at room temperature in a cool, dry place.

AGAVE

A sweetener derived from the agave plant (typically the same blue agave variety also used to make tequila), this Mexican syrup has a texture and flavor reminiscent of honey. The harvested sap is heated and filtered to obtain three different nectars of varying sweetness levels: light (mild), amber (moderate), and dark (strong, similar to maple syrup). There is also raw (actually minimally heated) agave nectar. Amber agave nectar is the most versatile of the three major varieties, and it can be found at natural food stores and most supermarkets. I use agave in cooking and as an alternative sweetener for simple syrup in cocktails.

CHILIES, DRIED

The dehydrated fruits of the capsicum plant, dried chilies are an essential ingredient in Mexican cuisine. Drying preserves the chile and concentrates its flavor. When a fresh chile is dried, its name changes. For example, when a fresh red jalapeño is smoked and dried, it becomes a chipotle, and a dried poblano is renamed an ancho.

Whole dried chilies are easily available at Latin markets and are showing up more and more at general supermarkets. Of course, they are easily purchased online, but it is most economical to buy them in bulk to save on postage. Stored in zip-top plastic bags in a cool, dry place, dried chilies maintain their flavor for about six months, or they can be frozen for up to a year.

There are many alternatives to whole dried chilies, such as pure ground ancho or chipotle chilies, cayenne pepper, and hot sauces. Virtually every supermarket now carries jars of ancho and chipotle powder in the spice aisle. (Chili powder is a spice blend of mild ground chile, cumin, oregano, and other seasonings for flavoring a pot of chili. It is not the same as pure ground chilies, which will have the chile variety clearly marked on the label.) These products can be used without soaking. Their minor drawback is that they don't add body to the sauces like the whole chilies. Flavor differences are a small issue because an ancho does not taste exactly like

> ## PREPARING DRIED CHILIES
>
> Whole dried chilies are sometimes toasted and soaked before using. The toasting brings out flavor nuances and soaking rehydrates the chilies for smooth puréeing.
>
> Cut off and discard the stem from each chile, if necessary. Tear or cut the chile open lengthwise, shake out the seeds, and cut away the ribs. Most of the heat is stored in the chile seeds and ribs, so if they are not removed, the finished dish will be too hot.
>
> Heat a medium heavy skillet, preferably cast iron, over medium-high heat. Add the split chilies and press them against the skillet surface with kitchen tongs. Cook, turning them occasionally, until the chilies are more pliable and give a toasty fragrance (but don't breathe in the fumes too deeply, as they can be irritating), 1 to 2 minutes. The chilies should be toasted in spots, but not burned.

a guajillo, but to the untrained palate, the difference will not be noticeable.

There are literally thousands of different chilies, but here is the core group used in this book:

Ancho: The dried version of the fresh poblano chile, the ancho is wide, wrinkled, and blackened red in color. Only moderately hot, with an underlying raisin-like sweetness, ancho is also available in supermarkets as a pure ground chile. Ancho, guajillo, and pasilla chilies are pretty similar in flavor, so it is no crime to substitute ground ancho for the other chilies in this trio when necessary.

Chile de árbol: Small chilies about the size of a pinky finger, these little guys are very hot, and are used when a noticeable heat is required.

Chipotle: Smoked red jalapeños, chipotles are fiery hot with lots of smoky flavor. They are commonly sold in canned, dried, and ground versions.

Canned chipotles packed in adobo have mainstreamed into a supermarket item. Leftover chilies, with the adobo (a vinegary red chile sauce), should be transferred to a covered container and refrigerated, where they will keep for a couple of months, as both the vinegar and chile act as natural preservatives and discourage molding. For longer storage, space individual chilies (with the adobo) on a parchment- or waxed paper–lined plate, and freeze until solid. Remove from the paper, transfer them to a zip-top plastic bag, and freeze for up to a few months. They only take a few minutes to thaw.

Dried chipotles are dark beige, and should be stemmed, seeded, and rehydrated before using. Morita (see entry) is a variation of dried chipotle.

Pure ground chipotle power is very useful as a substitute for other varieties of whole dried chilies.

Guajillo: Elongated, with a deep red, shiny skin, the guajillo is one of my favorite chilies. It has a fruity, berry-like flavor behind its warm (but not too hot) spiciness, which gives it a flavor profile similar to the ancho.

Morita: The morita chile has the dark purple color of a small mulberry (*morita* in Spanish). Related to the common dried chipotle, the morita is smoked for a shorter period of time, giving it a different color, softer texture, and fruitier flavor.

Pasilla: Also known as *chile negro*, this is the dried version of the chilaca chile, which is not used much in its fresh incarnation. Black and wrinkled, it is a bit narrower and more elongated than an ancho.

Soaking chilies: Place the toasted chilies in a small bowl just large enough to hold them. (If you wish, tear the chilies into pieces to help them fit into the bowl.) Add enough boiling water to cover them and let them stand until softened, 20 to 30 minutes. Drain the chilies, reserving the soaking water if the recipe requires. The chilies are now ready to be pureed or used as needed.

CHILE PASTES, PERUVIAN

American cooks are just discovering the delicious heat of the Peruvian chile (*ají*), of which over three hundred known varieties exist. These have not mainstreamed like Mexican chilies, and you cannot find the fresh versions in produce markets—yet. However, Peruvian chile pastes are sold in Latin markets and online. But if you are really interested in new flavors, search out the pastes, which are reasonably priced and, once opened, last for a few months in the refrigerator. You can always make a substitute with an equal amount of roasted and puréed bell peppers highly seasoned with hot sauce. The major types are:

Ají amarillo: A very hot, long yellow pepper, it is probably the most popular chile with Peruvian cooks and is used with everything from seafood to chicken. A substitute would be roasted yellow bell pepper purée seasoned to a fairly hot level with yellow or red hot pepper sauce.

Ají mirasol: This is the dried version of ají amarillo; a substitute would be roasted red bell pepper purée highly seasoned with red hot pepper sauce.

Ají panca: Because of its mild heat, this variety could be considered the poblano chile of Peruvian cuisine. If necessary, substitute roasted red bell pepper purée seasoned to a mild heat with ground ancho chile.

Ají rocoto: The fresh version of this fiery hot chile looks like a hot cherry pepper. It is the hottest of the commercially available pastes. You could substitute a roasted jalapeño (preferably red) purée or, if it is used in small quantities, Chinese chili sauce.

CHOCOLATE, MEXICAN

Mexican chocolate is different from American chocolate, as it is made to be melted with milk to become hot chocolate. Shaped into round disks that can be cut into individual wedges for single servings, it is gritty with sugar and flavored with a hint of cinnamon. Look for it in Latin markets in a hexagon-shaped yellow box. Two popular brands are Ibarra and Abuelita (which means "grandmother" in Spanish and has a little old lady on the label). If you need a substitute, use 3 ounces (85 g) semisweet (not bittersweet) chocolate with about 55% cacao content and a large pinch of ground cinnamon for every disk of Mexican chocolate. A standard American brand, such as Baker's or Hershey's, works perfectly. The cacao content is often listed on the label.

CURRY PASTE, THAI

This Southeast Asian style of curry seasoning comes in three different colors and corresponding flavors: yellow (with turmeric and other Indian spices and the Thai additions of shallot and lemongrass), green (based on fresh green chilies, Thai basil, and cilantro), and red (made from fresh red chilies). I use red curry paste in the Thai Chicken Empanadas on page 110. Look for it, sold in jars or small cans, at Asian groceries and well-stocked supermarkets and natural food stores.

DULCE DE LECHE

Many Mexican cooks make their own dulce de leche at home from milk and sugar slowly cooked until the milk solids in the mixture turn brown. (The sugars do not actually caramelize, a process that only happens at high heat.) It takes hours, but the good news is that canned or jarred dulce de leche is an excellent product and is becoming increasingly available in the Latin aisle of supermarkets.

FLOURS

Beyond the expected wheat flour, I use a few specialty flours in this book.

Almond flour: Also called almond meal, this used to be a specialty product only sold through baking supply companies, but the increased visibility of gluten-free foods has made it more readily available. It is no more than finely ground almonds. You'll find a reasonably priced, light brown version made from unskinned almonds at Trader Joe's. The ivory-colored type made from blanched almonds is more expensive. In the recipes in this book, it doesn't matter which one you use.

Arepas flour: Arepas, the Venezuelan and Colombian griddle cakes, require a special precooked cornmeal that doesn't have an American substitute—cornmeal just won't work. Sometimes labeled *masa para arepas*, it comes in white, yellow, and sweet yellow (made from a sweeter type of corn and not with added sugar) varieties. P.A.N., Areparina, and Goya (sold as Masarepa) are common brands. Latin markets carry it.

White rice flour: Milled from common white rice (although the one labeled "sweet rice flour" will work), this flour has no gluten, so it makes a particularly delicate batter for fried foods.

FURIKAKE

This colorful, flaky Japanese condiment looks like it would make a great cupcake topping, but it is savory and meant to be sprinkled on cooked rice. The main flavoring is dried fish flakes (either bonito or salmon) with seeds, seaweed, and other ingredients added to make at least six different kinds. I use a nori-and-sesame-seed furikake as a garnish for the Tuna Ceviche Nikkei on page 75, but you can experiment with other flavors.

GINGER, PICKLED

The pink, thin slices of sweet pickled ginger served with sushi can be purchased at Asian markets and in the specialty produce section of many supermarkets.

GUAVA PASTE (MEMBRILLO)

This thick and sticky paste made from guava pulp reduced with sugar products is often served in slices with cheese as a dessert or snack in Spanish-speaking countries.

HEARTS OF PALM

You might be able to find fresh hearts of palm in parts of Florida (where it is known as swamp cabbage), but most of us will have to settle for the canned kind. That's okay because they are still very good—firm stalks of pale yellow vegetable that just might remind you of firm asparagus. They should be drained and rinsed before using.

HERBS, DRIED, & SPICES

Latin cooks use a fairly tight range of herbs (the leaves of edible, aromatic plants, used either fresh or dried) and spices (the dried bark, fruits, seeds, roots, or nuts of similarly fragrant plants). It is interesting to note that there aren't many examples of plants that are both an herb and a spice, the exceptions being dill and cilantro. Chilies are spices, but I have provided separate listings for both dried and fresh chilies.

It wasn't too long ago when many cooks had to rely on dried herbs for seasoning food. We now use fresh herbs with abandon for their bright, fresh flavor. However, there are occasions when the concentrated flavor of a dried herb is appropriate. For example, dried oregano has more impact than fresh. On the other hand, dried cilantro and parsley taste so little like their fresh versions that there should be a law against selling them.

As dried herbs and spices age, their essential oils evaporate and lose flavor. Stored in a cool, dark place (never near a hot stove) in airtight containers, they should last about six months. Get in the habit of marking the date of purchase on your dried herbs and spices so you can keep track of when it is time to replace them. It is a temptation to buy herbs and spices in bulk to save money, but that is immaterial if you don't use them up soon enough and they have to be discarded because they have aged and lost their flavor. Especially in Latin markets, you will see herbs and spices sold in plastic bags. Once they are opened, be sure to transfer them to an airtight jar or bottle for further storage.

Here are the dried herbs and spices that I use the most often in this book:

Annatto seeds: These reddish, triangular seeds come from the fruit of the achiote tree, grown in subtropical regions around the world. While it has an earthy flavor, most Americans unknowingly eat annatto most often as a food coloring, for it is often the ingredient used to give an orange or yellow color to otherwise naturally white cheeses. In the Latin kitchen, annatto plays a much larger role as a flavoring. It is ground with other ingredients to make achiote, a versatile seasoning paste (see page 183).

Cumin, whole: The musky taste of cumin is found in many Latin recipes. While it is available ground, it is always at its best when the seeds are freshly toasted and pulverized in a spice grinder.

Oregano, Mexican: There are many varieties of oregano, all of which are members of the mint family. Most cooks are familiar with Mediterranean varieties, such as Greek or Italian. Mexican oregano is entirely different and has a bolder flavor, larger leaves, and a sharper aroma. While Mexican oregano is very easy to find at Latin markets and online, the Mediterranean variety can be substituted. However, for very little money and effort, you can bring this authentic Latin flavor to your cooking, so I encourage you to try it.

Paprika, sweet and smoked: The very best paprika comes from Spain and Hungary, but because the subject at hand is Latin cooking, let's limit our discussion to the Spanish variety (*pimentón*). Paprika is a very important flavor in Latin cooking and is used in everything from sauces to chorizo. You'll find two kinds commonly available: sweet (*dulce*, and the most versatile of the pair) and hot (*picante*). Smoked paprika (also labeled *pimentón de La Vera*, for its place of origin, a region south of Madrid) has been dried over smoldering oak and is a powerfully flavorful ingredient.

TOASTING & GRINDING SPICES

When whole spices are heated, their fragrant oils come to the surface and deliver deeper flavors. To do this, warm a small empty skillet over medium heat and add the whole spices. Cook, stirring almost constantly, until the aroma is distinct and the spices have turned a bit darker, about 2 minutes. In some cases, you may even see a wisp of smoke. Immediately transfer the spices to a plate to cool; if kept in the hot skillet, they will burn.

In Latin cooking, sometimes the spices are simmered in a sauce to soften, and then the entire mixture is ground in a blender. However, there are also instances where the toasted spices need to be ground without liquid. An electric coffee grinder (see entry in Equipment) with a rotating blade does the best job, as its small bowl contains the spices well. Surprisingly, a blender doesn't work as well.

HOISIN SAUCE

Sweet and salty, thick and deeply flavored with fermented soybeans, garlic, chilies, and spices, a spoonful of Chinese hoisin sauce is really a dipping sauce for Peking duck and moo shu pork, among other dishes. But with such a big flavor profile, it can also be used as a seasoning. Buy an imported brand at an Asian market (Lee Kum Kee is a good choice), and store it in the refrigerator for up to a year after opening.

JAMAICA (HIBISCUS BLOSSOMS)

Magenta-colored dried hibiscus blossoms (*jamaica*) can be brewed into hot or iced tea and are used in *ponche*, the warm Mexican Christmas punch.

KABAYAKI SAUCE

Sometimes labeled *unagi* (eel) sauce because it is the soy-based glaze used on barbecued (*kabayaki*) eel sushi, this sauce is easily found at Japanese markets and supermarkets in Asian communities. There is a homemade version on page 82.

MAGGI SEASONING

This salty seasoning is an umami bomb that will boost the flavors in your cooking. It is a close relative of the hydrolyzed vegetable protein that you see listed in many processed foods, and is basically sodium and monosodium glutamate (MSG) in a liquid form. The difference is that this MSG is naturally produced from processed soy (or wheat) and not artificially created. You may be shocked at its components, but used in small quantities, as I do, it is many a chef's secret ingredient. It is an especially popular seasoning with Mexican cooks. Soy sauce is an acceptable substitute.

MAYONNAISE

I use two kinds of mayonnaise in this book. For most recipes, a high-quality American brand, such as Hellman's or Best Foods, is perfect. When the recipe has an Asian inspiration, I recommend Kewpie, a Japanese product that has a creamier consistency and is less tart than American mayo, which can certainly be used instead.

MIRIN

Similar to sake, this sweetened rice wine gives luster to cooked Japanese sauces and is a flavor booster, too. (Alcohol is known to amplify the taste of the other ingredients in a dish, one reason why you find beer, wine, and other spirits as cooking liquids.) Mirin is now sold in the Asian section of most supermarkets. However, this industrial product (*aji-mirin*) is usually sweetened with corn syrup and does not have the depth of flavor of the traditional naturally fermented variety (*hon-mirin*). While hon-mirin is harder to find, most cooks find it is worth the effort to locate it at a Japanese market. Just look for brands without added sugar products or sweeteners, and you'll know that you are getting a superior mirin.

MOLE

This thick sauce of ground chilies, spices, nuts, seeds, and other ingredients dates back to Aztec times, and varies from region to region. You'll find green, black, orange, and yellow (and colors in between) at markets in Mexico. Stateside, you can buy basic brown mole (*mole poblano*) and green mole (*mole verde*) pastes at Latin markets. These are diluted with broth to make a mole sauce for meats or poultry. The oils from the nuts and seeds always rise to the top of the paste (like natural peanut butter), and must be stirred into the solids before using. This is easiest to do by scraping the contents of the jar into a small bowl and mashing it together with a fork. I sometimes use just a tablespoon or two of mole paste as a seasoning in a sauce. Any leftover mole can be frozen in an airtight container for up to three months.

PILONCILLO

Unrefined sugarcane juice dried and molded into a rectangle or cone, piloncillo is sometimes called *panela* to avoid confusion with *queso panela* cheese, and you will often see it labeled as such in Latin markets. The hard sugar with a strong molasses flavor must be crushed before using— chip away chunks from the rectangle with a meat pounder, and pound the chunks in a heavy-duty plastic storage bag until crushed. Raw sugar, such as demerara, is a good substitute, and dark brown sugar will suffice.

PONZU

This is a yuzu-flavored soy sauce used for dipping sushi, which I use as a seasoning. There are many good bottled brands, but it is also easy to make your own. Use the recipe on page 48.

RICE

While long-grain rice rules the roost in the American kitchen, short- and medium-grain rices are popular in other cuisines. In general, the shorter the grain, the starchier the rice. For example, Japanese cooks use sticky short-grain (sometimes labeled as medium-grain) rice to mold into sushi. (But this is not the sticky or sweet rice of Southeast Asian cuisine, which is even more adhesive.) Medium-grain arborio rice is essential for risotto because its starch releases into the cooking liquid to provide the proper creamy consistency. Long-grain rice cooks into individual grains that should not (when cooked properly) stick together. Latin cooks often prefer medium-grain rice because the clinging grains are easier to spoon out of a casserole. For example, paella is always made with medium-grain rice, such as Spanish Calaspara and Bomba.

SOY SAUCE

The ubiquitous Japanese brand of soy sauce, Kikkoman, may be an industrial product, but it is conscientiously made with highly consistent quality. There are countless Chinese brands, but they vary greatly. To know what you are getting every time (since it is easy to over- or under-season with an unfamiliar soy sauce) Kikkoman is a good choice. I also encourage using low-sodium soy sauce.

SWEET CHILI SAUCE, THAI

Another dipping sauce, great with spring rolls, egg rolls, and the Venezuelan tequeños on page 36. You can find it at supermarkets, although it is more reasonably priced at Asian markets.

TAMARIND

Valued for its tart flavor, tamarind is used in Latin, Southeast Asian, and Indian cuisines. While fresh tamarind is often sold at ethnic markets, the sticky flesh must be extracted from the tough brown pods, moistened with liquid, and strained through a sieve to remove the many seeds. It is more common to see tamarind pulp packed in blocks in the produce department of Latin markets. The pulp is added to liquids and then strained to remove any seeds. At Asian and Indian markets, look for tamarind concentrate, which is ready to use and requires no preparation.

TOGARASHI, SHICHIMI

While Mexican cooks are known for their way with chilies, *shichimi togarashi* (which translates to seven-flavor chile pepper) makes a claim for the Japanese talent with hot condiments. Sold in small (about .63-ounce or 18-gram) jars for easy transport, it is a beautifully fragrant spicy seasoning blend of coarsely ground red pepper with six of the following ingredients: ground *sansho* (also called Japanese peppercorn), dried or toasted orange or yuzu peel, black or white sesame seeds, hemp (but not cannabis!), ground ginger, dried shiso leaf, and black or white poppy seeds. It is a basic item at Japanese markets. Togarashi purchased online in bulk, instead of in the typical small jars, can be reasonably priced.

TORTILLAS

Flat cakes made from either wheat flour or lime-treated ground corn, tortillas are synonymous with Mexican cooking. Even though you can make them by hand, it is a labor of love. Whenever possible, choose refrigerated tortillas over the shelf-stable ones—they simply taste better and have better texture. There's a huge difference between brands, so experiment until you find one that you like (the tortillas should be flavorful and chewy and not dissolve easily on contact with sauce).

Corn tortillas come in just one size, about 6 inches (15 cm) in diameter. Flour tortillas are available from small to large diameters, but I use the small 6-inch (15-cm) size almost exclusively for soft tacos and serving with *queso fundido*.

VINEGAR

All vinegar is acetic acid made from the ethanol created by the fermentation of a base ingredient. The acid is then diluted with water, which is what the percentage number means on commercial vinegar labels. Vinegar is created either by a natural slow fermentation or by a fast fermentation where the base is inoculated with bacteria to make it sour quickly. Each vinegar has its own flavor, and they can easily bring variety to your cooking.

Cider vinegar is quite tart, and the apple cider provides a background fruity note to the acidic flavor.

Distilled white vinegar is not actually distilled but made from distilled alcohol, and is useful for its neutral color and taste.

Rice vinegar, a standard ingredient in Asian cuisine, is one of the mildest vinegars. Be sure to buy the unseasoned variety, and not the seasoned one with sugar and salt that is used to moisten rice for shaping into sushi.

Sherry vinegar is fermented from Spanish sherry, and has dark brown color and rounded, slightly sweet flavor.

White balsamic vinegar has the complex flavor of commercial balsamic vinegar, but not the dark coloring.

WASABI, POWDERED

Fresh wasabi is a rhizome related to horseradish. Peeled and grated, its green flesh is a condiment for sushi. Because the fresh version is perishable, dehydrated and ground wasabi is sold as a powder that can be reconstituted with water into a paste. I use it as a hot and spicy seasoning in some of my Nikkei dishes.

YUZU JUICE, BOTTLED

Yuzu is popular in Japanese cooking, with a bumpy orange-to-green peel and a unique tartness that is a cross between lime and grapefruit. Its juice is used to flavor everything from ponzu (the soy sauce dip) to vinegar. Fresh yuzu is a delicacy, and is only found in season at Japanese markets, although it is gaining ground with American chefs, so who knows when you might buy it as easily as pomegranates? Until that happens, use bottled yuzu juice, found in the vinegar section of Japanese markets, or fresh lime juice.

REFRIGERATED
AND
FROZEN

This is a listing of basic ingredients that should be stored in the refrigerator or freezer.

CHEESES, MEXICAN

Mexican cheeses play an important role in Latin cuisine—imagine your favorite enchiladas without a topping of creamy melted cheese. Imported Mexican cheeses are not widely distributed, even in Latin communities, but American-made cheeses in the same style are just as good. Yet even those you may not find easily. Don't worry, as the recommended substitutions work perfectly and you shouldn't think that you are taking a step down.

Chihuahua: A great melting cheese; substitute mild Cheddar.

Cotija: This firm, salty, off-white cheese is often crumbled over cooked food just before serving. Ricotta salata is a good substitute.

Cotija, grated: Aged cotija is sold refrigerated and pre-grated to sprinkle over food before cooking, similar to Italian grating cheeses like Romano, which is a fine substitute.

Queso fresco: Another semi-firm cheese that crumbles easily; substitute ricotta salata or a mild feta.

Oaxaca: Very similar to string cheese or mozzarella, this cheese melts smoothly.

Queso panela: This fresh cheese, shaped and drained in a small basket (*panela*), is often sautéed quickly in a hot nonstick skillet to give it a browned surface. You may find a similar cheese called *queso de freir* (frying cheese). Farmer's cheese and mozzarella can be prepared in the same way.

CHORIZO

Spicy with chilies and paprika and seasoned with vinegar, there are two distinct versions of this Latin sausage. **Spanish-style smoked chorizo** is sold in short or long links, and with a pepperoni-like texture, it is hard enough to slice or dice. **Mexican-style soft chorizo** has the texture of breakfast sausage and is sold in bulk or in plump links.

CREMA, MEXICAN

This is cream that has been naturally fermented to give it tang. Some cooks refer to crema as Mexican sour cream, but it is actually thinner and milder than the American product. Look for brands that have a Mexican name or labels with the Mexican flag's colors of red, green, and white because many Latin countries have a version of crema, and each is unique. To make a substitute for Mexican crema, thin ½ cup (120 ml) crème fraîche or sour cream with about 3 tablespoons whole milk to give the mixture a texture that is thin enough for drizzling.

FRUIT PURÉES, FROZEN

Latin markets carry a large selection of frozen fruit purées. These are much more economical than making them from scratch, and their flavor is excellent, as they are processed from fruit at its seasonal peak. I use mango and passion fruit in the recipes in this book.

MISO

Miso is a salty, umami-rich paste created from soy, with the addition of white or brown rice or barley. The array of misos at an Asian market can be confusing to the uninitiated. I only use white miso (*shiromiso*) in this book. Shiromiso isn't truly white, just light in color compared to the other varieties, which, depending on the amount of aging and its specific ingredients, can range from slightly red (*akamiso*) to deep chocolate brown. If the label says "medium-sweet," don't let that throw you, because it refers to the miso's relative saltiness and not its sugar level.

PRODUCE

These are the various fresh fruits and vegetables that can give your food Latin style.

CHILIES, FRESH

It wasn't too long ago that the only chile an American cook could buy at the supermarket was the canned green variety. Now you'll find a rainbow of fresh chilies in the produce aisle. (Young chilies are green and change to red as they age on the plant, their flavor mellowing along with the chameleon-like color change.) Along with the familiar Mexican varieties like jalapeño and serrano, you'll often find such popular Asian chilies as twisty cayenne or small (and incendiary) Thai bird chilies.

If you have sensitive skin, be sure to wear latex or rubber gloves to keep the irritating chile oils off your skin. If you do get burned, dab the area with milk, heavy cream, or yogurt, as capsaicin (the hot element in the chile) is not water soluble, but will disperse in butterfat. A cold beer will make your mouth feel better by numbing the area, even if it doesn't neutralize the capsaicin.

To chop fresh chilies, slice off the stem and cut the chile in half lengthwise. Using the tip of a small, sharp knife, cut away the thin ribs and seeds inside the chile. The chile is now ready for chopping into smaller pieces. If the recipe calls for chile rounds, cut the stemmed chile crosswise, and then remove the seeds and ribs from each round with the tip of the knife.

The skin of fresh chilies can be tough and not that pleasant to eat. In many cases, the chilies are roasted (actually, charred) before chopping to blacken and blister the skin to make it easier to remove. There are **three easy ways** to roast whole chilies (the stem, seeds, and ribs are removed after charring):

Broiler: This is an especially good method to roast a quantity of chilies. Position a broiler rack about 6 inches (15 cm) from the source of heat and preheat the broiler on high. Spread the whole chilies on the broiler rack and broil, occasionally turning the chilies with kitchen tongs, until the skins are blackened and blistered (but not burned through the flesh), about 10 minutes, depending on the heat of the broiler and the distance from the heat source.

Gas burner: An alternative way to roast chilies requires a gas range. It works well when you want to roast only a chile or two. Turn the burner on high and place the chile directly on the metal grate. Letting the flames touch the skin, turn the chile with tongs as needed until the skin is completely charred.

Grill: If you have an outdoor gas grill, it is a snap to grill a large number of chilies. (Don't bother to build a charcoal fire for this, unless you have subsequent grilling to do.) Preheat the grill on high for about 10 minutes. Spread the chilies on the grill grate. Cook, with the lid closed as much as possible, turning the chilies occasionally with tongs, until the skin is blackened and blistered, 10 to 15 minutes.

When the chilies are blackened, transfer them to a heatproof bowl. Cover the bowl with plastic wrap to create steam in the bowl. This will allow the chilies to cook a bit more and soften any skin that wasn't completely blackened by the heat. Let the chilies stand for about 15 minutes. Uncover the bowl, being careful of any steam. Using a small sharp knife, peel away the skin. Cut off the stem, slice the chile open, and discard the ribs and seeds. Do not clean the chilies under a stream of running water, as this only rinses away the flavor.

Because there are about twenty different kinds of commercially available chilies (and many more that can be grown in your garden), I'll only outline the ones used in this book.

Fresno: Very similar in appearance and flavor to the jalapeño, this chile has wider shoulders and a more pointed tip. It is sold in both red and green stages of ripeness, the red being older and slightly sweeter. Some cooks prefer using Fresno over the jalapeño because it has a thinner skin that makes for easier eating when used raw in salsas and the like.

Habanero: One of the hottest chilies, these have a wrinkled sphere shape and are sold in a mix of bright yellow, orange, red, and green colors; they add a particular flavor to the cooking of the Yucatan. Don't confuse it with the Scotch bonnet chile, which is more wrinkled and often somewhat larger, or the *ají dulce*, which is smaller; both of these are essentials in Caribbean cuisine. In a pinch, substitute Scotch bonnet for habanero.

Jalapeño: This is an excellent all-purpose chile for cooking in sauces and using raw in salsa. You'll find jalapeños at every supermarket.

Poblano: Deep dark green, with a shape like a flattened, elongated green bell pepper, this chile has a thicker flesh than other varieties, which makes it good for stuffing.

Serrano: This chile looks like a thinner jalapeño, and tastes a bit hotter.

CHAYOTE

This firm, pale green squash has a plump pear shape with vertical creases running down the skin. It should be peeled and its thick white seed removed before cooking. The flavor of chayote is mild and it works well with other vegetables. It releases a sticky juice when cut, so wash your hands after preparing the chayote.

GUAVA

Also called *guayaba*, the guava is a tropical fruit with a lovely sweet aroma and slightly acidic flavor. There is a range of varieties available at Latin, Indian, and Asian markets. Some have rough, bitter skin that must be pared away, while others have a thin skin that can be eaten like an apple. There are guavas with pink flesh and guavas with white interiors. Some are pear-shaped and some are round. And some people like to eat the crunchy seeds, while others find them too numerous to enjoy. The most common variety is pineapple guava, with pink flesh and not too many seeds. Guava should be ripened at room temperature until it "gives" when gently squeezed.

HERBS, FRESH

The lively flavor of fresh herbs is essential to good cooking. Don't underestimate their importance. Everyone knows that a sprinkle of chopped green herbs can rescue the appearance of dishes that are predominantly brown. But their main role is the bright taste they bring to food.

Cilantro: This herb embodies Latin cuisine, and it is also an important flavor in Southeast Asian cooking. Only a couple of decades ago, fresh cilantro was often labeled as coriander or Chinese parsley. But over the years, "cilantro" has come to mean the fresh herb, and "coriander" refers to the dried seeds used as a spice, with "Chinese parsley"

PREPARING FRESH HERBS

Getting herbs ready for cooking starts when they arrive home with you from the market. Cilantro should be stored in a glass of water on a refrigerator shelf, like a bouquet, with a plastic bag covering the bunch. This protects the leaves from the cold air of the refrigerator, and gives the herb a longer shelf life. Rosemary, thyme, and other less delicate herbs can be stored in a plastic bag in the humidifier drawer of the refrigerator for about a week.

Before chopping, fresh herbs must be completely clean and dry. To start, rinse them well in a large bowl or sink of cold water. This is especially important with cilantro, which can be sandy. Pick off the number of leaves you'll need from the stems and dry the leaves well in a salad spinner. Use a very sharp knife to cut the herbs, because if they are bruised and not cleanly cut, they'll turn black around the edges. To store chopped herbs for a few hours (and have them ready to sprinkle over a dish as a garnish), wrap them in a paper towel and refrigerate.

falling out of fashion altogether. Many produce markets sell cilantro with the roots still attached, which is a quick visual way to differentiate it from Italian parsley.

While I occasionally use other fresh herbs (such as mint and parsley), cilantro shows up a lot in my recipes. But let's face it: A lot of people don't like cilantro. There have been recent studies that link the aversion to a person's genes, so the dislike is pretty deep-seated and a cilantro hater isn't likely to become a cilantro lover. If you have a dinner guest with this dislike, it's no big deal. Just leave the cilantro out of the dish, and offer it on the side for the cilantro fans to sprinkle on their food to taste.

JÍCAMA

A squat tuber with a sweet flavor and crisp texture, jícama is peeled and usually served raw in salads.

LEMONGRASS

Fragrant with a strong citrus scent, this aromatic stalk is used a lot in Southeast Asian cooking. Buy moist-looking stalks with green tops and pale yellow bulbs and pass over any dried-out lemongrass. To prepare lemongrass, use a large knife to cut off and discard the upper woody top where it meets the paler, more bulbous lower stalk. Remove the first outer layer of the lemongrass bulb to expose the less tough inner flesh. The bulb can be sliced or chopped as required.

KAFFIR LIME LEAF

This very fragrant leaf is steeped in sauces to add its citrus flavor and aroma, and removed before serving. It is sold, fresh or frozen, at Asian groceries. If you can't find it, add the finely grated zest of a lime to the dish.

TOMATILLO

Sour and green with a papery husk, the tomatillo is more closely related to the gooseberry than the tomato. Its unusual taste is usually tempered with cilantro and chilies. Before cooking, remove the husk and rinse the tomatillo to remove its sticky natural coating. You will be sure to find tomatillos at Latin markets, although more and more supermarkets are stocking them.

YUCA

A tuber with scaly brown skin, yuca (also called cassava or manioc) is not attractive, but it is very tasty—even though it has a sticky texture that not everyone likes. Mashing and deep-frying are two common ways to cook fresh yuca, and it is also processed into tapioca and flour. Raw yuca is toxic, so don't nibble at the scraps during preparation. In spite of the sturdy-looking peel, yuca bruises easily, and is treated with a protective coating of wax before shipping. The peel, which is removed before cooking, is too tough for the average vegetable peeler, and must be pared away with a sturdy knife. After cooking, you will come across a tough cord in the center of the tuber, which should also be discarded.

EQUIPMENT

For my home cooking, I have a short list of what I consider to be essential appliances and utensils. Latin cuisine has its roots in rustic cooking, so when it comes to equipment, I prefer to do a lot with a little.

BLENDER

When it comes to Mexican cooking, the only electric appliance you really need is a blender. This handy, hard-working machine is required for puréeing the various ingredients in the many different chile sauces. A food processor is good for some jobs, but I don't use it nearly as much as my blender, as wet mixtures tend to seep through the processor's central hole, making a mess. Any blender will do the job, from a modestly priced model to a top-of-the-line super-mixer—as long as it has a glass container. The oils in dried chilies can stain, and could discolor a clear plastic blender jar. Handheld "stick" blenders are only okay, and not nearly as fast and efficient as the old-fashioned jar models.

One very important tip: Never purée hot food and always let it cool to tepid before processing in a blender. During puréeing, the hot mixture releases a vortex of pressurized steam that could blow the blender top off and shoot hot purée all over the kitchen (and your skin and clothes) in the bargain.

Some cooks vent the top hole in the blender lid to let the steam escape (or replace the lid with a kitchen towel to allow the steam to travel through the fabric weave), but I don't recommend a quick fix. To speed cooling, transfer the hot mixture to a heatproof bowl set in a larger bowl of iced water, and stir the food often to dissipate the steam.

SPICE GRINDER

Spices contain essential oils that are released by grinding. These oils begin to evaporate and lose flavor as soon as they are exposed to air, so freshly ground spices always taste better. Traditional Mexican cooking uses a *molcajete* (a stone mortar with a wooden or stone pestle) for this job, but an electric spice grinder is much faster.

The best spice grinder is actually an electric coffee grinder. Buy an inexpensive grinder with a rotary blade and dedicate it to spices. Don't use the same machine that grinds your coffee beans, or you'll end up with annatto-flavored java. To clean the grinder, process some raw rice or granulated sugar to absorb the residual spices. Toss out the rice mixture and brush the grinder bowl clean with a clean pastry brush.

You can also grind spices the old-fashioned way, with a molcajete or mortar and pestle and lots of elbow grease, but the investment in a time-saving electric grinder makes more sense for busy modern cooks.

HALF-SHEET PAN

Every professional kitchen has stacks of sturdy aluminum half-sheet pans for baking and roasting jobs. They do not have stacks of flimsy, thin cookie sheets! Half-sheet pans measure about 17 by 13 inches (43 by 33 cm) and are made to last. (A full sheet pan is very large and designed to fit in a commercial oven; a half-sheet is half its size.) When I use the term "rimmed baking sheet" in this book, I really mean a half-sheet pan, even if a lesser pan might get the job done.

FRUIT JUICER

I use a lot of fresh fruit juices in my cooking, so you will want to have an efficient, quick ream-type juicer. I like an inexpensive electric juicer—you'll have a cup of fresh orange juice in no time. At the very least, use a handheld citrus reamer. (See page 187 for more on fruit juicers for making drinks.)

V-SLICER

Professional chefs love plastic V-slicers to quickly cut ingredients into julienne or uniform slices. These lightweight tools are much easier to operate than a bulky metal mandoline. However, it is not an essential piece of equipment, and you can always cut the food by hand. Always use the holder to secure the food on the carriage—the blade is sharp and it is very easy to cut yourself, even if you are experienced. You can now purchase heavy gloves with protective mesh to wear while using a slicer. Even though a pair can cost as much as the slicer itself, I recommend at least one for the hand that will hold the food.

2
TAPAS
APPETIZE
&
SNACK

TOGARASHI TUNA
IN MINI WON TON BOWLS

Tuna con chile Japonés en tazones pequeños de wonton

FOR THE MINI WON TON BOWLS:

Canola oil, in a pump sprayer, or nonstick cooking oil spray

16 won ton wrappers

FOR THE MANGO-TOMATO SALSA:

½ ripe mango, cut into ½-inch (12-mm) dice

1 ripe plum tomato, seeded and cut into ½-inch (12-mm) dice

½ Fresno or jalapeño chile, preferably red, seeded and minced

1 tablespoon finely chopped pickled ginger

1 tablespoon minced fresh cilantro

Kosher salt and freshly ground black pepper

FOR THE SUSHI RICE:

2 tablespoons rice vinegar

2 tablespoons sugar

Kosher salt

½ cup (100 g) short-grain rice for sushi

6 ounces (170 g) skinless sushi-grade ahi tuna, cut into ½-inch (12-mm) dice

1 teaspoon shichimi togarashi

½ ripe Hass avocado, cut into ½-inch (12-mm) dice

½ cup (120 ml) Chipotle Aïoli (page 182), in a squeeze bottle

Japan meets Mexico in this tasty twist on the taco theme. Miniature won ton wrappers are baked into small bowls, then filled with sushi rice, grilled tuna, and mango salsa. Be sure to use short-grain sushi rice—the cooked rice should be somewhat sticky.

SERVES 6 TO 8 AS AN APPETIZER

1 **Make the won ton bowls:** Position a rack in the center of the oven and preheat it to 350°F (175°C). Spray 16 cups in two muffin tins with oil.

2 Fit a won ton wrapper into each cup, pleating the wrapper as needed to fit. Press the wrapper firmly into the bottom and corners of the cup. Bake until the wrappers are crisp and golden, about 7 minutes. Let them cool in the tins. Carefully remove the cooled cups from the tins. (The cups can be stored at room temperature for up to 4 hours.)

3 **Make the salsa:** Purée half of the mango in a blender. Transfer the purée to a medium bowl. Add the remaining mango, the tomato, chile, ginger, and cilantro and mix. Season to taste with salt and pepper. Cover and set aside. (The salsa can be stored at room temperature for up to 2 hours.)

4 **Make the sushi rice:** Heat the vinegar, sugar, and 1 teaspoon salt together in a small nonreactive saucepan over low heat, stirring constantly, just until the sugar and salt are dissolved. Transfer the mixture to a small bowl and set aside.

5 Rinse out the saucepan. Add the rice, 1 cup (240 ml) water, and ½ teaspoon salt and bring to a boil over high heat. Reduce the heat to low and tightly cover the saucepan. Cook until the rice is tender and has absorbed the liquid, about 20 minutes.

6 Transfer the hot rice to a shallow glass or ceramic bowl. (The rice will cool more quickly in a wide nonmetal container.) Using a wooden spatula, gradually stir in the vinegar mixture—the rice should be shiny and sticky with a salty sweet-and-sour flavor. Let it cool. (The rice can be covered and refrigerated for up to 4 hours. Remove it from the refrigerator 1 hour before using.)

7 Season the tuna all over with the togarashi. Heat a large nonstick skillet over high heat. Add the tuna and cook, stirring once, just until it is seared but still very rare, about 30 seconds. Transfer it to a bowl.

8 Divide the rice among the won ton bowls, followed by the tuna. Top each with a spoonful of salsa, a few pieces of diced avocado, and a squirt of the aïoli. Serve immediately.

These battered and sauced fried shrimp are a sure bet to serve to buddies during a Sunday afternoon game in front of the TV with a frosty cerveza. The only problem is that no one will pay attention to what's on the screen—these are that good. I use low-gluten flour to make the crispiest batter (a trick I learned from Japanese tempura masters). While the ají amarillo is my first choice for the sauce, it is certainly not the only option. Use whatever hot sauce you like, or even adobo from canned chipotles.

SERVES 4

1 **Make the ají amarillo mayonnaise:** Whisk together the mayonnaise, milk, ají amarillo, and vinegar in a medium bowl. Season to taste with salt and pepper. Cover and let it stand at room temperature for 1 hour. (The sauce can be refrigerated for up to 1 day. Let it stand at room temperature for 1 hour before using.)

2 **Make the crispy shrimp:** Toss the shrimp with the buttermilk in a medium bowl. Cover and refrigerate them for 30 minutes to 4 hours.

3 To serve, position a rack in the center of the oven and preheat it to 200°F (90°C). Place a wire cooling rack over a large rimmed baking sheet.

4 Sift the all-purpose flour, cornstarch, and rice flour together in a large bowl. Whisk in the salt and pepper. Drain the shrimp in a large colander, but do not rinse them.

5 Pour in enough oil to come halfway up the sides of a large saucepan and heat it over high heat until the oil reaches 350°F (175°C) on a deep-frying thermometer. In batches, toss the shrimp in the flour mixture, shake off the excess coating, and carefully add them to the hot oil. Deep-fry them until crisp and golden brown, about 2½ minutes. Using a wire spider or slotted spoon, transfer the shrimp to the wire rack and keep them warm in the oven while frying the remaining shrimp.

6 Transfer the fried shrimp to a large bowl. Dollop the ají mayonnaise over the shrimp and toss them together. Divide the shrimp evenly among four soup bowls. Sprinkle them with the jalapeños and cilantro. Serve immediately, with the lime wedges.

CRISPY
SHRIMP
WITH AJÍ
AMARILLO SAUCE

*Chicharrón de camarones
con salsa de ají amarillo*

FOR THE AJÍ AMARILLO MAYONNAISE:

½ cup (120 ml) mayonnaise

1 tablespoon condensed milk or heavy cream

1 tablespoon ají amarillo paste, or 2 teaspoons adobo from canned chipotle chilies or your favorite hot sauce

1 teaspoon rice vinegar

Kosher salt and freshly ground black pepper

FOR THE CRISPY SHRIMP:

1½ pounds (680 g) large (31 to 40 count) shrimp, peeled and deveined

1 cup (240 ml) buttermilk

¼ cup (35 g) quick-mixing all-purpose flour, such as Wondra

¼ cup (35 g) cornstarch

¼ cup (35 g) white rice flour

1 teaspoon kosher salt

½ teaspoon freshly ground black pepper

Canola oil, for deep-frying

½ cup (75 g) drained and coarsely chopped Pickled Jalapeños (page 181) or store-bought *jalapeños en escabeche* or nacho slices

Chopped fresh cilantro, for garnish

Lime wedges, for serving

Forget any opinions you may have about boring fast-food nachos. Moist brisket and homemade cheese sauce make the others pale in comparison to these super-nachos. One secret: For a smooth sauce with the right Tex-Mex flavor, Velveeta really is the key.

SERVES 4 TO 6

1 **Make the cheese sauce:** Heat the oil in a medium saucepan over medium heat. Add the onion and cook, stirring occasionally, until it is translucent, about 4 minutes. Add the tomato and chipotle and cook until the tomato is beginning to soften, about 2 minutes more. Add the cream and bring it to a simmer. Reduce the heat to very low. In batches, add the cheese product, stirring until it melts. Stir in the cilantro. Keep the sauce warm. (The sauce can be transferred to a bowl, cooled, covered, and refrigerated for up to 1 day. Reheat it over very low heat, whisking often.)

2 Position a rack in the center of the oven and preheat the oven to 350°F (175°C).

3 Spread the chips in a large heatproof serving dish. Bake until the chips are warm, about 5 minutes. Remove the dish from the oven. Scatter the shredded brisket over the chips. Drizzle them with the warm cheese sauce. Top with the pico de gallo, avocado, and jalapeños. Serve hot.

BRISKET NACHOS
WITH CHIPOTLE CHEESE SAUCE

Nachos de res con queso al chipotle

FOR THE CHIPOTLE CHEESE SAUCE:

1 tablespoon canola oil

½ cup (80 g) finely chopped yellow onion

1 small plum tomato, seeded and cut into ½-inch (12-mm) dice

1 canned chipotle chile in adobo, finely chopped

¾ cup (180 ml) heavy cream

8 ounces (225 g) pasteurized cheese product, such as Velveeta, coarsely chopped

2 tablespoons finely chopped fresh cilantro

One 8-ounce (225-g) bag tortilla chips

2 cups (600 g) Shredded Beef Filling with Tomatoes and Chilies (page 175), heated

1 cup (175 g) Pico de Gallo (page 179)

1 ripe Hass avocado, cut into ½-inch (12-mm) dice

3 tablespoons coarsely chopped Pickled Jalapeños (page 181) or store-bought *jalapeños en escabeche* or nacho slices

DEEP-FRYING

There is only one way to give food that irresistible crunchy texture that we all love: deep-frying. Latin cooks know this, and many classic dishes use this age-old cooking technique. There is also a historical reason for deep-frying food, as rural cooks often had stoves, but not ovens, so it was much more common to cook on the stovetop. Here are some tips for great deep-fried food every time.

THE RIGHT OIL: Just about any kind of standard cooking oil (canola, vegetable, and even olive) works well for deep-frying. Some cooks recommend grapeseed or peanut oil because of their high smoking points of above 450°F (230°C). The smoking point is the temperature where the heated oil begins to smoke and decompose, affecting its flavor. But deep-frying temperatures occur around 350°F (175°C), so there is no need to buy one of these more expensive oils.

KEEP IT DEEP: You can use either a large saucepan or a skillet for deep-frying. However, it is important that the oil is deep enough to float the food. Do not skimp on the oil! Pour in enough oil to come about halfway up the sides of the receptacle. If you are using a skillet, be sure that it has sides at least 2 inches (5 cm) high.

TAKING THE TEMPERATURE: Clip-on deep-frying thermometers have become antiquated. To get an oil temperature reading in seconds, use an instant-read thermometer dipped in the hot oil. Often, a classic clip-on thermometer won't give an accurate reading because the end of the probe doesn't dip far enough into the oil.

Even though I recommend using an instant-read thermometer, there are ways to tell if the oil is ready without one. First, the oil will shimmer slightly in the pan. Add a piece of food (a bit of tortilla or bread) to the oil—it should immediately float to the top of the oil and start to bubble. If the oil isn't hot enough, the food will sink.

DON'T CROWD THE FOOD: The food to be fried should be added to the hot oil in batches. If too much food is fried at the same time, the oil temperature will drop and the food will get soggy. Oil with the proper hot temperature (from 325° to 375°F/165° to 190°C) forces the moisture from the food's surface, making it crispy. Oil that is too cool will simply soak into the food. The right amount of food depends on the size of the cooking receptacle—the food should "swim" in the oil without crowding.

The oil temperature will lower a bit during cooking because of adding the cooler food. Always let the oil reheat to the proper temperature before adding another batch of food.

PRACTICE PROPER DRAINING: Draining on paper towels (or even a brown paper bag) is fine for crisp items like tortillas. But for breaded foods, skip the towels, as the steam given off by the coating will collect where it comes into contact with the paper and make the food soggy. The optimal way to drain fried food is on a wire cooling rack set over a large rimmed baking sheet, allowing the oil to drip off.

A wire spider is the best utensil for removing the fried food from the oil. You'll find this inexpensive tool, which looks like a small wire basket on a handle, at Asian markets (it is indispensible for cooking in a wok) and kitchenware shops. A slotted spoon is OK, but use one with large perforations so the oil quickly drains back into the saucepan.

KEEP IT WARM: Deep-fried food is always best served freshly cooked and warm. To hold the food for a few minutes while cooking subsequent batches, keep it warm on the cooling rack over the baking sheet in a very low oven set to 200°F (90°C).

TOSS THE OIL: It is a hassle to find room in the refrigerator to store leftover oil, which can go rancid before you use it again. Just dispose of the cooled used oil according to the advice of your local waste management authority.

I love how the combination of shrimp and bacon, two ingredients with slightly sweet flavors, plays off of spicy chilies. A quesadilla (or two or three) is a fun appetizer, but it is also a good lunch or supper dish.

SERVES 4

1 Cook the bacon in a large nonstick skillet over medium heat, turning occasionally, until it is crisp and browned, about 8 minutes. Transfer the bacon to paper towels to drain. Let it cool. Clean the pan and set it aside.

2 Toss together the shrimp, chili powder, oil, and salt in a medium bowl. Heat the skillet over medium heat. Add the shrimp and cook, stirring them occasionally, just until they turn opaque, about 3 minutes. Do not overcook. Spread the shrimp on a plate and put them in the freezer to quickly cool them, about 15 minutes.

3 Coarsely chop the bacon and shrimp and transfer them to a bowl. Mix in the cheese, scallions, jalapeños, mayonnaise, cilantro, lemon juice, and sesame seeds, if using. (The filling can be covered and refrigerated for up to 12 hours.)

4 Position a rack in the center of the oven and preheat it to 200°F (90°C).

5 Heat the skillet over medium heat. For each quesadilla, put a tortilla in the skillet and heat until the underside is hot, about 30 seconds. Flip the tortilla over. Spoon about $1/3$ cup (75 g) of the filling on the bottom half of the tortilla and fold it in half to cover the filling. Continue cooking, turning once, until the tortilla is lightly browned on both sides, about 1 minute. Transfer it to a baking sheet and keep it warm in the oven while cooking the remaining quesadillas.

6 To serve, cut each quesadilla into four wedges. Serve them immediately.

SHRIMP & BACON QUESADILLAS

Quesadillas con camarones y tocino

3 slices bacon

12 ounces (340 g) large (31 to 40 count) shrimp, peeled and deveined

2 tablespoons chili powder

1 tablespoon canola oil

¼ teaspoon salt

1 cup (115 g) shredded sharp cheddar cheese

2 scallions (white and green parts), thinly sliced

3 tablespoons coarsely chopped Pickled Jalapeños (page 181) or store-bought *jalapeños en escabeche* or nacho slices

3 tablespoons mayonnaise

2 tablespoons finely chopped fresh cilantro

1 tablespoon fresh lemon juice

1 teaspoon toasted sesame seeds (optional)

Twelve 6-inch (15-cm) flour tortillas

VENEZUELAN EGG ROLLS

WITH ROCOTO SWEET & SOUR SAUCE

Tequeños con salsa de ají rocoto agridulce

To a Venezuelan, a tequeño is a chunk of cheese wrapped in dough and fried on a stick. The term can also mean just about anything that is deep-fried and crispy. My tequeños, filled with shrimp, pork, and vegetables, are clearly influenced by Asian cooking.

SERVES 6; MAKES 12 EGG ROLLS

FOR THE ROCOTO SWEET & SOUR SAUCE:

⅔ cup (80 g) finely diced red bell pepper

½ cup (120 ml) canned pineapple juice

½ cup (120 ml) rice vinegar

½ cup (100 g) sugar

¼ cup (60 ml) ketchup

2 tablespoons ají rocoto paste or Sriracha

1 tablespoon cornstarch

FOR THE FILLING:

1 tablespoon canola oil

⅓ cup (40 g) finely diced carrot

⅓ cup (40 g) finely diced red bell pepper

1 tablespoon peeled and minced fresh ginger

1 scallion (white and green parts), minced

6 ounces (170 g) sweet Italian pork sausage, casings removed

6 ounces (170 g) large (31 to 40 count) shrimp, peeled, deveined, and finely chopped

¼ teaspoon kosher salt

1 **Make the sauce:** Bring the bell pepper, juice, vinegar, sugar, ketchup, and rocoto paste to a boil in a medium saucepan over medium heat, stirring often to dissolve the sugar. Sprinkle the cornstarch over 4 teaspoons water in a small bowl, whisk to dissolve, then whisk the mixture into the sauce. Return it to a full boil to thicken the sauce. Remove it from the heat and let it cool. (The sauce can be covered and refrigerated for up to 1 day. Bring it to room temperature before serving.)

2 **Make the filling:** Heat the oil in a large skillet over medium heat. Add the carrot and bell pepper and cover. Cook, stirring occasionally, until the carrot is crisp-tender, about 3 minutes. Stir in the ginger and cook until it is fragrant, about 1 minute. Transfer the mixture to a medium bowl and stir in the scallion. Let it cool completely. Stir in the sausage and shrimp. Season with the salt and pepper.

3 Line a large rimmed baking sheet with parchment or waxed paper. In a cup, whisk the cornstarch with 1 tablespoon water. For each tequeño, place an egg roll wrapper on a work surface with a corner facing you. Spoon about 3 tablespoons of the filling in a log about 2½ inches (6 cm) above the bottom wrapper corner. Fold up the bottom of the wrapper to completely cover the filling and tuck the wrapper snugly against the filling. Fold over the left and right sides of the wrapper. Tightly roll up the wrapper into a tight cylinder without any open gaps. Paste the exposed corner closed with a dab of the cornstarch mixture. Place the roll, seam-side down, on the parchment. Arrange the tequeños well apart so they don't touch. Loosely cover them with plastic wrap and refrigerate until you're ready to cook, up to 2 hours.

4 To serve, preheat the oven to 200ºF (90ºC). Place a wire cooling rack over a rimmed baking sheet near the stove.

5 Pour in enough oil to come halfway up the sides of a large saucepan and heat it over high heat until the oil reaches 325ºF (165ºC) on a deep-frying thermometer. In batches without crowding, deep-fry the tequeños, turning them occasionally, until they are golden brown, about 4 minutes. It is important to cook the tequeños at a moderate rate so the filling cooks through. Using a wire spider or slotted spoon, transfer the tequeños to the wire rack and keep them warm in the oven while frying the rest.

6 Pour the sauce into individual bowls for dipping. Serve the tequeños and sauce immediately.

¼ teaspoon freshly ground black pepper

1 tablespoon cornstarch

Twelve 6-inch (15-cm) egg roll wrappers

Canola oil, for deep-frying

CRISPY CHICKEN WINGS

WITH ORANGE ADOBO SAUCE

*Alitas de pollo crocantes
con adobo de naranja*

Think of these as Buffalo wings Latin-style, with fried chicken in a spicy sauce that will have you licking your fingers with abandon. The terrific sauce, based on the citrus and chile flavors of Yucatan, can be made almost entirely ahead, and quickly finished with some butter right before serving. Look for fresh (not frozen) wingettes or prep whole wings yourself as I describe below (the frozen ones retain too much moisture to brown properly). I've lightened the classic frying cooking method by roasting the wings at a high temperature. You still get crispy wings with falling-off-the-bone meat.

SERVES 6

FOR THE ORANGE ADOBO SAUCE:

2 cups (480 ml) fresh orange juice

1 cup (240 ml) distilled white vinegar

⅔ cup (165 ml) honey

3 guajillo chilies, seeded and torn into large pieces, or 3 tablespoons pure ground ancho chile

4 canned chipotle chilies in adobo, with their clinging sauce

2 tablespoons Achiote (page 183) or store-bought *condimento de achiote*

3 garlic cloves, crushed under a knife and peeled

½ cup (1 stick; 115 g) cold unsalted butter, thinly sliced

Kosher salt

FOR THE WINGS:

2 teaspoons kosher salt

2 teaspoons freshly ground black pepper

2 teaspoons sweet paprika

½ teaspoon granulated onion or onion powder

½ teaspoon granulated garlic or garlic powder

4¾ pounds (2.2 kg) fresh chicken wingettes, or 5 pounds (2.3 kg) chicken wings (see Note)

1 **Make the sauce:** Bring the juice, vinegar, honey, guajillos, chipotles, achiote, and garlic to a boil in a medium saucepan over medium-high heat, stirring often to dissolve the honey. Reduce the heat to medium and simmer briskly, stirring occasionally, until the sauce is reduced by half, about 30 minutes. Remove it from the heat and let it cool. Purée the mixture in a blender. You should have 2 cups (480 ml). The sauce base can be stored at room temperature for up to 4 hours.

2 **Make the wings:** Position a rack in the top third of the oven and preheat the oven to 425ºF (220ºC). Whisk together the salt, pepper, paprika, onion powder, and garlic powder in a small bowl. Put the wings in a large bowl and toss them with the spice mixture. Arrange the wings in a single layer on the baking sheet.

3 Bake until the wings are nicely browned and show no sign of pink when pierced at the bone with the tip of a small knife, about 40 minutes.

4 Just before the wings are done, finish the sauce. Return the sauce base in the saucepan to a boil over medium heat, stirring often. Reduce the heat to very low. One piece at a time, whisk in the butter, letting the first piece melt before adding another. Season it to taste with salt.

5 Transfer the wings to a large bowl. Add about half of the sauce and toss well. Transfer the wings to a platter. Serve them hot, with the additional sauce alongside for dipping; provide bowls for the bones and plenty of napkins.

NOTE To prepare whole wings: Using a large heavy knife or cleaver, chop off the wing tips at the joint. (Reserve the wing tips to make chicken stock, if desired.) Cut the remaining wing in half at the "elbow" joint.

These fries with mojo (Caribbean garlic sauce) are a good way to get to know yuca, the flavorful tuber that is the source of tapioca. Note the two-step cooking process, with an initial boiling before the final frying. Roasted garlic makes a mellow mojo without the heat of raw cloves.

YUCA FRIES

WITH ROASTED GARLIC MOJO

Yuca frita con mojo de ajo

SERVES 6 TO 8

1 **Make the mojo:** Preheat the oven to 275°F (135°C). Cut each garlic head in half crosswise. Drizzle the cut surfaces with oil and sprinkle them with a pinch each of salt and pepper. Put the halves back together to return the garlic to its original shape and wrap each in aluminum foil. Bake until the garlic flesh is tender and beige, about 1¼ hours. Let the garlic cool completely. Squeeze the cloves out of the hulls into a bowl and mash them coarsely with a fork. You should have about ¼ cup (120 g).

2 Transfer the roasted garlic to a blender. Add the lemon juice and purée. Transfer the purée to a bowl and stir in the parsley. Generously season it with salt and pepper, cover, and refrigerate to blend the flavors, at least 1 hour. (The mojo can be refrigerated for up to 3 days.)

3 Bring a large pot of salted water to a boil over high heat. Trim the ends from the yuca and cut it into 5-inch (12.5-cm) lengths. One at a time, stand a yuca length on end. Using a large sharp knife, cut off the thick waxed bark where it meets the flesh. Cut the yuca lengthwise into sticks about 5 inches (12.5 cm) long and ¾ inch (2 cm) square. You should have about 30 yuca sticks.

4 Add the yuca to the water and boil it over medium heat until barely tender, 12 to 15 minutes. Drain the yuca and rinse it under cold running water to stop the cooking. Spread the sticks on clean kitchen towels to drain and cool completely. Discard any tough thin cords running lengthwise in the yuca sticks. (The yuca can be stored at room temperature for up to 4 hours.)

5 Preheat the oven to 200°F (90°C). Place a wire cooling rack over a rimmed baking sheet.

6 Pour in enough oil to come halfway up the sides of a large saucepan and heat it over high heat until the oil reaches 350°F (175°C) on a deep-frying thermometer. In batches without crowding, deep-fry the yuca sticks, turning them as needed, until they are golden brown, about 3 minutes. Using a wire spider or slotted spoon, transfer them to the cooling rack and keep them warm in the oven while frying the remaining yuca.

7 Divide the mojo among six to eight ramekins. For each serving, divide the fries among six to eight plates and add a ramekin to each. Serve hot.

FOR THE ROASTED-GARLIC MOJO:

2 large, plump heads of garlic

Olive oil

Kosher salt and freshly ground black pepper

⅔ cup (165 ml) fresh lemon juice

2 tablespoons coarsely chopped fresh flat-leaf parsley

2½ pounds (1.2 kg) long, narrow yuca (see Note)

Vegetable oil, for deep-frying

NOTE Yuca comes in a wide range of sizes. The elongated, narrow tubers are best for this recipe because they are more tender and easier to peel.

HAM CROQUETTES

WITH CHINESE MUSTARD DIP

*Croquetas de jamón
con salsa de mostaza China*

**FOR THE CHINESE
MUSTARD DIP:**

¼ cup (25 g) dry mustard powder

¼ cup (60 ml) soy sauce

¼ cup (60 ml) rice vinegar

2 tablespoons honey

4 teaspoons sugar

½ cup (120 ml) canola oil

2 teaspoons sesame seeds, toasted

1 scallion (green part only),
very thinly sliced

FOR THE FILLING:

4 tablespoons (½ stick; 55 g)
unsalted butter

½ cup (65 g) all-purpose flour

1 cup (240 ml) heavy cream,
heated to steaming

2 ounces (55 g) cream cheese,
at room temperature

½ cup (85 g) finely chopped
white onion

2 garlic cloves, minced

12 ounces (340 g) smoked ham,
finely minced in a food processor

1 cup (115 g) shredded Emmenthaler
cheese

2 tablespoons fresh lime juice

1 tablespoon finely chopped
fresh cilantro

2 teaspoons Sriracha

Ham croquettes are among the most beloved of all tapas. My version has unexpected Asian flavors that you are not likely to find in a Spanish restaurant. Bite into one of these walnut-size balls, and you'll first encounter a crunchy panko coating, which then gives way to a creamy, warm filling. Start these early in the day (or even the day before) so the filling is firm enough for shaping.

SERVES 6 TO 8; MAKES 24 CROQUETTES

1 **Make the mustard dip:** Whisk the mustard and ¼ cup (60 ml) cold water together in a small bowl. Pour them into a blender and add the soy sauce, vinegar, honey, and sugar. With the blender running, gradually add the oil through the hole in the lid to make a thick dip. Return it to the bowl and stir in the sesame seeds and scallion. Cover and let the dip stand for at least 1 hour before serving. (The dip can be refrigerated for up to 3 days. Return it to room temperature before serving.)

2 **Make the filling:** Melt 2 tablespoons of the butter in a medium saucepan over medium heat. Whisk in the flour to make a lumpy paste. (It will not look like the typical roux.) Gradually whisk in the cream and bring it to a boil over medium heat, whisking often to dissolve the lumps, to make a very thick sauce. Pour the sauce into a medium bowl. Let the sauce cool, whisking it occasionally, until warm, about 15 minutes. Whisk in the cream cheese until smooth. Let the sauce cool, whisking often, until it cools to room temperature, about 1 hour. Do not worry if the butter separates from the sauce.

3 Melt the remaining 2 tablespoons butter in a small skillet over medium heat. Add the onion and garlic and cook, stirring often, until the onion is translucent and tender, about 3 minutes. Whisk it into the cooled sauce. Add the ham, cheese, lime juice, cilantro, and Sriracha and mix well. Season the filling to taste with salt and pepper. Cover and refrigerate it until congealed and easier to shape, 1 to 2 hours.

4 Line a baking sheet with parchment or waxed paper. Using a generous tablespoon for each croquette, shape the ham mixture into 24 balls and place them on the paper. Cover them with plastic wrap and freeze until completely frozen, at least 2 hours or up to 1 day.

5 **Make the coating:** Line another baking sheet with parchment or waxed paper. Spread the flour in a shallow bowl. Beat the eggs well in a second shallow bowl. Spread the panko in a third shallow bowl. One at a time, roll a frozen croquette in the flour, shaking off the excess flour, then in the eggs, and finally in the panko, shaking off the excess panko. Place them on the paper.

6 Preheat the oven to 200ºF (90ºC). Place a wire cooling rack over a large rimmed baking sheet. Pour in enough oil to come halfway up the sides of a large saucepan and heat it over high heat until the oil reaches 325ºF (165ºC) on a deep-frying thermometer. In batches without crowding, deep-fry the croquettes, turning them occasionally, until they are golden brown, 3 to 4 minutes. Adjust the heat so the croquettes bubble in the oil but the panko doesn't brown too quickly, as the filling must heat through. Using a wire spider or slotted spoon, transfer the croquettes to the rack and keep them warm in the oven while frying the rest.

7 Pour the mustard dip into a bowl. Transfer the croquettes to a platter and serve them hot, with the dip alongside.

Kosher salt and freshly ground black pepper

FOR THE COATING:

1 cup (130 g) all-purpose flour

3 large eggs

1½ cups (90 g) panko

Canola oil, for deep-frying

POTATOES BRAVAS

WITH SMOKED ROMESCO & CHORIZO

Patatas bravas con romesco ahumado y chorizo

FOR THE SMOKY CHIPOTLE ROMESCO:

3 plum tomatoes

½ small yellow onion, cut into ¼-inch (6-mm) rings

Olive oil

1 garlic clove, crushed and peeled

5 drained piquillo peppers (see Notes), or 1 roasted red pepper, coarsely chopped

2 tablespoons slivered almonds, toasted (see Notes)

2 tablespoons fresh bread crumbs

1 tablespoon sherry vinegar

1 canned chipotle chile in adobo, with clinging sauce

1 teaspoon smoked paprika (pimentón)

Kosher salt

2 pounds (910 g) fingerling or small red-skinned potatoes, scrubbed but unpeeled, halved lengthwise

3 tablespoons olive oil

5 ounces (140 g) smoked Spanish-style chorizo, cut into ½-inch (12-mm) dice

3 scallions (white and green parts), thinly sliced

This is how I make patatas bravas, crispy potatoes that have been made "angry" (*brava*) with the addition of a spicy sauce. The exact kind of sauce varies from cook to cook—some use aïoli, others a paprika-spiced tomato sauce. I lean toward this red pepper romesco, one of the classic sauces of Spain, which I make smoky with chipotle and smoked paprika. The potatoes are traditionally deep-fried, but they are just as tasty when roasted, as I do here. Serve them as tapas, or try them as a side dish (with or without the chorizo) to a simple main course, such as roast pork or chicken.

SERVES 6

1 **Make the romesco:** Position a broiler rack about 6 inches (15 cm) from the source of heat and preheat the broiler on high.

2 Toss the tomatoes and onion rings with oil and spread them on the broiler rack. Broil, turning occasionally, until the onion rings are lightly charred, about 4 minutes. Remove the onion rings. Continue broiling the tomatoes until the skins are split and charred, about 4 minutes more. Transfer them to a bowl. Let the tomatoes cool. Remove the skins and seeds.

3 Transfer the tomatoes, onion, and garlic to a food processor. Add 2 tablespoons olive oil, the peppers, almonds, bread crumbs, vinegar, chipotle, and paprika. Process the romesco until it is smooth. Season to taste with salt. Transfer the romesco to a bowl, cover, and let it stand for at least 1 hour to blend the flavors. (The romesco can be refrigerated for up to 3 days. Let it stand at room temperature for 1 hour before serving.)

4 Position a rack in the top third of the oven and preheat the oven to 425º (220ºC). Spread the potatoes on a large rimmed baking sheet. Drizzle them with 2 tablespoons of the oil and toss to coat. Arrange the potatoes with the cut side down. Bake, turning the potatoes after 25 minutes, until they are tender and golden brown, about 15 minutes longer.

5 Meanwhile, heat the remaining 1 tablespoon oil in a medium skillet over medium heat. Add the chorizo and cook, stirring it occasionally, until it is browned, about 6 minutes. Remove it from the heat and cover with the lid to keep it warm.

6 To serve, add the romesco and chorizo to the potatoes on the baking sheet and toss to combine them. Divide the potato mixture among six small bowls, sprinkle with scallions, and serve hot.

NOTES Piquillo peppers, one of the glories of Spanish cuisine, are small red peppers roasted and packed in olive oil, vinegar, and brine, and are sold at specialty food stores and many supermarkets. Their name means "little beak," and you can see how they got it from their long, pointed shape. They are richly flavored to begin with, and roasting heightens their taste, which is a little hotter and more complex than your average red bell pepper.

To toast almonds and other nuts, heat an empty small skillet over medium heat. Add the almonds and cook, stirring occasionally, until they are toasted and golden brown, 2 to 3 minutes. Immediately transfer them to a plate and let them cool completely.

CLASSIC GUACAMOLE

Guacamole clásico

2 ripe Hass avocados, coarsely chopped

1 plum tomato, seeded and cut into ½-inch (12-mm) dice

¼ cup (40 g) finely chopped white or yellow onion

½ jalapeño, or 1 serrano chile, seeded and minced

2 tablespoons fresh lime juice

Kosher salt

Tostaditas (see page 50) or store-bought tortilla chips, for serving

Put out a bowl of great guacamole, and the party can begin! What makes great "guac"? Start by choosing the right avocados, which are the pebbly skinned varieties such as Hass and Fuerte, originally grown as a domestic crop in California, and now augmented year-round with imports from Mexico, Peru, and Chile. This is the classic recipe, which should always be chunky and never made in a blender or food processor. Avocados by themselves are bland, so don't be shy with the salt.

SERVES 4 TO 6

Mash the avocados, tomato, onion, chile, and lime juice together in a medium bowl with a large serving fork or a potato masher. Be sure to keep the guacamole chunky. Season it generously to taste with salt. Serve it immediately, with the chips. (The guacamole can be covered with a piece of plastic wrap pressed directly on its surface and refrigerated for up to 8 hours.)

There are many cooks, professional and otherwise, who would put bacon on *anything* edible. (I have seen bacon ice cream on menus.) I use bacon in many of my dishes, too, because with just a few minutes' cooking time, you can add a crispy, chewy, salty, slightly sweet flavor that is addictive. Here I add bacon to guacamole, and they were clearly made for each other. Think outside of the tortilla chips box (or bag) and try pork rinds with this guacamole.

SERVES 4 TO 6

1 Cook the bacon in a large skillet over medium heat, turning occasionally, until it is crisp and browned, about 8 minutes. Transfer it to paper towels to drain. Coarsely chop the bacon.

2 Put the guacamole in a serving bowl. Top it with the bacon, cheese, and jalapeños. Serve it immediately, with the pork rinds for dipping.

BACON
GUACAMOLE

Guacamole con tocino

4 slices bacon

1 recipe Classic Guacamole (page 44)

½ cup (60 g) crumbled fresh cotija cheese or ricotta salata

3 tablespoons coarsely chopped Pickled Jalapeños (page 181) or store-bought *jalapeños en escabeche* or nacho slices

Fried pork rinds or store-bought tortilla chips, for serving

AHI TUNA GUACAMOLE

Guacamole con atún

FOR THE WON TON CHIPS:

Canola oil, for deep-frying

12 won ton wrappers, cut into halves

FOR THE JÍCAMA TOPPING:

¾ cup (85 g) peeled and thinly julienned jícama (use a mandoline or V-slicer)

1 tablespoon fresh lime juice

1 tablespoon chopped fresh cilantro

Kosher salt

8 ounces sushi-grade ahi steaks, cut into ¼-inch (6-mm) dice

1 tablespoon Ponzu, homemade (page 48) or store-bought

3 tablespoons mayonnaise

1½ teaspoons adobo from canned chipotle chilies in adobo

1 recipe Classic Guacamole (page 44)

½ teaspoon sesame seeds, toasted

Here is an upscale version of layered dip, a lowbrow Tex-Mex favorite that a lot of people love in spite of its humble ingredients. I start with chunky guacamole, add diced fresh tuna marinated in ponzu, spread it with spicy mayonnaise, and finish it off with crisp jícama. Served on crunchy won ton chips, it shows how well Latin and Asian cuisines can complement each other . . . and how you can take a good thing and make it better. You can also assemble the ingredients on individual chips and pass them as hors d'ouevres.

SERVES 6

1 **Make the won ton chips:** Pour in enough oil to come halfway up the sides of a large saucepan and heat it over high heat until the oil reaches 350°F (175°C) on a deep-frying thermometer. Line a baking sheet with paper towels. In small batches, deep-fry the won ton wrapper pieces, turning them after 5 seconds, until they are golden brown, about 15 seconds total. (They brown very quickly, so you may want to do a test strip to judge the timing for your particular brand.) Using a wire spider or slotted spoon, transfer the chips to the paper towels to drain. The won ton chips can be stored uncovered at room temperature for up to 8 hours.

2 **Make the jícama topping:** Toss together the jícama, lime juice, and cilantro in a small bowl. Season them to taste with salt.

3 Toss together the tuna and ponzu in a small bowl. Mix the mayonnaise and adobo together in another small bowl.

4 Spread the guacamole in a wide layer about 1 inch (2.5 cm) thick on a serving platter. Top it with the tuna. Spread it with the aïoli. Scatter the jícama over the aïoli and sprinkle the top with the sesame seeds. Serve the dip immediately, with the won ton chips.

PONZU

MAKES ABOUT ⅞ CUP (210 ML)

While ponzu is becoming increasingly available at supermarkets, here is a recipe for a homemade version.

½ cup (120 ml) mirin

2 tablespoons sake

2 tablespoons rice wine vinegar

One 3-inch (7.5-cm) square kombu (dried seaweed for cooking), rinsed under cold water

⅛ teaspoon hot red pepper flakes

½ cup (120 ml) soy sauce

2 tablespoons bottled yuzu or fresh lime juice

Bring the mirin, sake, vinegar, kombu, and pepper flakes to a simmer in a small nonreactive saucepan over medium heat. Reduce the heat to low and simmer for 5 minutes. Remove the pan from the heat and stir in the soy sauce and yuzu juice. Strain the ponzu into a small bowl, discarding the kombu. Let it cool. Cover and refrigerate the sauce for up to 2 weeks.

When people share food from the same vessel, there is no choice but for everyone to get close—both physically and in their frame of mind. This version of queso fundido is upgraded from the standard model with sautéed mushrooms and a trio of cheeses.

SERVES 4 TO 6

1 Heat the oil, garlic, thyme, and oregano together in a medium ovenproof skillet, preferably cast iron, over medium heat until the garlic begins to brown, about 2½ minutes. Add the mushrooms and season to taste with salt and pepper. Increase the heat to medium-high and cook, stirring occasionally, until the mushrooms are tender but moist, about 6 minutes. (The mushrooms can be transferred to a bowl and cooled, covered, and refrigerated for 1 day. Reheat them in a skillet over medium heat.)

2 Position a broiler rack about 6 inches (15 cm) from the source of heat and preheat the broiler on high.

3 Mix the Gouda, Chihuahua, and Oaxaca cheeses together. Stir them into the mushrooms in the skillet. When the cheese begins to melt, transfer the skillet to the broiler. Broil until the cheese is fully melted and beginning to brown in spots, about 3 minutes. Watch the queso fundido carefully during browning because it can burn quickly.

4 Immediately bring the skillet to the table and place it on a trivet. Using a serving spoon, scoop the queso fundido directly from the pan and spread it on the tortillas. (Alert your guests not to touch the hot skillet.)

VARIATION **Chorizo Queso Fundido:** Omit the mushrooms. Cook 4 ounces (115 g) soft Mexican-style chorizo, casings removed, in the skillet over medium heat, stirring often and breaking up the meat with a wooden spoon, until the chorizo is lightly browned, about 7 minutes. Drain off the excess fat from the skillet. Continue with the recipe as directed. This is especially good served with Tomatillo-Jalapeño Green Salsa (page 179).

QUESO FUNDIDO

WITH WILD MUSHROOMS

Queso fundido con setas silvestres

2 tablespoons canola oil

3 garlic cloves, smashed under a knife and peeled

Three 3-inch (7.5-cm) sprigs fresh thyme

Three 3-inch (7.5-cm) sprigs fresh oregano

10 ounces (280 g) cremini, stemmed shiitake, or other full-flavored mushrooms, coarsely chopped

Kosher salt and freshly ground black pepper

¾ cup (95 g) shredded Gouda cheese

¾ cup (95 g) shredded Chihuahua or mild cheddar cheese

¾ cup (95 g) shredded Oaxaca, string, or mozzarella cheese

Flour tortillas, heated according to package directions, for serving

COOKED TOMATO SALSA
WITH TORTILLA CHIPS

*Salsa de molcajete
con tostaditas*

FOR THE MOLCAJETE SALSA:

1 pound (455 g) ripe plum tomatoes

2 tablespoons canola oil

½ small yellow onion, coarsely chopped

1 serrano chile, or ½ jalapeño, seeded and minced

2 garlic cloves, minced

1 teaspoon adobo from canned chipotle chilies in adobo

2 tablespoons finely chopped fresh cilantro

Kosher salt

FOR THE TOSTADITAS:

Canola oil, for deep-frying

8 corn tortillas, cut into 6 wedges each

Tomato salsa and tortilla chips can be memorable when the salsa is homemade from ripe tomatoes and the chips are freshly fried. Broiling the tomatoes adds a bit of smoky flavor to the salsa, and cooking the vegetables gives the salsa a clinging texture that is perfect for dipping. In Mexico, many cooks crush the vegetables in a molcajete, the classic mortar and pestle made from volcanic rock, but a food processor works well and is much easier to clean!

MAKES 2 CUPS (480 ML) SALSA; SERVES 6 TO 8

1 **Make the salsa:** Position a broiler rack about 6 inches (15 cm) from the source of heat and preheat the broiler on high. Place the tomatoes on a broiler pan and broil, turning them occasionally, until the skins are blackened and blistered, about 8 minutes. Let them cool until they are easy to handle. Peel off and discard the blackened tomato skins and poke out the seeds with your finger.

2 Meanwhile, heat the oil in a large skillet over medium heat. Add the onion, chile, and garlic and cook, stirring often, until the onion is tender but not browned, about 3 minutes. Let it cool.

3 Pulse the tomatoes, onion mixture, and adobo in a food processor until they are smooth but not puréed. Add the cilantro and pulse just to combine. Season to taste with salt. Transfer the salsa to a covered container. (It can be refrigerated for up to 3 days. Remove it from the refrigerator 1 hour before serving.)

4 **Make the tostaditas:** Pour in enough oil to come halfway up the sides of a large deep skillet and heat it over high heat until the oil is shimmering and reaches 350°F (175°C) on a deep-frying thermometer. Line a large rimmed baking sheet with a double thickness of paper towels.

5 In batches, add the tortilla wedges and deep-fry them until golden brown, about 1 minute. Using a wire spider or slotted spoon, transfer the tortilla chips to the paper towels. (The chips can be stored in a paper bag for up to 12 hours.)

6 Transfer the salsa to a serving bowl and serve it with the chips.

Make this chunky dip once for a party, and expect to make it again for your next bash. It's that good. And with an outdoor grill, it is also very easy to smoke the swordfish. Use applewood chips, as the smoke gives off a sweet, not-too-strong aroma that works well for delicate foods like fish. The smoking can also be done in the kitchen.

MAKES ABOUT 3 CUPS (660 G); SERVES 8

1 Prepare an outdoor grill for indirect grilling over low heat. For a charcoal grill, let the coals burn until they are covered with pale gray ash and you can hold your hand about 1 inch (2.5 cm) above the grill grate for 3 to 4 seconds. Push the coals to one side of the grill, leaving the other side empty. For a gas grill, preheat the grill on high. Turn one burner off, then adjust the heat to 325°F (165°C). Place a double-thick piece of aluminum foil directly on the heat source (under the grate) to hold the drained chips. (Or use a smoker box according to the manufacturer's directions.)

2 Tear off a 12-inch (30.5-cm) square of foil and pierce an area the shape of the swordfish steak with a meat fork. Brush the swordfish with the oil, season it with ½ teaspoon salt and ½ teaspoon pepper, and place it on the pierced area of the foil.

3 Drain the wood chips and scatter them on the coals (or place them on the foil or smoker box on the gas grill). Close the grill and allow the chips to build up a head of smoke. Place the swordfish on its foil on the empty (or turned-off) area of the grill. Close the grill and cook until the swordfish looks barely opaque when flaked with the tip of a knife, 30 to 40 minutes. Let the swordfish cool completely.

4 Remove the swordfish skin. Flake the flesh and transfer it to a medium bowl. Stir in the tomato, onion, mayonnaise, jalapeños, lime juice, and cilantro. Season to taste with salt and pepper. Cover and refrigerate the mixture until chilled, at least 2 hours and up to 1 day.

5 Serve it chilled, with the tortillas for dipping.

NOTE To smoke the swordfish indoors, line a Dutch oven with aluminum foil, pressing the foil flat against the bottom of the Dutch oven. Add the drained chips. Place an oiled steamer basket over the chips. Heat the Dutch oven over high heat until the chips begin to smoke, about 5 minutes. Add the swordfish to the basket. Cover the Dutch oven with a large sheet of aluminum foil and the lid to make a tight seal. Lower the heat to medium so the chips are smoking steadily. Cook until the swordfish is opaque when pierced with the tip of a knife, about 30 minutes.

APPLEWOOD-SMOKED SWORDFISH DIP

Dip de pez espada ahumado

One 1-pound (455-g) swordfish steak, cut about 1 inch (2.5 cm) thick

Olive oil, for brushing

Kosher salt and freshly ground black pepper

1 large handful applewood chips, soaked in cold water for at least 1 hour

1 medium tomato, seeded and cut into ½-inch (12-mm) dice

⅔ cup (105 g) finely chopped white onion

½ cup (120 ml) mayonnaise

½ cup (75 g) drained and coarsely chopped Pickled Jalapeños (page 181) or store-bought *jalapeños en escabeche* or nacho slices, or more to taste

2 tablespoons fresh lime juice

2 tablespoons finely chopped fresh cilantro

Tortilla chips, for serving

There is no way that you can eat just one of these crunchy and spicy nuts. The seven ingredients in shichimi togarashi have been magically combined to arouse your appetite, and they certainly work their sorcery here. Although I don't have salt in this recipe, you can add a generous sprinkle if you wish. One important tip: Do not drain the warm glazed nuts on paper towels, or they will stick. Be sure to wait until they are cooled, and then spread them on paper towels to remove any excess oil. The cocktail in the photo is the Pisco Sour (page 207).

GLAZED TOGARASHI PECANS

Nueces glaseadas con chile Japonés

2½ cups (500 g) granulated sugar

4 cups (450 g) pecan halves

¾ cup (90 g) confectioners' sugar

Canola oil, for deep-frying

One .63-ounce (18-g) jar shichimi togarashi

MAKES ABOUT 4 CUPS (450 G)

1 Bring the sugar and 2½ cups (600 ml) water to a boil in a large saucepan over high heat, stirring often to be sure that the sugar dissolves. Boil for 1 minute. Add the pecans and return them to a boil. Cook until the pecans soften, about 2 minutes. Drain them well in a colander.

2 Toss the pecans in the colander, sprinkling them with the confectioners' sugar until they are coated. Spread the pecans on a large baking sheet lined with parchment paper and let them dry for at least 2 hours.

3 Pour in enough oil to come one-third up the sides of a large saucepan and heat it over high heat until the oil reaches 350°F (175°C) on a deep-frying thermometer. Line another large rimmed baking sheet with parchment paper.

4 Deep-fry half of the pecans until they turn a shade darker, about 1 minute. (You may want to do a test run with couple of pecans to get the timing right. They should develop a thin glaze, and color lightly, but not burn.) Using a wire spider or slotted spoon, transfer the nuts, letting as much oil as possible drain back into the saucepan, to the parchment paper to drain. Let the oil return to 350°F (175°C) and repeat with the remaining pecans. Let the pecans drain for about 2 minutes; they should be warm and slightly sticky.

5 Transfer the pecans to the unlined baking sheet. Stir the pecans and sprinkle them with the togarashi to coat. Let them cool completely. Store them in an airtight container at room temperature for up to 1 month.

3

ALADS,

BIG

SMALL

CRISPY FRIED CALAMARI SALAD
WITH HABANERO-ORANGE GLAZE

Ensalada de calamar frito con glaseado de naranja y chile habanero

FOR THE HABANERO-ORANGE GLAZE:

5 cups (1.2 L) fresh orange juice, preferably blood orange

2 habanero chilies, seeded and coarsely chopped

1 teaspoon honey, as needed

FOR THE CALAMARI:

1 pound (455 g) cleaned calamari, bodies cut into ½-inch (12-mm) rings, tentacle sections cut in half

1 cup (240 ml) buttermilk

1 cup (130 g) all-purpose flour

2 teaspoons chili powder

1 teaspoon Spanish or Hungarian sweet paprika

1 teaspoon kosher salt

½ teaspoon freshly ground black pepper

½ teaspoon cayenne pepper

Canola oil, for deep-frying

FOR THE SALAD:

¼ cup (60 ml) fresh lime juice

¼ cup (60 ml) avocado or olive oil

Salt

5 ounces (140 g) baby salad greens

1 large navel orange, segmented

½ cup (10 g) coarsely chopped fresh cilantro

1 small red onion, finely chopped

Fried calamari with a spicy dip has got to be one of the most popular appetizers on the planet. Served with a cool green salad, it also makes a claim for fame in the salad department. The sauce is a reduction of fresh oranges and ultra-hot habanero chilies. The flavor and consistency of the reduction will change according to the season, so add sugar if needed to adjust the sweetness or cook it longer for a thicker texture. I like to make this with blood oranges when they are in season, but navel oranges are more readily available and are delicious.

SERVES 4

1 Make the glaze: Bring the orange juice and habaneros to a boil in a medium saucepan over high heat, being sure that the mixture doesn't boil over. Cook until it has reduced to about 1¼ cups (300 ml), about 20 minutes. Let it cool. Taste and adjust the tartness with honey as needed. (The glaze can be covered and refrigerated for up to 2 days.)

2 Make the calamari: Combine the calamari and buttermilk in a medium bowl. Cover and refrigerate them for 30 minutes to 1 hour. Whisk the flour, chili powder, paprika, salt, pepper, and cayenne together in another medium bowl.

3 Position a rack in the center of the oven and preheat the oven to 200°F (90°C). Place a wire cooling rack over a large rimmed baking sheet.

4 Pour in enough oil to come halfway up the sides of a large saucepan and heat it over high heat until the oil reaches 350°F (175°C) on a deep-frying thermometer.

5 Reserve 2 tablespoons of the glaze for the salad dressing. Divide the remaining glaze among four ramekins.

6 Drain the calamari in a colander. In batches, add the calamari to the flour mixture and toss to coat it. Shaking off the excess flour, add the calamari to the oil, and deep-fry until it is golden brown, about 2 minutes. Using a wire spider or slotted spoon, transfer the calamari to the wire cooking rack and keep them warm in the oven while frying the remaining calamari.

7 Make the salad: Whisk the lime juice, reserved orange glaze, and oil together in a large bowl. Season them to taste with salt. Add the salad greens, orange, cilantro, and onion and toss. Divide the salad among four serving bowls, placing the salad on one side of each bowl. Add the calamari to the empty sides of the bowls. Serve immediately, with the glaze alongside for dipping.

This is another interesting green salad that delivers more than expected. The warm avocado is a surprise against the cool greens, and the spicy pico de gallo gets a sweet note from the corn. I guarantee that the grilled avocado will be a subject of conversation as guests discuss how the heat enhances its flavor. If you can find them at an Asian market, substitute pea shoots for the baby salad greens—the shoots' vegetal flavor plays well with the other ingredients.

SERVES 4

1 **Make the dressing:** Whisk together the lime juice, salt, and pepper in a large bowl. Gradually whisk in the oil. Set the bowl aside.

2 **Make the pico de gallo:** Mix the pico de gallo and corn together in a medium bowl and set them aside. (The dressing and pico de gallo can be kept at room temperature for up to 2 hours before serving.)

3 Prepare an outdoor grill for direct cooking over medium-high heat. For a charcoal grill, let the coals burn until they are covered with white ash and you can hold your hand 1 inch (2.5 cm) above the cooking grate for about 3 seconds. For a gas grill, preheat the grill on high and adjust the heat to 450ºF (230ºC).

4 Lightly brush the cut sides of the avocados with the canola oil and season them lightly with salt and pepper. Brush the grill grate clean. Place the avocados on the grill, cut sides down. Cook, with the lid closed, until they are seared with grill marks, 3 to 4 minutes. Turn the avocados over and cook them with the lid closed until the flesh is beginning to shrink away from the skins, about 4 minutes more. Transfer the avocado halves to a cutting board.

5 Protecting your hand from the hot avocado skins with a clean kitchen towel, use a large serving spoon to scoop out the flesh from each half in one piece. Cut each avocado half into four wedges.

6 Add the salad greens to the bowl with the dressing and toss. Divide the salad mixture among four dinner plates. Top each with four avocado wedges and about ½ cup (100 g) of the pico de gallo. Drizzle additional avocado oil over each salad, garnish with a lime wedge or two, and serve.

GRILLED AVOCADO
WITH BABY GREENS & CORN PICO DE GALLO

Aguacate a la parilla con hojas de lechuga y pico de gallo de maíz

FOR THE LIME DRESSING:

3 tablespoons fresh lime juice

½ teaspoon kosher salt

½ teaspoon freshly ground black pepper

1/3 cup plus 1 tablespoon (90 ml) avocado or extra-virgin olive oil, plus more for drizzling

FOR THE CORN PICO DE GALLO:

1 recipe Pico de Gallo (page 179)

½ cup (110 g) roasted corn kernels from 1 small ear of corn (see Note, page 59)

2 ripe but firm Hass avocados, halved lengthwise and pitted, but not peeled

Canola oil, for brushing

Kosher salt

Freshly ground black pepper

5 ounces (140 g) mixed baby greens

Lime wedges, for serving

SOLTERITO OF GREEN VEGETABLES

WITH AVOCADO–WHITE BALSAMIC DRESSING & QUESO FRESCO

Solterito de verduras verdes con aguacate y aderezo de vinagre blanco balsámico y queso fresco

FOR THE AVOCADO–WHITE BALSAMIC DRESSING:

1 ripe Hass avocado, coarsely chopped

¼ cup (60 ml) white balsamic vinegar

¼ cup (60 ml) extra-virgin olive oil

2 tablespoons fresh lime juice

Kosher salt and freshly ground black pepper

1 Persian cucumber, thinly sliced

1 tablespoon white balsamic vinegar

1 chayote, peeled, hard core removed, cut into ½-inch (12-mm) dice

6 ounces (170 g) sugar snap peas, cut into ½-inch (12-mm) pieces, about 2 cups

1 cup (125 g) thawed frozen edamame, lima beans, or fava beans

1 large red-skinned potato, scrubbed but unpeeled, cut into ½-inch (12-mm) dice

2 heads romaine lettuce hearts, coarsely chopped into bite-size pieces

1 Zebra or other tomato, seeded and cut into ¾-inch (2-cm) dice

¼ cup (5 g) thinly sliced fresh mint leaves

Kosher salt and freshly ground black pepper

½ cup (115 g) crumbled queso fresco

Solterito means "little bachelor" in Spanish, and could refer to the way this salad is often tossed together with whatever vegetables are on hand for a quick meal. I've carefully chosen the ingredients here to make a gorgeous all-green salad. Be sure to use a sturdy lettuce, to stand up to the thick, tasty dressing. I purposely make it with white balsamic vinegar, as the standard balsamic darkens the bright color.

SERVES 6

1 Make the dressing: Purée the avocado with ¼ cup (60 ml) water and the vinegar, oil, and lime juice. Season it to taste with salt and pepper. Transfer it to a bowl and cover. (The dressing can be refrigerated for up to 12 hours.)

2 Toss the cucumber and vinegar together in a small bowl, cover, and refrigerate them for 1 to 2 hours to lightly pickle the cucumber. Drain the pickled cucumbers before using.

3 Bring a medium saucepan of salted water to a boil over high heat. Prepare a bowl of ice water. Add the chayote to the pan and cook until it is crisp-tender, about 3 minutes. Using a wire spider or slotted spoon, transfer the chayote to the ice water, leaving the water boiling. Add the peas and edamame to the water and cook until they turn a brighter shade of green, about 1 minute. Using the spider, transfer them to the ice water.

4 Add the potato to the water and return it to a boil. Reduce the heat to medium-low and simmer until the potato is tender but not falling apart, about 12 minutes. Drain and transfer it to the ice water and let it stand for 2 minutes. Drain the vegetable mixture.

5 Toss the lettuce, pickled cucumber, and avocado dressing together in a very large bowl. Add the vegetable mixture, tomato, and mint and toss again. Season the salad to taste with salt and pepper. Sprinkle it with the queso fresco and serve it immediately.

Chile-seasoned food often needs a cool and refreshing side dish to balance the spiciness. This colorful and versatile slaw does the trick with lots of Latin flavors that pair nicely with Mexican main courses.

SLAW

WITH CORN & RADISHES

Col con maíz y rábanos

SERVES 4 TO 6

1 Whisk the lime zest and juice, agave, and garlic together in a large bowl. Gradually whisk in the oil.

2 Add the cabbage, carrots, radishes, scallions, and corn, if using, and toss well. Season the salad to taste with salt and pepper. Cover and refrigerate it for at least 30 minutes and up to 4 hours to blend the flavors before serving.

NOTE Roasting corn on the cob toasts the kernels and brings out their sweetness. One small ear of corn yields about ½ cup (100 g) of kernels. The corn can be roasted on a grill or in a broiler. Prepare an outdoor grill for direct cooking over medium-high heat. For a charcoal grill, let the coals burn until they are covered with white ash and you can hold your hand about 1 inch (2.5 cm) over the grate for about 3 seconds. For a gas grill, preheat the grill on high, then reduce the heat to 450°F (230°C). For a broiler, position the broiler rack about 8 inches (20 cm) from the source of heat and preheat it on high. Husk the corn and remove the silks. Grill (or broil) the corn, turning it occasionally, until some of the kernels are toasted to dark brown, about 10 minutes. Let the cobs cool.

To cut the kernels from the cob, stand the ear on its wide end in a wide bowl. (If you wish, trim the wide end from the cob to give it a steady base.) Using a large sharp knife, cut down the ear where the kernels meet the cob, letting the kernels fall into the bowl.

Trader Joe's sells frozen roasted corn kernels that are a very good substitute for the freshly roasted corn.

Finely grated zest of ½ lime

¼ cup (60 ml) fresh lime juice

2 tablespoons amber agave syrup

2 garlic cloves, minced

⅓ cup (75 ml) olive oil

4 cups (260 g) packed shredded Savoy cabbage (about ½ small head)

2 medium carrots, shredded

6 radishes, shredded

2 scallions (white and green parts), finely chopped

1 cup (220 g) roasted corn kernels (see Note; optional)

Kosher salt and freshly ground black pepper

ROASTED BEETS

WITH ANCHO-HONEY GLAZE & SPICED PECANS

Remolachas asadas con glaseado de chile ancho, miel y nueces

6 medium beets, about 1½ pounds (680 g) total, leaves trimmed, scrubbed but unpeeled

FOR THE ANCHO-HONEY GLAZE:

1 ancho chile, split, seeded, and toasted (see page 23)

Boiling water

⅓ cup plus 2 tablespoons (105 ml) honey

¼ cup (60 ml) sherry vinegar

Kosher salt

½ small red onion, cut into very thin rings

¼ cup (60 ml) red wine vinegar

5 ounces (140 g) baby arugula

1 cup (115 g) crumbled queso fresco or ricotta salata

1 Granny Smith apple, unpeeled and cut into julienne

⅓ cup (40 g) coarsely chopped Glazed Togarashi Pecans (page 53) or store-bought glazed walnuts or pecans

2 tablespoons finely chopped fresh mint leaves

Kosher salt and freshly ground black pepper

This great-looking salad will surprise your palate with every bite, with crunchy glazed nuts, strips of tart apple, crumbles of cheese, and fragrant mint. But the stars of the show are the roasted beets, as their naturally sweet flavor is enhanced by the spicy honey glaze.

SERVES 6

1 **Roast the beets:** Position a rack in the center of the oven and preheat it to 400°F (205°C).

2 Wrap each beet in aluminum foil. Put them on a baking sheet and bake until the beets are tender when pierced with a meat fork, about 1¼ hours, depending on the age of the beets. Unwrap them and let them cool until they are easy to handle. Slip the skins off the warm beets. Let them cool completely. Cover and refrigerate them until chilled, at least 2 hours.

3 **Make the glaze:** Put the chile in a small bowl and add boiling water to cover. Let it stand until the chile softens, about 20 minutes. Purée the chile and 2 tablespoons of its soaking water in a blender. Add the honey and sherry vinegar and process again until smooth. Season the glaze to taste with salt. Transfer it to a bowl, cover, and set aside. (The glaze can be stored at room temperature for up to 6 hours.)

4 Put the onion and wine vinegar in a small bowl, cover, and let them stand for at least 30 minutes and up to 2 hours. Drain well.

5 Spread the arugula on a large platter. Arrange overlapping slices of the beets over the arugula. Drizzle the beets and arugula with the glaze. In this order, top with the cheese, apples, red onion, and pecans, and finish with a sprinkling of mint. Season the salad to taste with salt and pepper. Serve it immediately.

Serve this easy salad alongside grilled meats and poultry. You won't believe how much the roasting brings out the flavors and makes something new out of an old favorite. If you wish, use cilantro instead of the parsley for a stronger Latin note.

■ SERVES 6 ■

1 Position a rack in the center of the oven and preheat it to 425°F (220°C).

2 Toss the potatoes and corn with about 1 tablespoon oil on a rimmed baking sheet. Transfer the corn to a plate; set aside. Season the potatoes with 1 teaspoon salt. Roast, turning the potatoes occasionally, for 20 minutes. Add the corn to the baking sheet and continue roasting, turning everything occasionally, until the vegetables are tender, about 15 minutes more. Let them cool. Cut the kernels from the cobs and set them aside.

3 Transfer the potatoes and corn kernels to a medium bowl. Sprinkle them with the lime juice. Add the mayonnaise, parsley, and jalapeño and mix well. Season the salad to taste with salt and pepper. Cover and refrigerate it to blend the flavors, at least 1 hour or overnight. Remove it from the refrigerator and let it stand at room temperature for 30 minutes before serving.

ROASTED
FINGERLING
&
CORN
SALAD

Papas fingerling asadas con ensalada de maíz

2 pounds (910 g) fingerling potatoes, scrubbed but unpeeled

2 ears corn, husked

Olive oil

Kosher salt

2 tablespoons fresh lime juice

⅓ cup (75 ml) mayonnaise

2 tablespoons finely chopped fresh flat-leaf parsley or cilantro

2 tablespoons seeded and minced jalapeño

Freshly ground black pepper

The concept of grilled romaine hearts can seem counterintuitive, as we are so used to the idea of chilled lettuce for salad. But give this a try—the grill's heat brings out the sweetness in the lettuce, which is balanced by a tart buttermilk dressing.

SERVES 6

1 **Make the dressing:** Purée the mayonnaise, buttermilk, cilantro, jalapeño, lime juice, vinegar, celery seeds, onion powder, garlic powder, and pepper together in a blender. Season the dressing to taste with salt. Transfer it to a covered container and refrigerate until it is chilled, at least 1 hour.

2 Prepare an outdoor grill for direct cooking over medium-high heat. For a charcoal grill, let the coals burn until they are covered with white ash and you can hold your hand about 1 inch (2.5 cm) above the cooking grate for about 3 seconds. For a gas grill, preheat it on high and adjust the heat to 450°F (230°C).

3 Brush the lettuce halves all over with olive oil. Brush the grill grate clean. Place the lettuce halves on the grill. Cook, turning them occasionally, just until they are lightly browned and wilted, 4 to 6 minutes. Transfer them to a platter.

4 Pour about one-third of the dressing over the lettuce leaves. Top with the corn, tomatoes, and onion. Sprinkle with the cilantro and serve the salad immediately, with the remaining dressing passed on the side. (Leftover dressing can be refrigerated for up to 3 days.)

GRILLED
ROMAINE HEARTS
WITH CILANTRO RANCH DRESSING

Corazones de lechuga romana asadas con aderezo cilantro ranch

FOR THE CILANTRO RANCH DRESSING:

1¼ cups (300 ml) mayonnaise

½ cup (120 ml) buttermilk

½ cup (10 g) packed fresh cilantro leaves

1 jalapeño or serrano chile, seeded and coarsely chopped

2 tablespoons fresh lime juice

2 tablespoons red wine vinegar

1 teaspoon celery seeds

1 teaspoon onion powder

½ teaspoon garlic powder

½ teaspoon freshly ground black pepper

Kosher salt

3 romaine hearts, each cut in half lengthwise

Olive oil, for brushing

1 cup (145 g) fresh or grilled (see page 59) corn kernels

2 plum tomatoes, cut into ½-inch (12-mm) dice

½ medium white onion, thinly sliced

Chopped fresh cilantro, for garnish

HOUSE SALAD

WITH CHIPOTLE-BALSAMIC DRESSING, GOAT CHEESE & DRIED CRANBERRIES

Ensalada de la casa con aderezo de vinagre balsámico con chipotle, queso de cabra, y arándanos secos

FOR THE CHIPOTLE-BALSAMIC DRESSING:

1 canned chipotle chile in adobo, with clinging sauce

1 tablespoon balsamic vinegar

1 tablespoon rice vinegar

1 tablespoon fresh lemon juice

1 tablespoon honey

1 tablespoon soy sauce

1 tablespoon dark sesame oil

½ cup (120 ml) olive oil

Kosher salt and freshly ground black pepper

10 ounces (280 g) mixed baby greens

¾ cup (85 g) crumbled goat cheese

½ cup (70 g) dried cranberries

½ cup (70 g) slivered almonds, toasted (see page 43)

Whenever I serve this salad dressing, guests always chime in with compliments. The secret is a combination of rice vinegar, balsamic vinegar, and lemon juice instead of just the single note of one acidic ingredient. It is worth making in a double batch and storing in the refrigerator for a couple of nights' worth of green salads.

SERVES 6

1 **Make the dressing:** Purée the chipotle, balsamic and rice vinegars, lemon juice, honey, soy sauce, and sesame oil in a blender. With the blender running, slowly pour in the olive oil through the hole in the lid. Season the dressing to taste with salt and pepper. (The dressing can be refrigerated in a covered container for up to 1 week. Whisk it well before using.)

2 Toss the greens and dressing together in a large bowl. Add the cheese, cranberries, and almonds. Toss again. Divide the salad equally among six salad plates and serve it immediately.

We may treat tomatoes and avocados like vegetables, but they are fruits, and this salad uses them with other ingredients for a very interesting summer dish for your outdoor barbecue. Browned panela is a nice touch, but if you can't find that cheese, just add coarsely crumbled ricotta salata or sliced fresh (preferably imported buffalo-milk) mozzarella to the salad, and skip the browning.

SERVES 6 TO 8

1 **Make the dressing:** Bring the vinegar, syrup, lime zest and juice, and tequila to a simmer in a small saucepan. Let them cool. Combine the vinegar mixture and papaya purée in a blender. With the machine running, gradually add the oil through the hole in the lid to make an emulsified dressing. Season the dressing to taste with salt and pepper.

2 **Make the salad:** Heat a medium nonstick skillet over medium heat. Add the cheese and cook until it is seared light brown on the underside, about 1 minute. Turn and sear the other side for 1 minute more. Transfer it to a plate and let it cool. Chop the cheese into ¼-inch (6-mm) dice.

3 Purée the avocado and crema together in a blender. Transfer them to a bowl and season to taste with salt and pepper. (The dressing, cheese, and avocado crema can be separately covered and refrigerated for up to 1 day.)

4 Toss the apple strips with the lime juice. Spread the avocado crema in the center of a large serving platter. Arrange the watercress around the edge of the platter. Arrange overlapping and alternating slices of the tomato and watermelon over the crema. Sprinkle them with the cheese, apple, and onion. Drizzle some of the dressing on top. Serve the salad immediately, with the remaining dressing passed on the side.

HEIRLOOM TOMATO & WATERMELON SALAD
WITH PAPAYA-TEQUILA DRESSING

Ensalada de jitomate y sandía con aderezo de papaya y tequila

FOR THE PAPAYA-TEQUILA DRESSING:

¼ cup (60 ml) cider vinegar

¼ cup (60 ml) agave syrup

Finely grated zest of ½ lime

¼ cup (60 ml) fresh lime juice

2 tablespoons tequila reposado

⅔ cup (165 ml) fresh or thawed frozen papaya purée

½ cup (120 ml) canola oil

Kosher salt and freshly ground black pepper

FOR THE SALAD:

One ½-inch (12-mm) slice round panela (cut crosswise from an entire cheese)

1 ripe Hass avocado, coarsely chopped

2 tablespoons crema or sour cream

Kosher salt and freshly ground black pepper

1 Granny Smith apple, cut into julienne

1 tablespoon fresh lime juice or cider vinegar

One 6-ounce (170-g) bunch watercress, tough stems removed

4 large heirloom tomatoes, cut into ¼-inch (6-mm) rounds

½ seedless baby watermelon, peeled and cut into ¼-inch (6-mm) wedges

2 tablespoons finely chopped red onion

4

CEVICHE & TIRADITOS

A ceviche in the classic Peruvian style, this is marinated in a mixture of fish broth (or clam juice) and lime called *leche de tigre* ("tiger milk"). The Incas actually preserved fish in citrus juice, although today the fish is prepared this way simply because it tastes good.

SERVES 4

1 **Make the sweet potatoes:** Combine all of the ingredients in a small saucepan, being sure the liquid covers the sweet potatoes. Bring them to a boil over high heat. Reduce the heat to medium-low and simmer until the sweet potatoes are almost tender, about 15 minutes. Remove the pan from the heat and let the sweet potatoes cool in the liquid. Drain and cut the sweet potatoes into ½-inch (12-mm) dice. Transfer them to a bowl and cover. (The sweet potatoes can be stored at room temperature for up to 4 hours.)

2 **Make the ceviche:** Process the clam juice, lime juice, celery, 1 tablespoon of the cilantro, and the garlic in a blender to finely chop the celery. Strain the mixture through a wire sieve into a medium bowl. Cover and refrigerate the liquid until chilled, at least 1 hour.

3 Add the sea bass to the juice mixture and mix well. Using a slotted spoon, divide the fish slices among four chilled dinner plates with rims. Add the onion, chile, and remaining 2 tablespoons cilantro to the juice mixture in the bowl and mix again. Divide the juice mixture with the solids over each serving. Garnish with the sweet potatoes and choclo. (Or, if you wish, toss the ingredients together and serve family style.) Serve chilled.

NOTE Choclo is a large-kernel variety of Peruvian corn. You'll find it frozen in Latin markets. Cook the choclo in lightly salted boiling water until it is heated through, about 5 minutes, then drain and rinse it under cold running water. Let it cool before using it for ceviche. If you wish, substitute standard corn kernels, cut from the cob, and boil them for 3 minutes.

CLASSIC CEVICHE

WITH SEA BASS, GLAZED SWEET POTATOES & PERUVIAN CORN

Ceviche clásico de robalo con batatas glaseadas y choclo

FOR THE GLAZED SWEET POTATOES:

1 medium sweet potato, peeled and cut into ½-inch (12-mm) rounds

1 cup (240 ml) fresh orange juice

¼ cup (50 g) sugar

1 tablespoon fresh lime juice

1 star anise

One 1½-inch (4-cm) piece cinnamon stick

FOR THE CEVICHE:

½ cup (120 ml) bottled clam juice

¼ cup (60 ml) fresh lime juice

¼ celery rib, coarsely chopped

3 tablespoons chopped fresh cilantro

½ garlic clove, sliced

1 pound (455 g) skinless sea bass or corvina fillet, cut into ¾-inch (2-cm) chunks

½ small red onion, cut into thin half-moons

1 Fresno or jalapeño chile, seeded and minced

1 cup (130 g) chilled cooked choclo (see Note)

STRIPED BASS TIRADITO

WITH PONZU, APPLE & RADISH

Tiradito de lubina rayada con salsa ponzu, manzana y rábano

½ Granny Smith apple, peeled

2 large radishes, trimmed

14 ounces (400 g) skinless striped bass, cut on a diagonal into ¼-inch (6-mm) slices

½ cup (120 ml) Ponzu, homemade (page 48) or store-bought, chilled

Finely grated zest of 1 large lemon

Sriracha, for serving

A tiradito is the South American version of ceviche, and it often has Asian influences, such as the ponzu in this recipe. It is one of the lightest (and quickest) first courses you'll ever make, yet at the same time, it is one of the most flavorful. There are many good brands for sale, but it is also easy to make your own (page 48), and it is worth the minimal effort for this recipe, where it plays such a big role.

SERVES 4

1 Just before serving, use a V-slicer or mandoline to cut the apple and radishes into julienne. (You can also use a chef's knife.) Combine them in a small bowl.

2 For each serving, fan the bass on a chilled serving plate with a rim. Spoon 2 tablespoons of the ponzu around, but not on, the bass. Top each with one-quarter of the apple mixture and the grated lemon zest. Serve immediately, with the Sriracha on the side.

You'll recognize this as the ceviche that most people are familiar with, consisting of raw fish and citrus juice with a spark of chile heat. Mahi mahi is a good choice, or try red snapper, sea bass, or tuna instead. The important thing is that it is sparkling fresh and bought from the best fish market in your area.

━━━━━━━━━━ SERVES 4 ━━━━━━━━━━

1 Mix the mahi, lime juice, and ½ teaspoon salt in a medium nonreactive bowl. Refrigerate it until the mahi loses its translucent look, about 20 minutes. Stir the onion, tomato, cilantro, and minced chile into the mahi mixture. Season it to taste with black pepper.

2 Mix 1 teaspoon salt and the ground chile together in a small bowl.

3 Divide the mahi mixture and its liquid among four serving bowls. Garnish each serving with avocado slices and sprinkle them with the chipotle salt. Serve the ceviche cold, with the tortilla chips.

MEXICAN-STYLE MAHI MAHI CEVICHE

WITH TOMATO, CUCUMBER & CHILE

Ceviche de mahi mahi estilo Mexicano con tomate, pepino y chile

14 ounces (400 g) skinless mahi mahi fillets, cut into ¾-inch (2-cm) chunks

½ cup (120 ml) fresh lemon juice

Kosher salt

½ medium white onion, finely chopped

1 ripe plum tomato, seeded and cut into ¼-inch (6-mm) dice

3 tablespoons chopped fresh cilantro leaves

1 serrano or ½ jalapeño chile, seeded and minced

Freshly ground black pepper

¼ teaspoon pure ground chipotle chile

1 ripe Hass avocado, sliced

Tortilla or yuca chips, for serving

AHI TUNA CEVICHE
IN MOLE VERDE BROTH

*Ceviche de atún en
caldo de mole verde*

FOR THE ADOBO PEPITAS:

1 teaspoon sugar

1 teaspoon pure ground ancho chile

½ teaspoon ground cumin

¼ teaspoon fennel seed, ground

Large pinch of cayenne pepper

1 teaspoon canola oil

½ cup (60 g) skinned pepitas
(pumpkin seeds)

Kosher salt

FOR THE MOLE VERDE BROTH:

½ cup (120 g) Mole Verde (page 180)

½ cup (120 ml) extra-virgin olive oil

½ ripe Hass avocado, coarsely chopped

Finely grated zest of 1 lime

¼ cup (60 ml) fresh lime juice

¼ cup (60 ml) rice vinegar

¼ cup (5 g) packed fresh cilantro leaves

2 teaspoons honey

Kosher salt

12 ounces (340 g) sushi-grade ahi tuna,
cut into ¾-inch (2-cm) chunks

1 ripe mango, cut into ½-inch (12-mm) dice

½ small red onion, thinly sliced into half-
moons

1 jalapeño or serrano chile, seeded
and minced

2 tablespoons finely chopped fresh cilantro

Lime wedges, for serving

Hot chili-sesame oil, for serving

Plantain chips, for serving

The adage about eating with our eyes will be confirmed in spades when you serve this high-style dish to your guests. The deep pink tuna against the bright green mole sauce looks beautiful and is matched by the flavor. When you are looking for a real showstopper of a first course, consider this. Make the individual components ahead of time, and the final assembly takes only a few minutes.

SERVES 4

1 Make the pepitas: Combine the sugar, ancho chile, cumin, fennel, and cayenne in a small bowl. Heat the oil in a medium nonstick skillet over medium heat. Add the pepitas and cook, stirring often, until they begin to brown, about 2 minutes. Sprinkle the pepitas with the sugar mixture and cook, stirring often, just until the spices smell toasted, about 30 seconds. Transfer the pepitas to a small plate. Season them to taste with salt.

2 Make the broth: Purée the mole with the oil, ½ cup (120 ml) water, the avocado, lime zest and juice, vinegar, cilantro, and honey in a blender. Season it to taste with salt. Transfer the mixture to a bowl, cover, and refrigerate until it is chilled, at least 1 hour or up to 2 days.

3 Combine the tuna, mango, onion, jalapeño, cilantro, and ¼ cup (30 g) of the pepitas in a large bowl. Add the mole verde broth and toss.

4 Divide the ceviche mixture and the broth among four soup bowls. Garnish each serving with lime wedges, drizzle with the chili oil, and sprinkle with the remaining pepitas. Serve them immediately, with the plantain chips.

This excellent ceviche shows why Nikkei (the name given to the first wave of Japanese immigrants to Peru) cuisine is so fascinating. When I serve it, my guests can't quite pinpoint the flavors, but they all agree that the dish is delicious. It has the traditional Peruvian garnish of sweet potatoes and choclo (large corn kernels), but regular corn works well, too.

SERVES 4

1 **Make the broth:** Process the clam juice, yuzu juice, celery, ponzu, cilantro, sesame oil, garlic, and ice cubes in a blender and pulse to chop the ice cubes. Strain the mixture into a medium bowl.

2 Add the tuna, scallions, avocado, cucumber, onion, cilantro, and ginger to the broth and mix well. Season the ceviche to taste with salt.

3 Divide the tuna mixture and its broth among four serving bowls. Garnish each bowl with two sweet-potato slices and one-quarter of the choclo, and finish with a sprinkling of furikake. Serve it immediately.

PERUVIAN DINNER MENU

Pisco Sours (PAGE 207)

Crispy Shrimp with Ají Amarillo Sauce (PAGE 31)

Striped Bass Tiradito with Ponzu, Apple, & Radish (PAGE 72)

Chicken Skewers with Nikkei Glaze (PAGE 108)

Steamed Quinoa

Chilean Riesling

Piloncillo Pots de Crème (PAGE 170)

TUNA CEVICHE NIKKEI
WITH YUZU BROTH

Ceviche de tuna Nikkei en caldo de yuzu

FOR THE CEVICHE NIKKEI BROTH:

⅓ cup (75 ml) bottled clam juice

⅓ cup (75 ml) bottled yuzu juice or fresh lime juice

¼ celery rib, coarsely chopped

2 tablespoons Ponzu, homemade (page 48) or store-bought

2 teaspoons chopped fresh cilantro

1 teaspoon Asian sesame oil

½ garlic clove, peeled

2 ice cubes

12 ounces (340 g) sushi-grade ahi tuna, cut into ¾-inch (2-cm) chunks

2 scallions (white and green parts), julienned

1 ripe Hass avocado, cut into ½-inch (12-mm) dice

¼ seedless cucumber, cut into ½-inch (12-mm) dice

½ small red onion, finely chopped

2 tablespoons finely chopped fresh cilantro

1 tablespoon finely chopped pickled ginger (optional)

Kosher salt

8 slices glazed sweet potato (see page 71)

1 cup (130 g) cooked and chilled choclo (see Note, page 71)

Furikake or puffed rice cereal, for garnish

TUNA TIRADITO

WITH LEMON-WASABI DRESSING & AVOCADO

Tiradito de atún con aderezo de limón y wasabi con aguacate

FOR THE TUNA:

2 tablespoons shichimi togarashi

2 teaspoons kosher salt

12 ounces (340 g) sushi-grade ahi tuna, cut in half lengthwise across the grain

FOR THE LEMON-WASABI DRESSING:

½ cup (120 ml) canola oil

2 tablespoons coarsely chopped shallot

2 teaspoons wasabi powder

⅓ cup (75 ml) soy sauce

3 tablespoons sugar

3 tablespoons rice vinegar

2 tablespoons fresh lemon juice

1 tablespoon mirin

2 teaspoons peeled, micro-grated fresh ginger

1 teaspoon bottled yuzu juice or fresh lime juice

5 ounces (140 g) mixed spring greens

1 ripe Hass avocado, sliced

3 tablespoons coarsely chopped fresh cilantro

Kosher salt

1 scallion (white and green parts), very thinly sliced

1 piece peeled fresh ginger, for micro-grating as garnish

This tiradito is almost a main-course salad, with slices of seared tuna served on a bed of mixed baby greens. The Japanese-inspired dressing has a little heat from the wasabi, and is a great vinaigrette to add to your repertoire to serve on other salads. Because this tiradito is such a good option for a summer lunch, I suggest serving it on a platter instead of in individual portions.

SERVES 4

1 **Make the tuna:** Mix the togarashi and salt together on a plate. Roll the tuna pieces in the spice mixture to coat them completely.

2 Heat a large dry nonstick skillet over high heat. Add the tuna and cook, turning it occasionally, just until it is seared on all sides but still raw inside, about 2 minutes. Transfer it to a plate, cover loosely with plastic wrap, and refrigerate it until chilled, at least 2 hours.

3 **Make the dressing:** Heat 1 tablespoon of the oil in a small skillet over medium heat. Add the shallot and cook, stirring often, until it is browned, about 3 minutes. Transfer it to a blender. Mix the wasabi and 1 tablespoon water together in a small bowl to dissolve the wasabi. Add them to the blender with the soy sauce, sugar, vinegar, lemon juice, mirin, ginger, and yuzu juice and process until everything is smooth. With the machine running, pour the remaining 7 tablespoons (105 ml) oil through the hole in the blender lid to make an emulsified dressing. (The dressing can be refrigerated in a covered container for up to 2 days.)

4 To serve, toss the greens, avocado, and cilantro with ½ cup (120 ml) of the dressing. Transfer the salad to a large serving platter. Sprinkle the scallions on the salad. On a cutting board, cut the tuna across the grain into slices about ¼ inch (6 mm) thick. Arrange the tuna on the salad. Drizzle about 2 tablespoons more of the dressing over the tuna. Top the tuna with a few gratings of fresh ginger. Serve it immediately, with the remaining dressing passed on the side.

Here is another cooked ceviche, and this one has three different kinds of seafood and a trio of citrus for a combination of colors, flavors, and textures. A fourth kind of fish, dried bonito flakes (an essential ingredient in Japanese cooking), can be sprinkled on top as a garnish. This ceviche should be served bracingly cold, so have all of the components well chilled before assembly. It makes six servings, so it is a good choice for a larger dinner party.

SEAFOOD CEVICHE
WITH THREE CITRUS & HEARTS OF PALM

Ceviche de mariscos en un trío de cítricos y palmitos

████████████ SERVES 6 ████████████

1 **Make the seafood.** Bring 2 quarts (2 L) salted water and the lemon rounds to a boil in a large saucepan over high heat. Add the calamari, shrimp, and scallops and cook (the water does not have to return to a boil) just until they turn opaque, about 2 minutes. Drain the seafood in a colander. Let it cool until tepid. Transfer it to a bowl, cover tightly, and refrigerate until it is chilled, at least 2 hours and up to 1 day (you can keep it for 1 day).

2 **Make the sauce:** Whisk together the orange zest and juice, lime juice, lemon juice, sugar, honey, ají panca paste, and yuzu juice and chili-garlic paste, if using, in a medium bowl to dissolve the sugar. Add the tomatoes. Cover and refrigerate until the sauce is chilled, at least 1 and up to 4 hours.

3 Add the chilled seafood, orange segments, hearts of palm, corn kernels, and chile to the sauce and mix gently. Divide the seafood mixture and its sauce among six chilled serving bowls. Sprinkle each with cilantro and scallions. Serve the seafood chilled.

FOR THE SEAFOOD:

Kosher salt

1 lemon, cut into thick rounds

8 ounces (225 g) cleaned calamari bodies, cut into ¼-inch (6-mm) rings

8 ounces (225 g) extra-large (26 to 30 count) shrimp, peeled and deveined, tails removed

8 ounces (225 g) bay scallops

FOR THE SAUCE:

Finely grated zest of 1 orange

½ cup (120 ml) fresh orange juice

⅓ cup (75 ml) fresh lime juice

2 tablespoons fresh lemon juice

2 tablespoons sugar

2 tablespoons honey

1 tablespoon ají panca paste, or 1½ teaspoons adobo from canned chipotles in adobo

1 tablespoon bottled yuzu juice (optional)

1 teaspoon Chinese chili-garlic paste or Sriracha (optional)

2 plum tomatoes, seeded and cut into ½-inch (12-mm) dice

1 navel orange, cut into segments

One 14-ounce (400-g) can hearts of palm, drained and cut into ¼-inch (6-mm) rounds

1 ear corn, roasted (see Note, page 59), kernels cut from the cob

1 serrano or jalapeño chile, cut into thin rings

Chopped fresh cilantro, for serving

1 scallion, thinly sliced for serving

There isn't a rule that says ceviche must be made with raw fish, and this one—truly a crowd-pleaser—is made with cooked shrimp. It shows the kind of high-flavor cooking that I like to serve to my guests, and if one of them is an unadventurous eater who doesn't like raw fish, I'll make this and everyone will rest easy. Tomatoes, oranges, and habanero chilies are an amazingly refreshing combination, and really create the perfect appetizer to excite the palate.

SERVES 4

1 **Make the shrimp:** Bring 2 quarts (2 L) salted water and the lemon slices to a boil in a large saucepan over high heat. Add the shrimp and cook until they turn opaque, about 3 minutes. Drain and rinse them under cold running water. Transfer them to a bowl and refrigerate until they are chilled, at least 1 hour and up to 1 day.

2 **Make the broth:** Process the orange zest and juice, lemon juice, tomato, onion, garlic, habanero, and honey in a blender until smooth. With the blender running, gradually pour the oil through the hole in the lid to make an emulsified broth. Season it to taste with salt. Pour it into a medium nonreactive bowl, cover, and refrigerate until it is chilled, at least 2 hours and up to 1 day. Whisk the broth well before using.

3 To serve, stir the shrimp, avocado, tomato, orange, and cilantro into the broth. Divide the shrimp and broth equally among four wide soup bowls. Top each with three pickled onion rings and serve them immediately.

SHRIMP CEVICHE
WITH TOMATO-HABANERO BROTH

Ceviche de camarón con caldo de tomate y habanero

FOR THE SHRIMP:

Kosher salt

1 large lemon, sliced

1 pound (455 g) extra-large (26 to 30 count) peeled and deveined shrimp, tails removed

FOR THE TOMATO-HABANERO BROTH:

Grated zest of ½ orange

⅔ cup (165 ml) fresh orange juice

½ cup (120 ml) fresh lemon juice

1 ripe plum tomato, seeded and coarsely chopped

3 tablespoons chopped yellow onion

1 small garlic clove, coarsely chopped

½ habanero chile, seeded and coarsely chopped

2 tablespoons honey

½ cup (120 ml) canola oil

Kosher salt

1 ripe Hass avocado, cut into ½-inch (12-mm) dice

1 small plum tomato, seeded and cut into ½-inch (12-mm) dice

1 navel orange, cut into segments, each segment cut in half

2 tablespoons chopped fresh cilantro

12 Pickled Red Onions (page 182) or raw red onion rings

5
SEAFOO

Miso has become a popular marinade for rich, oily fish, such as the black cod that I use here—it's also excellent with salmon. But this dish also has the sweet and savory flavors from the kabayaki glaze and lemon aïoli. The fish is finished off with garnishes of the glaze and aïoli, so you'll need two plastic squeeze bottles.

SERVES 4

1 Make the kabayaki sauce: Bring 1½ cups (360 ml) water, the sake, soy sauce, sugar, and mirin to a boil in a medium saucepan over high heat. Reduce the heat to low and simmer, stirring often to be sure the sugary mixture does not burn, until it is reduced by about three-quarters and thickened into a syrup, about 20 minutes. Remove it from the heat and let the sauce cool. (The sauce will thicken more as it cools.) The kabayaki sauce can be refrigerated for up to 1 week.

2 Make the marinade: Purée the miso, sugar, mirin, sake, and chipotles in a blender. Pour them into a 1-gallon (3.8-L) zip-top plastic bag. Add the cod and seal the bag. Refrigerate it, turning the bag occasionally, for at least 4 hours or overnight.

3 Make the togarashi aïoli: Whisk the mayonnaise, togarashi, sake, lemon juice, and garlic together in a medium bowl. Season them to taste with salt and pepper.

4 Position a broiler rack about 8 inches (20 cm) from the source of heat and preheat the broiler on high. If the broiler is in the oven, position an oven rack in the center of the oven. Otherwise, preheat a separate oven to 500°F (260°C).

5 Toss the asparagus with the oil on a large rimmed baking sheet. Spread the asparagus in a single layer in the pan.

6 Remove the cod from the marinade and discard the marinade. Oil the broiler rack. Add the cod, skinned-side up. Broil until it is lightly browned, about 4 minutes. Turn it skinned-side down and continue cooking for 2 minutes. Brush it with the glaze until the flesh looks barely opaque when pierced in the thickest part with the tip of a knife, 8 to 10 minutes. During the last 5 minutes of cooking, add the asparagus and cook, turning it occasionally, until it is crisp-tender. Remove the cod and asparagus from the oven.

7 For each serving, transfer a cod fillet to a dinner plate. Remove any protruding bones, if necessary. Spoon the aïoli and kabayaki sauce over the fillets. Add the asparagus. Sprinkle the chives over each plate and serve immediately.

MISO BLACK COD
WITH LEMON-TOGARASHI AÏOLI

Bacalao con alioli de limón y chile Japonés

FOR THE KABAYAKI SAUCE:

¾ cup (180 ml) Junmai-shu sake, such as Gekkeikan Traditional

¾ cup (180 ml) soy sauce

¾ cup (150 g) sugar

7 tablespoons (105 ml) mirin

FOR THE CHIPOTLE-MISO MARINADE AND BLACK COD:

⅓ cup (100 g) white miso

¼ cup (50 g) sugar

2 tablespoons mirin

2 tablespoons sake

2 canned chipotle chilies in adobo, with clinging sauce

Four 6-ounce (170-g) skinless black cod or center-cut salmon fillets

FOR THE LEMON-TOGARASHI AÏOLI:

½ cup (120 ml) mayonnaise, preferably Kewpie

2 teaspoons shichimi togarashi

2 teaspoons sake

1½ teaspoons fresh lemon juice

1 garlic clove, very finely minced

Kosher salt and freshly ground black pepper

1½ pounds (680 g) asparagus, woody stems snapped off, stalks peeled with a vegetable peeler

1 tablespoon extra-virgin olive oil

2 tablespoons thinly sliced fresh chives

GRILLED MAHI MAHI TACOS

WITH POBLANO TARTAR SAUCE

Tacos de mahi-mahi con salsa tártara de chile poblano

FOR THE POBLANO TARTAR SAUCE:

1 cup (240 ml) mayonnaise

1 poblano chile, roasted, seeded, and cut into ½-inch (12-mm) dice

Finely grated zest of ½ lime

1 tablespoon fresh lime juice

1 garlic clove, minced

FOR THE LEMON-ACHIOTE MARINADE AND MAHI MAHI:

½ cup (120 ml) mayonnaise

¼ cup (60 ml) fresh lemon juice

1½ tablespoons Achiote (page 183) or store-bought *condimento de achiote* (see Note; optional)

1 teaspoon honey

Kosher salt and freshly ground black pepper

1½ pounds (680 g) skinless mahi mahi fillets

FOR THE FISH TACO SLAW:

2 cups (130 g) packed shredded green cabbage

2 tablespoons finely chopped fresh cilantro

1 tablespoon fresh lime juice

The classic fish taco hails from Baja, California, where most versions are battered and deep-fried. They are good in their own way, but I prefer this recipe with marinated and grilled mahi mahi. A perforated grill pan will help keep the fish fillets from sticking to the grate. This recipe is also great with other firm fish fillets, such as snapper, grouper, or striped bass.

SERVES 4 TO 6

1 **Make the tartar sauce:** Mix the mayonnaise, chile, lime zest and juice, and garlic together in a small bowl. Cover and refrigerate the sauce for at least 1 hour and up to 3 days.

2 **Make the marinade:** Whisk the mayonnaise, lemon juice, achiote, if using, and honey together in a medium bowl. Season them to taste with salt and pepper. Transfer the marinade to a 1-gallon (3.8-L) zip-top plastic bag and add the mahi. Refrigerate it, turning the bag occasionally, for at least 2 hours and up to 1 day.

3 **Make the slaw:** Mix the cabbage, cilantro, and lime juice together in a medium bowl. Season them to taste with salt and pepper. Cover and refrigerate the slaw for no longer than 1 hour, or it will lose its crispness.

4 Meanwhile, prepare an outdoor grill for direct cooking over medium-high heat. For a charcoal grill, let the coals burn until they are covered with white ash and you can hold your hand about 1 inch (2.5 cm) above the cooking grate for 2 to 3 seconds. For a gas grill, preheat it on high and adjust the heat to 450°F (230°C). Heat a perforated grill pan on the grate.

5 Remove the mahi from the marinade, letting the marinade cling to the fish. Place the mahi on the grill. Cook it, with the lid closed as much as possible, until the underside of the mahi is browned and releases easily from the grate, about 3 minutes. Turn the mahi over and cook to brown the other side, about 3 minutes more. Transfer it to a cutting board and tent it with aluminum foil to keep warm.

6 Remove the grill pan and quickly brush the grill grates clean. Place the tortillas on the grill and cook, turning them occasionally, until they are lightly browned on both sides and heated through, about 1 minute. Transfer them to a napkin-lined bowl and wrap them in the napkin to keep warm.

7 Put the avocado slices and lime wedges in separate bowls. Cut the mahi across the grain into ½-inch (12-mm) slices and transfer them to a bowl. Put the bowls of fish, tortillas, tartar sauce, avocado, and the cabbage mixture on the table. Let each person make a taco, adding the fish, sauce, cabbage, and avocado to a tortilla, folding it in half. Eat them immediately, with a squeeze of lime juice.

NOTE If you wish, substitute 1 tablespoon tomato paste, 1 minced garlic clove, ¼ teaspoon ground cumin, ¼ teaspoon ground black pepper, and a pinch of ground cloves for the achiote.

Kosher salt and freshly ground black pepper

Twelve 6-inch (15-cm) flour tortillas

1 ripe Hass avocado, thinly sliced

Lime wedges, for serving

ACHIOTE SALMON

WITH
CHIPOTLE AÏOLI

*Salmón con achiote
y alioli de chipotle*

**FOR THE ACHIOTE-PONZU
BROTH:**

½ cup (120 ml) fresh orange juice

2 tablespoons Achiote (page 183)
or store-bought *condimento
de achiote*

One 3-inch (7.5-cm) square piece of
kombu (dried seaweed for cooking),
rinsed under cold water

¼ cup (60 ml) mirin

¼ cup (60 ml) Ponzu, homemade
(page 48) or store-bought

Kosher salt

**FOR THE CHAYOTE-MUSHROOM
SAUTÉ:**

2 slices bacon, cut into 1-inch (2.5-cm)
lengths

2 tablespoons canola oil

8 ounces (225 g) cremini mushrooms,
thinly sliced

1 chayote, hard center trimmed, cut
into julienne (use a mandoline, V-slicer,
or large knife)

Kosher salt and freshly ground black
pepper

The aïoli for this requires the Achiote on page 183, but this is exactly the kind of interesting dish with unusual ingredient that will have your guests wondering about the source of the delicious flavors.

███████████████ SERVES 4 ███████

1 **Make the broth:** Process the orange juice and achiote together in a blender until smooth. Set them aside.

2 Bring ½ cup (120 ml) water to a boil in a medium saucepan over high heat. Remove it from the heat, add the kombu, and let it stand for 30 minutes. Strain the mixture through a wire sieve into a bowl, discarding the kombu. Rinse out the saucepan and return the liquid to the saucepan. Add the mirin, ponzu, and the reserved orange juice mixture and bring them to a simmer over medium heat. Season the broth to taste with salt. (The broth can be cooled, covered, and refrigerated for up to 3 hours. Reheat it gently without boiling before serving.)

3 **Make the sauté:** Cook the bacon in a medium skillet over medium heat, stirring it occasionally, until it is crisp and browned, about 8 minutes. Using a slotted spoon, transfer the bacon to paper towels to drain. Discard the bacon fat and wipe out the skillet.

4 Heat 1 tablespoon of the oil in the skillet over medium heat. Add the mushrooms and cook, stirring often, until they are beginning to brown, about 8 minutes. Transfer them to a bowl. (The bacon and mushrooms can be stored at room temperature for up to 2 hours.)

5 **Make the marinade:** Process the achiote, Sriracha, vinegar, ginger, garlic, and ¼ cup (60 ml) water together in a blender until smooth. Put the salmon in a nonreactive baking dish and add the marinade. Cover it with plastic wrap and refrigerate it for at least 30 minutes and up to 1 hour.

6 **To finish the sauté:** Heat the remaining 1 tablespoon oil in the skillet over medium-high heat. Add the chayote and cook, stirring it occasionally, until it is crisp-tender, about 3 minutes. Return the mushrooms and bacon to the skillet and cook, stirring them often, until they are heated through, about 1 minute more. Season the sauté to taste with salt and pepper. Remove it from the heat and cover it, with the lid ajar, to keep warm.

7 Meanwhile, to cook the salmon, position a broiler rack about 6 inches (15 cm) from the source of heat and preheat the broiler on high. Lightly oil the broiler pan.

8 Remove the salmon from the marinade and place it on the broiler pan. Broil until the top of the salmon turns opaque, about 3 minutes. Turn the salmon over and cook it until the top is turning opaque, about 3 minutes more. Remove the broiler pan from the oven and pipe random zigzags of the aïoli across the top of the salmon. Return it to the broiler and cook until the aïoli is browned, about 1 minute more.

9 To serve, divide the chayote mixture among four deep, wide soup bowls. Top each with a salmon fillet. Ladle equal amounts of the broth around each fillet. Serve them hot.

FOR THE SALMON AND MARINADE:

3 tablespoons Achiote (page 183) or store-bought *condimento de achiote*

3 tablespoons Sriracha

1 tablespoon rice vinegar

1 tablespoon peeled and minced fresh ginger

2 garlic cloves, crushed and peeled

Four 6-ounce (170-g) skinless salmon fillets

¼ cup (60 ml) Chipotle Aïoli (page 182) in a plastic squeeze bottle

SEAFOOD ENCHILADAS
WITH GREEN TOMATILLO SALSA

*Enchiladas de mariscos con
salsa de tomatillo y jalapeño*

FOR THE SEAFOOD FILLING:

½ cup plus 2 tablespoons (135 ml) canola oil, plus more for the baking dish

¾ cup (115 g) finely chopped white onion

2 cups (130 g) well-washed, coarsely chopped spinach leaves

8 ounces (225 g) large (31 to 40 count) shrimp, peeled, deveined, and coarsely chopped

8 ounces (225 g) crab meat, picked over for cartilage

1 cup (230 g) mascarpone cheese

2 poblano chilies, roasted, peeled, seeded, and chopped

Kosher salt and freshly ground black pepper

2 recipes Tomatillo-Jalapeño Green Salsa (page 179)

12 corn tortillas

1 cup (115 g) shredded Muenster or Chihuahua cheese

Filled with shrimp, crab, spinach, and mascarpone, these first-class seafood enchiladas could become a go-to dinner party dish. If you wish, use either crab or shrimp, but the combination is a winner. Be careful not to fully cook the shrimp when sautéing, as they will cook more in the oven. The enchiladas can be rolled, sauced, and refrigerated for a few hours and baked just before serving, giving you another reason for putting them on the short list for party entrées.

SERVES 4

1 **Make the filling:** Heat 1 tablespoon of the oil in a medium skillet over medium heat. Add the onion and cook, stirring occasionally, until it is translucent, about 3 minutes. Add the spinach and cook, stirring often, until it is wilted and tender. Transfer the mixture to a wire sieve and press hard on it to extract excess moisture. Transfer it to a medium bowl.

2 Add another 1 tablespoon of the oil to the skillet and heat it over medium-high heat. Add the shrimp and cook just until they turn opaque, about 1½ minutes. Do not overcook. Add them to the spinach mixture. Stir in the crab meat, mascarpone, and poblano. Season the filling to taste with salt and pepper. (The filling can be covered and refrigerated for up to 4 hours.)

3 Lightly oil a 10-by-15-inch (25-by-38-cm) baking dish. Spread 3 tablespoons of the salsa in the bottom of the dish.

4 Heat the remaining ½ cup (120 ml) oil in a medium skillet over medium heat until the oil is hot but not smoking. One at a time, add a tortilla to the hot oil and cook just until it is pliable, about 10 seconds. Using tongs, lift the tortilla from the oil, letting the excess oil drip back into the skillet, and transfer the softened tortilla to a plate. Spoon about ¼ cup (65 g) of the filling into the center of the tortilla, roll it up, and transfer it, seam-side down, to the baking dish. Repeat with the remaining tortillas and filling. Spread the remaining salsa over the enchiladas. (The enchiladas can be covered with plastic wrap and refrigerated for up to 4 hours. Uncover them before baking.)

5 Position a rack in the upper third of the oven and preheat it to 350°F (175°C).

6 Sprinkle the cheese over the enchiladas. Bake until the salsa is bubbling and the cheese is melted, about 20 minutes. Serve the enchiladas hot.

At Mexican beachside communities, you'll find pescado zarandeado, whole fish cooked in a grill basket. You don't really need the basket if you use fish fillets, and the flavor is just as great. (A perforated grill grate is the more modern way to keep fish from sticking to the grill.) The garam masala may seem like an odd addition, but it has just the right mix of warm spices to give distinction to the marinade.

■■■■■■■■■■■■■■■ SERVES 4 ■■■■■■■■■■

1 **Make the marinade:** Process the orange juice, oil, achiote, garam masala, cumin, garlic, and chile in a blender until thick and smooth. Season the marinade to taste with salt. Pour it into a shallow nonreactive baking dish. Add the snapper fillets, turn to coat them, cover, and refrigerate them for 15 to 30 minutes.

2 **Make the chayote and carrot slaw:** Using caution (the peeled chayote is slippery), cut the chayote into julienne on a mandoline or V-slicer. Repeat with the carrot. Transfer the vegetables to a medium bowl. Add the onion. Sprinkle them with the lime juice and cilantro and season to taste with salt. Cover and refrigerate the slaw for up to 1 hour.

3 Prepare an outdoor grill for direct cooking over high heat. For a charcoal grill, let the coals burn until they are covered with white ash and you can hold your hand about 1 inch (2.5 cm) above the cooking grate for only 1 or 2 seconds. For a gas grill, preheat it on high and adjust the heat to 550°F (285°C). Heat a perforated grill pan on the grate.

4 Remove the fillets from the marinade, letting the marinade cling to the fish. Place them on the grill pan, flesh-side down. Cook them, with the lid closed as much as possible, for 3 minutes. Flip the fillets and cook them until the fish is opaque when pierced in the thickest part with the tip of a small sharp knife, about 3 minutes more (or less for small fillets). Transfer the fish fillets to a platter and tent them with aluminum foil to keep warm.

5 Brush the grates clean again. Place the tortillas on the grill and cook, turning them occasionally, until they are lightly browned on both sides and heated through, about 1 minute. Transfer them to a napkin-lined bowl and wrap them in the napkin to keep warm.

6 Serve bowls of the fish, slaw, aïoli, avocado, tortillas, and lime wedges. Let each guest make a taco with the desired ingredients.

FOR THE MARINADE AND SNAPPER:

½ cup (120 ml) fresh orange juice

3 tablespoons olive oil

2 tablespoons Achiote (page 183) or store-bought *condimento de achiote*

1 teaspoon garam masala

1 teaspoon toasted cumin seeds

3 garlic cloves, peeled

1 guajillo chile, seeded, stemmed, and toasted, or 1 tablespoon pure ground ancho chile

Kosher salt

2 pounds (910 g) skinless red snapper fillets

FOR THE CHAYOTE AND CARROT SLAW:

1 chayote, peeled, hard central part removed

1 large carrot

½ small red onion, cut into thin half-moons

2 tablespoons fresh lime juice

2 tablespoons finely chopped fresh cilantro

Kosher salt

12 corn tortillas, heated

1 cup (240 ml) Chipotle Aïoli (page 182)

1 ripe Hass avocado, thinly sliced

Lime wedges, for serving

ANCHO-PISTACHIO TUNA STEAKS

WITH MOLE VERDE & APPLE-CILANTRO SALAD

Filetes de atún con chile ancho y pistachos con mole verde y ensalada de manzana, cilantro

FOR THE APPLE-CILANTRO SALAD:

1 Granny Smith apple, cored and cut into julienne

½ small red onion, cut into very thin half-moons

2 tablespoons fresh lime juice

1 tablespoon finely chopped fresh cilantro

Kosher salt and freshly ground black pepper

FOR THE TUNA:

4 dried ancho chilies, stemmed and seeded (see Note)

1 teaspoon sugar

½ cup (60 g) shelled pistachios

Four 6-ounce (170-g) ahi tuna steaks, each cut 1 inch (2.5 cm) thick

Canola oil

Kosher salt

¾ cup (240 g) Mole Verde (page 180)

Fresh cilantro sprigs, for garnish

Tuna's firm texture and full flavor are as much turf as surf, and these qualities can hold their own against strong seasonings. As a comparison, you wouldn't want to use this bold ancho-and-pistachio crust on flounder.

SERVES 4

1 **Make the salad:** Mix the apples, onion, lime juice, and cilantro together in a medium bowl. Season them to taste with salt and pepper. Cover and refrigerate the salad for up to 3 hours.

2 **Make the tuna:** Process the chilies and sugar together in a food processor until the chilies are roughly chopped, about 1 minute. In batches, transfer the mixture to an electric spice (coffee) grinder and process it to a coarse powder.

3 Add the pistachios and chile mixture to the food processor and pulse until the pistachios are finely ground but not a powder. Transfer the pistachio mixture to a wide bowl, and set aside 1 tablespoon for a garnish. Brush the tuna all over with oil and season with salt. Coat the tuna steaks on all sides with the pistachio mixture and transfer them to a plate.

4 Heat a very large nonstick skillet over medium-high heat. Add 2 tablespoons oil and heat until it is hot but not smoking. Add the tuna and reduce the heat to medium-low. Cook, adjusting the heat as needed so the tuna cooks steadily without burning the crust, until the underside is crispy, about 3 minutes. Turn and brown the other side for 3 minutes more for rare tuna. Transfer the tuna to a cutting board and let it stand for 2 minutes.

5 Meanwhile, heat the mole verde and 3 tablespoons water in a small saucepan over medium heat until simmering. Reduce the heat to very low to keep the mole warm.

6 Cut each steak across the grain into ½-inch (12-mm) slices. For each serving, spread about 3 tablespoons of the mole on a dinner plate. Using a slotted spoon, top each with one-quarter of the apple salad. Spread a tuna steak, fanning out the slices, over the salad. Garnish with a cilantro sprig. Sprinkle the reserved pistachio mixture over the plate as a garnish and serve the tuna immediately.

NOTE If you wish, substitute 3 tablespoons pure ground ancho chile. Although it is already ground, add it to the pistachios in the food processor before grinding the nuts, as the chile will help keep the pistachios from processing into butter.

MUSSELS

WITH BEER, CHORIZO, ORANGE & BASIL

Mejillones con cerveza, chorizo, naranja y albahaca

2 tablespoons canola oil

8 ounces (225 g) smoked Spanish-style chorizo, cut into ½-inch (12-mm) dice

1 medium white onion, finely chopped

5 tablespoons (70 g) unsalted butter, thinly sliced

2 garlic cloves, smashed under a knife and peeled

Two 12-ounce (340-ml) bottles dark beer, such as Negra Modelo

2 tablespoons honey

4 pounds (1.8 kg) cultivated mussels, such as Prince Edward Island, or sea-harvested mussels (see Note)

⅓ cup (10 g) loosely packed coarsely chopped fresh basil

Finely grated zest of 1 large orange

Kosher salt and freshly ground black pepper

In Mediterranean cuisine, mussels are often cooked with white wine. In Mexico, where I grew up, the hot climate is much more friendly to growing the ingredients for beer, so I use that as the liquid for my mussels. The beer's bitterness is balanced by the sweet flavors of orange, basil, and honey. Be sure to serve this with crusty bread to sop up every drop of the sauce.

SERVES 4

1 Heat the oil in a large pot over medium-high heat. Add the chorizo and cook until it is beginning to brown, about 1 minute. Stir in the onion and 1 tablespoon of the butter and reduce the heat to medium. Cook, stirring often, until the onion is translucent but not browned, about 4 minutes.

2 Stir in the garlic and cook for 1 minute. Add the beer and honey and bring the liquid to a simmer over high heat. Add the mussels and tightly cover the pot. Cook, occasionally shaking the pot by its handles, until the mussels have opened, about 5 minutes. Remove them from the heat.

3 Using a wire sieve, scoop up the mussels and other solids from the pot, discarding any that have not opened, and divide them among four large soup bowls. Add the remaining butter, the basil, and orange zest to the pot and whisk until the butter has melted and lightly thickened the sauce. Season it to taste with salt and pepper. Ladle equal amounts of the sauce over the mussels. Serve them immediately.

NOTE Cultivated mussels, such as the ones raised on Prince Edward Island near Nova Scotia, now dominate the marketplace. The traditional sea-harvested mussels attach themselves to rocks with thick cords (called beards) that must be pulled off before cooking. Cultivated mussels don't have beards, making their preparation much easier—just rinse and cook.

To prepare sea-harvested mussels, scrub them well under cold running water, discarding any mussels that are not tightly closed or feel very heavy (as they may be dead and filled with mud). Transfer the mussels to a bowl of salted ice water and let them stand for 1 hour to expel any grit. Drain well. Using pliers, pull off and discard the thick, hairy beard from each mussel.

Garlic shrimp is a recipe that you'll find in just about every Latin cuisine from Puerto Rico to Spain. You won't find two recipes that are exactly alike. Mine has heat from chilies de árbol, acidity and fragrance from lemons, and white wine to pull it all together. Serve it on crusty rolls and you'll get to savor every bit of the sauce.

GARLIC SHRIMP TORTAS

Tortas con camarones al ajillo

SERVES 4

1 Season the shrimp with 1 teaspoon salt and ½ teaspoon pepper. Heat the oil, garlic, bay leaf, and chilies in a very large skillet over medium-high heat, stirring often, until the garlic begins to brown, about 1½ minutes. Add the shrimp and cook, stirring often, just until the shrimp turn opaque, about 4 minutes. Transfer the shrimp to a serving bowl.

2 Add the wine and lemon juice to the skillet and bring them to a boil over high heat. Cook until the liquid is reduced by half, about 3 minutes. Return the shrimp to the skillet and cook to reheat them, about 1 minute. Remove the pan from the heat and add the butter, parsley, and lemon zest. Stir until the butter has melted and lightly thickened the sauce. Season the sauce to taste with salt and pepper.

3 Place a roll on each dinner plate. Spoon the shrimp and sauce over the bottom half of each roll. Top each with a few tomato slices and a handful of arugula, and place the top half on each roll. Cut the rolls in half and serve them immediately.

1½ pounds (680 g) large (31 to 40 count) shrimp, peeled and deveined

Kosher salt and freshly ground black pepper

3 tablespoons olive oil

6 garlic cloves, thinly sliced

1 large bay leaf, broken in half

3 dried chilies, such as chilies de árbol, stemmed and seeded, each cut in half

1½ cups (360 ml) dry white wine

3 tablespoons fresh lemon juice (zest the lemon first)

4 tablespoons (½ stick; 55 g) unsalted butter, thinly sliced

2 teaspoons finely chopped fresh flat-leaf parsley

Finely grated zest of 1 lemon

4 crusty rolls, split lengthwise and toasted

2 ripe plum tomatoes, thinly sliced

1 cup (40 g) baby arugula

These sweet sea scallops are capped with a golden brown crust that gives them a five-star appearance, but they are really very easy to make. You will need the biggest (colossal) scallops for this recipe to be sure that they don't get overcooked. The scallops could also be served simply with a sprinkle of cilantro and lemon wedges.

PARMESAN-CRUSTED SCALLOPS

WITH LIME BUTTER SAUCE & CILANTRO

Vieiras con cubierta crocante de queso parmesano con salsa de mantequilla de limón y cilantro

━━━━━━━━━ SERVES 4 ━━━━━━━━━

1 **Make the butter:** At least 4 hours before serving, use a rubber spatula to mash the panko, cheese, and butter together in a medium bowl until they are completely combined. Spoon the butter onto a 12-inch (30.5-cm) sheet of plastic wrap. Using the wrap as an aid, shape the butter into a log about 10 inches (25 cm) long. The diameter of the log should be about the same width as the scallops. Twist the ends of the plastic wrap and freeze it until the butter is firm, at least 4 hours.

2 **Make the sauce:** Finely grate the peel from 1 lime; set the zest aside. Juice the limes; you should have 3 tablespoons. Bring the lime juice, wine, and shallot to a boil in a small nonreactive saucepan over high heat. Boil until the wine has reduced to about 2 tablespoons, about 5 minutes. Reduce the heat to very low. A few cubes at a time, whisk in the butter, whisking constantly to let each addition soften into a creamy mass before adding more cubes. The butter should not actually melt into a liquid, but emulsify into a sauce. Strain the sauce into a small bowl and stir in the zest; discard the shallot. Season the sauce to taste with salt and pepper. Return it to the saucepan. (The sauce can be prepared to this point and kept at room temperature for up to 1 hour. Whisk it over very low heat until barely warm.) About 20 minutes before cooking, remove the Parmesan butter from the freezer and let it soften slightly. Cut the butter into twenty equal slices about ½ inch (12 mm) thick.

3 Position a broiler rack about 8 inches (20 cm) from the source of heat and preheat the broiler on high. Season the scallops with the salt and pepper.

4 Heat a very large skillet (the scallops should fit in a single layer) with an ovenproof handle over medium-high heat. Add the oil, swirl it in the skillet, and heat until the oil is very hot but not smoking. Stand the scallops, flat-side down, in the skillet. Cook, turning them once, until they are golden brown on both sides, about 5 minutes. Quickly top each scallop with a slice of the Parmesan butter. Transfer the skillet to the broiler and cook, watching carefully to avoid burning, until the panko crust is nicely browned (it will hold its shape and not melt), about 1 minute.

5 Divide the scallops among four dinner plates. Spoon the sauce around the scallops and sprinkle them with the cilantro. Serve immediately.

FOR THE PARMESAN-PANKO BUTTER:

1 cup (60 g) panko

1 cup (115 g) freshly grated Parmigiano-Reggiano cheese

½ cup (1 stick; 115 g) unsalted butter, at room temperature

FOR THE LIME BUTTER SAUCE:

2 limes

½ cup (120 ml) dry white wine

2 tablespoons finely chopped shallot

1 cup (2 sticks; 230 g) cold unsalted butter, cut into ½-inch (12-mm) cubes

Kosher salt and freshly ground white pepper

20 colossal-size sea scallops, patted dry with paper towels

½ teaspoon kosher salt

½ teaspoon freshly ground white pepper

2 tablespoons canola oil

3 tablespoons whole fresh cilantro leaves

SEAFOOD & BACON GRATINÉE TACOS

*Tacos de mariscos y
tocino glaseado*

FOR THE ADOBO MARINADE:

4 guajillo chilies, stemmed, seeded, and coarsely chopped

3 tablespoons chopped white onion

1 garlic clove, smashed under a knife and peeled

¼ teaspoon ground cumin

Pinch of ground cinnamon

Kosher salt

12 ounces (340 g) large sea scallops

12 ounces (340 g) medium (41 to 50 count) shrimp, peeled and deveined

FOR THE CHILE DE ÁRBOL AÏOLI:

1 tablespoon canola oil

¼ cup (35 g) finely chopped yellow onion

3 garlic cloves, minced

¼ cup (65 g) tomato paste

3 chilies de árbol, stemmed, seeded, and coarsely chopped

5 black peppercorns

1 cup (240 ml) chicken stock or reduced-sodium chicken broth

1 cup (240 ml) mayonnaise

When people share food from a common platter, the sense of community and conviviality is heightened. Tacos of marinated seafood and crisp bacon, glazed with a chile aïoli, are really a sophisticated dish served in a rustic manner. And it could become one of your favorite party dishes (as it is mine) because it takes just a final few minutes to assemble, broil, and serve.

■ SERVES 4 TO 6 ■

1 Make the marinade: Put the chilies, onion, garlic, cumin, and cinnamon in a small saucepan and add enough cold water to barely cover them. Bring them to a boil over high heat. Reduce the heat to low and simmer until the chilies are very tender but not falling apart, about 30 minutes. Strain the mixture through a wire sieve into a heatproof bowl, reserving the liquid. Transfer the chile mixture to a blender. With the blender running, pour in enough of the reserved liquid to make a smooth marinade. Season with salt. Pour the marinade into a 1-gallon (3.8-L) zip-top plastic bag and let it cool completely.

2 Add the scallops and shrimp to the cooled marinade and seal the bag. Refrigerate it, turning the bag occasionally, for at least 1 and up to 4 hours.

3 Make the aïoli: Heat the oil in a small skillet over medium heat. Add the onion and garlic and cook, stirring them occasionally, until the onion is translucent, about 4 minutes. Add the tomato paste, chilies, and peppercorns and reduce the heat to low. Cook, stirring often, until the tomato paste has turned a deeper shade of red, making sure the tomato paste does not burn, about 10 minutes. Stir in the stock, scraping up the paste with a wooden spoon. Return the heat to medium and simmer the liquid briskly, stirring often, until the mixture is reduced to a few tablespoons, about 10 minutes more. Let it cool completely. Transfer it to a blender and purée to grind the peppercorns. Add the mayonnaise and process again until it is combined. Transfer the aïoli to a bowl, cover, and refrigerate it for up to 8 hours.

4 Make the slaw: Toss the cabbage with the lime juice and season it to taste with salt and pepper. Stir in the cilantro, if using. Cover and refrigerate it until ready to use, up to 2 hours. (The cabbage slaw should be crisp, so don't refrigerate it longer than 2 hours, or it will wilt.)

5 Cook the bacon in a medium skillet, turning it occasionally, until it is crisp and brown, about 8 minutes. Transfer it to paper towels to drain and cool. Chop the bacon into ¼-inch (6-mm) pieces. Cover and refrigerate it until ready to use.

6 Drain the scallops and shrimp in a colander to remove any excess marinade. Pat the seafood dry with paper towels. Heat a large nonstick skillet over high heat. Add the scallops and shrimp and cook, stirring them occasionally, until they are seared, about 2 minutes. Transfer them to a plate and let them cool. Cover the plate with plastic wrap and refrigerate it until chilled, at least 1 and up to 3 hours.

7 Position the broiler rack about 8 inches (20 cm) from the source of heat and preheat the broiler on high.

8 Toss the chilled seafood with the aïoli in a large bowl. Transfer it to an ovenproof serving dish large enough to hold the mixture in a single layer. Broil the seafood until the aïoli is golden brown, about 2 minutes. Sprinkle the crushed tortilla chips and bacon on top.

9 To serve, allow the guests to make their own tacos, filling a tortilla with a spoonful of the seafood mixture topped with the slaw.

FOR THE CABBAGE-LIME SLAW:

2 cups (130 g) shredded cabbage

2 tablespoons fresh lime juice

Kosher salt and freshly ground black pepper

2 tablespoons finely chopped fresh cilantro (optional)

4 slices bacon

1 cup (80 g) coarsely crushed tortilla chips, coarsely ground in a blender

Twelve 8-inch (20-cm) flour tortillas, heated according to package directions

CRISPY SHRIMP LETTUCE WRAPS

WITH TAMARIND SAUCE

Camarón crocante envuelto en lechuga con salsa de tamarindo

FOR THE TAMARIND DIP:

1 tablespoon canola oil

½ small yellow onion, finely chopped

1 small garlic clove, minced

½ red or green jalapeño, seeded and minced

1 cup (240 ml) Thai sweet chili sauce

½ cup (140 g) tamarind concentrate

2 teaspoons pure ground ancho chile

1 tablespoon distilled white vinegar

1 tablespoon coarsely chopped fresh mint

1½ teaspoons coarsely chopped fresh cilantro

½ teaspoon Sriracha or other hot red pepper sauce

Kosher salt

FOR THE CRISPY SHRIMP FILLING:

2 tablespoons Thai sweet chili sauce

2 tablespoons Chinese XO or oyster sauce

1 cup (140 g) cornstarch

2 tablespoons all-purpose flour

1¼ pounds (570 g) shelled jumbo (21 to 25 count) rock shrimp or peeled and deveined jumbo standard shrimp

2 tablespoons canola oil

When eating this incredible Asian stir-fry, you will discover a huge range of flavors and textures—crispy, sweet, sour, spicy, salty, tender, and a few more! As when cooking all stir-fried dishes, organization is key. Once everything is prepped, your final assembly is accomplished in just a few minutes. Learn how to make this dish, because you will want to cook it again.

SERVES 4

1 Make the dip: Heat the oil in a medium saucepan over medium heat. Add the onion, garlic, and jalapeño and cook, stirring them occasionally, until the onion is translucent, about 3 minutes. Transfer the onion mixture to a blender. Add the chili sauce, tamarind, ground chile, vinegar, mint, cilantro, and Sriracha and process until they are smooth. Season the dip to taste with salt. Transfer it to a bowl and let it cool completely. (The sauce can be covered and refrigerated for up to 3 days.)

2 Make the filling: Position a rack in the center of the oven and preheat the oven to 200°F (90°C). Place a wire cooling rack over a rimmed baking sheet.

3 Whisk ¾ cup (180 ml) of the tamarind dip with the chili sauce and XO sauce in a small bowl to combine; set it aside. Divide the remaining tamarind sauce among four ramekins to use as a dip.

4 Pour in enough oil to come halfway up the sides of a large saucepan and heat it over high heat until the oil reaches 350°F (175°C) on a deep-frying thermometer. Whisk the cornstarch and flour together. Whisk in enough water, about ½ cup (120 ml), to make a thick, clinging batter for the shrimp. In batches, coat the shrimp in the batter. Lift the shrimp from the batter, letting the excess drip back into the bowl, and transfer the coated shrimp to the oil. Deep-fry the shrimp until golden brown, about 2½ minutes. Using a wire spider or slotted spoon, transfer the shrimp to the wire cooling rack and keep them warm in the oven while frying the remaining shrimp.

5 Heat a large wok or skillet over high heat. Add the oil and swirl to coat the inside of the pan. Add the chorizo and stir-fry until it is beginning to brown, about 30 seconds. Add the shallot and stir-fry until it is softened, about 15 seconds. Add the tamarind sauce mixture, peanuts, and cilantro and stir-fry until the sauce is simmering, about 30 seconds. Add the shrimp and stir-fry just until they are coated with the sauce, about 15 seconds. Remove the skillet from the heat.

6 For each serving, place three lettuce leaves on a dinner plate. Divide the filling equally among the leaves. Serve at once, with ramekins of sauce for dipping. (Remove the shrimp tails, if attached, before eating.)

5 ounces (140 g) smoked Spanish-style chorizo, cut into ½-inch (12-mm) dice

¼ cup (35 g) chopped shallot

⅓ cup (45 g) coarsely chopped roasted unsalted peanuts

2 tablespoons chopped fresh cilantro

12 Bibb lettuce leaves

SPANISH-STYLE RISOTTO
WITH SEAFOOD

Arroz con mariscos

Three 8-ounce (240-ml) bottles clam juice

4 tablespoons (60 ml) olive oil

8 ounces (225 g) jumbo (21 to 25 count) shrimp, peeled and deveined

8 ounces (225 g) calamari bodies and tentacles, cleaned, bodies cut into ½-inch (12-mm) rings

Kosher salt and freshly ground black pepper

5 ounces (140 g) Spanish-style smoked chorizo, cut into ½-inch (12-mm) dice

4 tablespoons (½ stick; 55 g) unsalted butter

¾ cup (105 g) finely chopped shallots

2 garlic cloves, minced

1¾ cups (350 g) Arborio rice

1 cup (240 ml) dry white wine

¼ teaspoon crumbled saffron threads

2 pounds (910 g) cultivated mussels, such as Prince Edward Island, or littleneck clams, scrubbed under cold water (see Note, page 92)

8 cherry tomatoes, halved

Finely chopped chives, for garnish

Paella meets risotto in this comforting stovetop rice dish. It is a myth that risotto requires constant stirring. You do want to stir it often to release the starches in the arborio rice to give the dish its famous creamy texture, and a heavy saucepan to prevent scorching is a good idea. If I have some lobster meat in the refrigerator, I like to add it to the risotto along with the cherry tomatoes and butter at the end.

SERVES 4

1 Bring the clam juice and 1 cup (240 ml) water to a simmer in a medium saucepan over high heat. Reduce the heat to very low and keep it warm.

2 Heat 2 tablespoons of the oil in a large skillet over medium-high heat. Add the shrimp and calamari and cook, stirring them often, just until they turn opaque, about 2 minutes. Do not overcook. Season the seafood mixture to taste with salt and pepper. Transfer the shrimp mixture to a bowl and tent it with aluminum foil to keep it warm.

3 Heat 1 tablespoon of the oil in a large heavy-bottomed saucepan over medium heat. Add the chorizo and cook, stirring occasionally, until it is beginning to brown, about 2 minutes. Add 1 tablespoon of the butter with ½ cup (70 g) of the shallots and the garlic and cook, stirring often, until the shallots are softened but not browned, about 2 minutes. Add the rice and cook, stirring often, until it turns chalky white and feels heavier in the spoon, about 2 minutes. Stir in the wine and saffron and cook, stirring often, until the wine is almost absorbed by the rice mixture, about 2 minutes.

4 Spoon ¾ cup (180 ml) of the hot clam juice into the rice and adjust the heat so the liquid is at a steady simmer. Stir almost constantly, until the liquid is about three-quarters reduced, about 2½ minutes. Add another ¾ cup (180 ml) of the juice and stir until the liquid reaches the same point of reduction, about 2½ minutes more. Repeat the procedure, until the rice is barely tender and has a loose, flowing consistency, 15 to 20 minutes more. If you run out of the hot clam juice, use hot water.

5 About 7 minutes before the rice is done, heat the remaining 1 tablespoon oil in a large pot over medium heat. Add the remaining ¼ cup (35 g) shallots and cook until they are softened, about 2 minutes. Add the mussels, cover the pot tightly, and increase the heat to high. Cook, shaking the pan occasionally, until the mussels open, about 5 minutes. Set the pot aside with the lid ajar.

6 When the rice is done, stir in the remaining 3 tablespoons butter. Stir in the shrimp and calamari with any collected juices and the cherry tomatoes. Season the rice mixture with salt and pepper.

7 Divide the rice mixture among four deep bowls. Use tongs to add equal amounts of the mussels to each bowl. (The mussel cooking liquid can be reserved for another use as seafood stock.) Sprinkle the tops with the chives and serve the risotto hot.

CASUAL SEAFOOD SUPPER

Ginger Fizzes (PAGE 193)

Perfect Palomas (PAGE 191)

Shrimp and Bacon
Quesadillas (PAGE 35)

Seafood Enchiladas with
Green Tomatillo Salsa (PAGE 88)

Grilled Avocado with
Baby Greens & Corn
Pico de Gallo (PAGE 57)

Mexican Beer

Chocolate Dulce de Leche
Roulade (PAGE 152)

6
POULTRY

GRILLED CHICKEN BREASTS

WITH ORANGE-CHILE MARINADE

Pechuga de pollo asada con adobo de naranja y chile

FOR THE ORANGE-CHILE MARINADE:

1 small yellow onion, coarsely chopped

⅓ cup (75 ml) fresh orange juice

3 tablespoons pure ground ancho chile

1 tablespoon Achiote (page 183) or store-bought *condimento de achiote*

1 tablespoon distilled white vinegar

3 garlic cloves, crushed and peeled

1 teaspoon kosher salt

1 teaspoon cumin seeds, toasted

1 teaspoon dried Mexican oregano

½ teaspoon ground allspice

¼ teaspoon freshly ground black pepper

⅛ teaspoon ground cinnamon

⅓ cup (75 ml) canola oil

Six 8-ounce (225-g) boneless, skinless chicken breast halves

I will be very surprised if this citrus-and-spice marinade does not become a favorite at your house. Just toss the ingredients in a blender, and you are good to go (the recipe is easily doubled for big parties). The thick marinade clings to the food so the flavor really stands out after cooking. It's just as good on pork chops as it is on chicken. While this is outstanding by itself, you can knock it out of the park by brushing on some Mole BBQ Sauce (see page 107) during the last few minutes of grilling.

SERVES 6

1 Make the marinade: Purée the onion, orange juice, ancho, achiote, vinegar, garlic, salt, cumin, oregano, allspice, pepper, and cinnamon in a blender. With the motor running, pour the oil through the hole in the lid and process, occasionally scraping down the marinade, until it is emulsified. Season it to taste with salt and pepper.

2 Pour half of the marinade into a 1-gallon (3.8-L) zip-top plastic bag and add the chicken. Seal the bag and refrigerate it for at least 1 and up to 4 hours. (The remaining marinade can be refrigerated for up to 1 week.)

3 Prepare an outdoor grill for direct cooking over medium-high heat. For a charcoal grill, let the coals burn until they are covered with white ash and you can hold your hand about 1 inch (2.5 cm) above the cooking grate for 2 to 3 seconds. For a gas grill, preheat the grill on high, then adjust the heat to 450°F (230°C).

4 Remove the chicken from the marinade. Brush the grill grates clean. Place the chicken on the grill. Cook it, with the lid closed as much as possible, flipping the chicken occasionally, until it is firm to the touch and opaque to the center, 10 to 12 minutes. Transfer the chicken to a carving board.

5 Let the chicken stand for 5 minutes. Cut it across the grain into ½-inch (12-mm) slices. Transfer them to a platter and serve them hot.

There is no one way to make these tacos—you'll often see them made with crisp corn tortillas, like tostadas, sprinkled with queso fresco and topped with avocados. But this is the way that I like them, with the tender chicken melding with the black bean purée in soft flour tortillas. It's a great meal for a cold winter night.

CHICKEN TINGA TACOS

Tacos de tinga de pollo

SERVES 4; MAKES 12 TACOS

1 Make the purée: Heat the oil in a medium saucepan over medium heat. Add the bacon and cook, stirring it occasionally, until it is crisp and browned, about 6 minutes. Add the onion, jalapeño, and garlic and cook, stirring them occasionally, until the onion is tender, about 3 minutes. Stir in the cumin and oregano. Add the beans and broth and bring them to a simmer. Reduce the heat to low and simmer until the liquid has reduced slightly, about 15 minutes. Remove the mixture from the heat and let it cool until tepid.

2 Drain the bean mixture and reserve the liquid. Process the bean mixture in a blender, adding enough of the broth to make a smooth, spreadable purée. Season it to taste with salt and pepper. Return it to the saucepan and reheat it over medium heat, stirring often, until it is hot, about 2 minutes. Transfer the purée to a serving bowl.

3 Serve bowls of the bean purée, chicken tinga, tortillas, lettuce, and crema. Let the guests make their own tacos with the desired ingredients.

FOR THE BLACK BEAN PURÉE:

1 tablespoon canola oil

1 slice bacon, cut into 1-inch (2.5-cm) lengths

1 small onion, chopped

½ jalapeño, seeded and minced

1 garlic clove, minced

¼ teaspoon ground cumin

Pinch of dried oregano, preferably Mexican

Two 15.5-ounce (445-g) cans black beans, drained and rinsed

1½ cups (360 ml) reduced-sodium chicken broth

Kosher salt and freshly ground black pepper

1 recipe Chicken Tinga Filling (page 176)

Twelve 6-inch (15-cm) flour tortillas, heated according to package directions

¼ head iceberg lettuce, shredded, for serving

Crema or sour cream, for serving

BACKYARD PARTY

Sangría Tinta Roja **(PAGE 219)**

Cooked Tomato Salsa with Tortilla Chips **(PAGE 50)**

Grilled Chicken with Mole BBQ Sauce **(PAGE 107)**

Mexico City–Style Corn on the Cob **(PAGE 149)**

Grilled Romaine Hearts with Cilantro Ranch Dressing **(PAGE 63)**

Mexican Chocolate & Raspberry Tart **(PAGE 156)**

For a surefire barbecued grilled chicken that will be the hit of a backyard party, you have got to try this version. The rub and sauce share many of the same ingredients, so it all comes together pretty quickly. The sauce, in particular, is a keeper, and you'll use it for steaks, chops, and burgers, too. Any leftover sauce will keep for a couple of weeks in the fridge.

GRILLED CHICKEN
WITH MOLE BBQ SAUCE

Pollo a la plancha con salsa de mole barbacoa

SERVES 6 TO 8

1 **Make the BBQ sauce:** Bring the ketchup, 1 cup (240 ml) water, the sugar, chocolate, liquid smoke, chipotles with adobo, garlic powder, onion powder, ancho, paprika, mustard, cumin, oregano, and pepper to a boil in a medium saucepan over medium-high heat. Reduce the heat to low and simmer, stirring often, until the sauce is slightly reduced, about 15 minutes. Season it with salt and let it cool. Purée the mixture in a blender, adding more chipotles, if you wish.

2 **Make the rub:** Mix the salt, ancho, mustard, cumin, oregano, pepper, garlic powder, and onion powder together in a small bowl.

3 Arrange the chicken on a large rimmed baking sheet and brush it all over with oil. Season it on both sides with the rub. Let it stand at room temperature while heating the grill. (Or cover and refrigerate the chicken for up to 12 hours; let it stand at room temperature for 30 minutes before cooking.)

4 Prepare an outdoor grill for indirect cooking over medium-high heat. For a charcoal grill, let the coals burn until they are covered with white ash and you can hold your hand about 1 inch (2.5 cm) above the cooking grate for about 2 seconds. Leave the coals in the center of the grill. For a gas grill, preheat the grill on high. Turn the burner(s) off on one side of the grill, and adjust the heat to 450°F (230°C).

5 Brush the grill grates clean. Arrange the chicken pieces on the empty areas of the grill, placing them around the coals in the center of the charcoal grill, or on the off side of the gas grill. Cook them, with the lid closed as much as possible, flipping the chicken occasionally, until the chicken shows no sign of pink when pierced at the drumstick bone, 50 minutes to 1 hour. For a charcoal grill, after 25 minutes, add six to eight more pieces of charcoal to maintain the heat. During the last 10 minutes, occasionally turn the chicken and generously brush it on all sides with about half of the BBQ sauce.

6 Transfer the chicken to a platter and serve it hot, with the remaining sauce passed on the side. (The remaining BBQ sauce can be stored in a covered container in the refrigerator for up to 2 weeks.)

FOR THE MOLE BBQ SAUCE:

1 cup (315 g) tomato ketchup

¼ cup (50 g) packed light brown sugar

2 ounces (55 g) unsweetened chocolate, coarsely grated

¼ cup (60 ml) mesquite-flavored liquid smoke

4 canned chipotle chilies in adobo, with clinging sauce, coarsely chopped, or more to taste

1 teaspoon garlic powder

1 teaspoon onion powder

1 teaspoon pure ground ancho chile

1 teaspoon sweet paprika

1 teaspoon dry mustard powder

1 teaspoon ground cumin

1 teaspoon dried Mexican oregano

1 teaspoon freshly ground black pepper

Kosher salt

FOR THE ANCHO RUB:

1 tablespoon kosher salt

2 teaspoons pure ground ancho chile

1 teaspoon dry mustard powder

1 teaspoon ground cumin

1 teaspoon dried Mexican oregano

1 teaspoon freshly ground black pepper

1 teaspoon garlic powder

1 teaspoon onion powder

Two 4-pound (1.8-kg) chickens, cut into 4 drumsticks, 4 thighs, 4 wings, 4 breast halves, and 2 backs

Olive oil, for coating the chicken

CHICKEN
SKEWERS
WITH NIKKEI
GLAZE

Anticuchos de pollo con glaseado de Nikkei

FOR THE NIKKEI MARINADE AND CHICKEN:

½ cup (130 g) ají panca (see page 14)

½ cup (120 ml) canola oil

3 tablespoons kabayaki sauce (also called eel sauce)

3 tablespoons distilled white vinegar

4 garlic cloves, coarsely chopped

½ teaspoon dried oregano

½ teaspoon cumin seeds

2¼ pounds (1.1 kg) skinless boneless chicken thighs, cut into 24 pieces about 1½ inches (4 cm) square

FOR THE NIKKEI DIPPING SAUCE:

¾ cup (180 ml) kabayaki sauce (also called eel sauce)

2 tablespoons peeled and minced fresh ginger

1 tablespoon rice vinegar

1 tablespoon peanut or canola oil

1 tablespoon fresh lime juice

½ habanero or jalapeño chile, seeded and minced

1 small garlic clove, minced

2 medium zucchini, cut into 1-inch (2.5-cm) lengths

Canola oil, for brushing the zucchini

SPECIAL EQUIPMENT:

4 long metal grilling skewers

Kabayaki is a Japanese cooking method for eel in which it is butterflied, grilled, and glazed with a sweet soy-based sauce. In my exploration of Nikkei cuisine, I discovered that kabayaki sauce is also terrific in a chicken marinade and glaze. This recipe shows why Nikkei cooking is getting so much attention from American cooks wanting to expand their horizons. There is a recipe for homemade kabayaki sauce on page 82. It makes a large batch, but it keeps for weeks in the fridge.

SERVES 4

1 **Make the marinade:** Whisk together the ají panca, oil, kabayaki sauce, vinegar, garlic, oregano, and cumin in a medium bowl. Reserve 2 tablespoons of the marinade. Pour the remaining marinade into a 1-gallon (3.8-L) zip-top plastic bag and add the chicken. Seal the bag and refrigerate it, turning the bag occasionally, for at least 4 and up to 12 hours.

2 **Make the dipping sauce:** Whisk together the kabayaki sauce, reserved marinade, ginger, vinegar, oil, lime juice, chile, and garlic in a medium bowl. Cover and let the sauce stand until ready to serve, for up to 8 hours.

3 Prepare an outdoor grill for direct cooking over medium-high heat. For a charcoal grill, let the coals burn until they are covered with white ash and you can hold your hand about 1 inch (2.5 cm) above the coals for about 3 seconds. For a gas grill, preheat it on high and adjust the heat to 450°F (230°C).

4 Remove the chicken from the marinade. Brush the zucchini with oil. Thread the chicken and zucchini onto the skewers (do not pack the ingredients together on the skewers, and leave a little space between them). Brush the grill grates clean. Cook the chicken, turning it once or twice, until it is browned and shows no sign of pink when pierced with the tip of a small sharp knife, 12 to 15 minutes.

5 Divide the sauce among four ramekins. Divide the skewers among four dinner plates. Serve them immediately, with the sauce for dipping.

NOTE To broil the chicken skewers, position a broiler rack about 8 inches (20 cm) from the source of heat and preheat the broiler on high. Lightly oil a broiler pan. Grill the chicken skewers, turning them occasionally, until they are cooked through, about 15 minutes.

This is Mom's homemade chicken soup . . . if your mother is Mexican and she wants to cook a deliciously hearty soup in under an hour. Part of the fun of this comforting dish is the unexpected bits of chayote, tomato, red onion, and avocado, with a surprise kick of smoky chipotle. One trick with this recipe: The potato in the soup base is purposely overcooked to break up and thicken the cooking liquid.

MEXICAN CHICKEN-VEGETABLE SOUP

Caldo de pollo y vegetales estilo Mexicano

■■■ SERVES 4 TO 6 ■■■

1 **Make the soup base:** Put the chicken in a large saucepan, meaty-side down. Add the stock, sliced potato, and chipotles. Pour in enough cold water to barely cover the chicken. Bring it to a simmer over high heat. Reduce the heat to medium-low and simmer it, partially covered, until the potato has fallen apart and an instant-read thermometer inserted in the thickest part of the chicken reads 165°F (74°C), about 35 minutes. Using kitchen tongs, transfer the chicken to a carving board and set it aside to cool.

2 Meanwhile, strain the soup base into a large heatproof bowl, discarding the solids. Return the soup base to the saucepan. Add the diced potato, carrot, and chayote and bring them to a simmer over high heat. Reduce the heat to medium-low and simmer until the potato is tender, about 20 minutes.

3 Discard the chicken skin and bones and shred the chicken meat into bite-size pieces. Stir it into the simmering soup with the tomatoes and red onion and cook until they are all heated through, about 2 minutes. Season the soup to taste with salt and pepper.

4 Divide the soup among four to six soup bowls. Top them with equal amounts of the avocado and cilantro and serve hot.

NOTE If you wish, substitute 1 large zucchini, cut into ½-inch (12-mm) dice, for the chayote, adding it to the soup after the potato and carrot have simmered for 10 minutes.

FOR THE SOUP BASE:

1½ pounds (680 g) bone-in chicken breast halves with skin

6 cups (1.4 L) chicken stock or reduced-sodium chicken broth

1 large baking potato, peeled and cut into very thin rounds

2 canned chipotle chilies in adobo

FOR THE SOUP:

1 large baking potato, peeled and cut into ½-inch (12-mm) dice

1 large carrot, cut into ½-inch (12-mm) dice

1 medium chayote, peeled, pitted, and cut into ½-inch (12-mm) dice (see Note)

2 plum tomatoes, seeded and cut into ½-inch (12-mm) dice

½ small red onion, finely chopped

Kosher salt and freshly ground black pepper

1 ripe Hass avocado, cut into ½-inch (12-mm) dice

2 tablespoons finely chopped fresh cilantro

THAI CHICKEN EMPANADAS

WITH MANGO–RED CURRY SAUCE

Empanadas de pollo Tailandés con salsa de mango y curry rojo

SPECIAL EQUIPMENT:

One 5-inch (12-cm) cookie cutter or saucer, for cutting out the pastry

FOR THE EMPANADA DOUGH:

2¼ cups (295 g) unbleached all-purpose flour, plus more for kneading

¼ teaspoon fine salt

3 tablespoons unsalted butter, melted

1 tablespoon canola oil

FOR THE MANGO–RED CURRY SAUCE:

1 tablespoon canola oil

1 small yellow onion, finely chopped

2 tablespoons peeled and finely minced fresh ginger

3 garlic cloves, minced

3 tablespoons tomato paste

1 cup (240 ml) canned coconut milk

One 4-ounce (115-g) container Thai red curry paste

¼ cup (50 g) packed light brown sugar

1 stalk lemongrass, tender bottom part only, finely chopped

1 Kaffir lime leaf (optional)

¾ cup (180 ml) fresh or thawed frozen mango purée

Kosher salt

These handheld pies are known by a variety of names throughout the Latin world, and the savory ones are stuffed with everything from chicken to tuna. (A dessert version with apples and Manchego cheese is on page 159.) Here they are made with Southeast Asian ingredients to give new life to an old favorite. One of the many reasons why empanadas are so beloved is that they can be made well ahead of baking, or you can warm up prebaked empanadas. The curry-sauce dip makes these "not your abuela's empanadas." Serve these with a hearty salad for a great supper.

SERVES 5; MAKES 10 EMPANADAS

1 Make the dough: Whisk together the flour and salt in a medium bowl. Make a well in the center. Pour in the butter, oil, and ⅔ cup (165 ml) cold water. Stir them together to make a rough dough. Turn it out onto a lightly floured work surface and knead it a few times, just until the dough is smooth. Flatten it into a thick disk, wrap it in plastic wrap, and refrigerate until the dough is chilled, at least 2 hours and up to 1 day.

2 Have ready 10 pieces of waxed paper to separate the dough disks. Cut the dough into 10 equal pieces and roll each piece into a ball. (A kitchen scale comes in very handy for dividing the dough equally.) On a lightly floured work surface, roll out each piece of dough into a thin round about 6 inches (15 cm) in diameter. Using a 5-inch (12-cm) round pastry cutter or a saucer, cut out a pastry disk, discarding the trimmings. Transfer it to a plate and top it with a piece of waxed paper. Continue with the remaining dough, layering the rounds with waxed paper. Cover them loosely with plastic wrap and refrigerate them again until they are chilled, at least 30 minutes or up to 2 hours.

3 Meanwhile, make the sauce: Heat the oil in a medium saucepan over medium heat. Add the onion, ginger, and garlic and cook, stirring occasionally, until the onion is translucent, about 3 minutes. Push the onion mixture to one side of the saucepan. Add the tomato paste on the empty side of the saucepan and cook until it turns dark brown, about 2 minutes. Add ½ cup (120 ml) water with the coconut milk, curry paste, sugar, lemongrass, and lime leaf, if using. Bring everything to a simmer, whisking often to combine. Reduce the heat to low and simmer, whisking often, until the sauce has reduced by about one-third, about 30 minutes. Let it cool. Discard the lime leaf if you used it. Pour the sauce into a blender, add the mango purée, and process until it is smooth. Season it to taste with salt. (The sauce can be stored at room temperature for up to 2 hours. Or transfer it to a covered bowl and refrigerate it for up to 2 days. Return it to room temperature before using.)

4 **Make the filling:** Heat the oil in a medium skillet over medium heat. Season the chicken on both sides with salt and pepper. Add the chicken to the skillet and cook until the underside is lightly browned, about 3 minutes. Flip the chicken over and continue cooking until it feels firm when pressed with a fingertip, about 3 minutes more. Transfer to a cutting board and let cool completely.

5 Using a large knife, chop the chicken into ¼-inch (6-mm) dice. Transfer to a medium bowl. Add the poblano, cheese, cilantro, and sweet chili sauce and mix well. Season the filling to taste with salt and pepper.

6 Line a large rimmed baking sheet with parchment paper. For each empanada, place a disk on the work surface. Brush the edge of the disk with some of the beaten egg, reserving the rest for later. Spoon about 2 tablespoons of the filling on the bottom half of the disk, leaving a ½-inch (12-mm) border. Fold it in half and seal the open edges closed with the tines of a fork. Transfer the empanada to the baking sheet and cover it loosely with plastic wrap. Repeat with the remaining dough and filling. Refrigerate the empanadas for at least 15 minutes and up to 3 hours.

7 Meanwhile, position racks in the top third and center of the oven and preheat the oven to 350°F (175°C).

8 Brush the top of each empanada with more of the egg mixture. Bake until the empanadas are golden brown, about 25 minutes. (The baked empanadas can be cooled, covered, and refrigerated for up to 1 day. Reheat them on a baking sheet in a preheated 350°F/175°C oven for about 15 minutes.)

9 Divide the sauce among five wide ramekins. For each serving, place two empanadas and a ramekin of sauce on a dinner plate.

FOR THE THAI CHICKEN FILLING:

1 tablespoon canola oil

One 8-ounce (225-g) boneless, skinless chicken breast half, cut in half lengthwise

Kosher salt and freshly ground black pepper

1 large poblano chile, roasted, peeled, seeded, and finely chopped (see page 23)

½ cup (60 g) shredded Oaxaca or mozzarella cheese

2 tablespoons coarsely chopped fresh cilantro

2 tablespoons Thai sweet chili sauce

1 large egg, beaten until foamy

"DIVORCED" ENCHILADAS

Enchiladas "divorciadas"

Variety is the spice of life, especially when you make your enchiladas with two kinds of sauce. These enchiladas are "divorced" because of the separate green and red sauces, a combination that makes this a good dish for a Christmas party. I often top each serving with Pico de Gallo (page 179) for a fresh contrast to the baked enchiladas, but the lettuce and red onion also provide balance with their crisp texture.

FOR THE CHICKEN:

1 tablespoon canola oil

2¼ pounds (1.1 kg) bone-in chicken breast halves with skin

1 medium yellow onion, sliced

2 garlic cloves, coarsely chopped

2 teaspoons kosher salt

6 black peppercorns

1 recipe Tomato-Chipotle Sauce (page 178)

1 recipe Tomatillo-Jalapeño Green Salsa (page 179)

Canola oil, for the baking dish

12 corn tortillas

⅓ cup (35 g) grated aged cotija or Romano cheese

2 cups (75 g) shredded iceberg lettuce

1 small red onion, cut into thin rings

SERVES 4

1 **Make the chicken:** Heat the oil in a large deep saucepan over medium heat. Add the chicken, skin-side down, and cook until the skin is lightly browned, about 5 minutes. Transfer the chicken to a plate. Add the yellow onion and garlic to the saucepan and cook until they are softened, about 3 minutes. Return the chicken to the saucepan and add enough water to cover it, about 2½ quarts (2.5 L). Add the salt and peppercorns and bring the water to a boil over high heat. Reduce the heat to medium-low and partially cover the saucepan. Simmer until an instant-read thermometer inserted in the thickest part of the chicken reads 165°F (74°C), about 35 minutes. Remove it from the heat and let the chicken cool in the liquid.

2 Transfer the chicken to a carving board. (Strain the chicken broth and reserve it for another use.) Remove the skin and bones from the chicken and shred the meat into bite-size pieces. Divide the chicken between two bowls. Moisten the chicken in one bowl with about ⅓ cup (75 g) of the tomato-chipotle sauce, and stir about ⅓ cup (75 g) of the tomatillo sauce into the other bowl of chicken.

3 Position a rack in the center of the oven and preheat it to 350°F (175°C). Lightly oil a 10-by-15-inch (25-by-38-cm) baking dish.

4 Heat a medium nonstick skillet over medium heat. You want six tortillas made with each color of filling. Add a tortilla to the skillet and heat, turning it occasionally, just until it is soft and pliable, about 10 seconds. Transfer the tortilla to a plate. Add about 3 tablespoons of the chicken mixture from one bowl to the bottom half of the tortilla, roll it up, and place it, seam-side down, in the baking dish. Repeat with five more tortillas, arranging them side by side in the dish. Continue with the remaining six tortillas, using the other bowl of filling. Cover each group of tortillas with the remaining matching sauce. Sprinkle them with the cheese.

5 Bake the enchiladas until the sauce is bubbling, about 30 minutes.

6 To serve, transfer three enchiladas to each dinner plate, being sure to serve at least one of each color. Top with a handful of lettuce and a few onion rings. Serve them immediately.

Most people associate mole with the black version of Oaxaca, but there are really many different types of this sauce created from various chilies, seeds, and spices. I am especially fond of this quick version, which gets its thick texture and fruity flavor from an unexpected source—dried plums (aka prunes). This dish would be a fantastic alternative to roast turkey at a holiday meal. The mole can be made well ahead of serving, leaving only the simple job of roasting the turkey breasts. This is a heck of a lot easier than making American gravy!

TURKEY BREAST
WITH DRIED-PLUM MOLE

Pechuga de pavo con mole de ciruelas secas

SERVES 8 TO 10

1 **Make the mole:** Heat 3 tablespoons of the oil in a medium saucepan over medium heat. Add the onion and garlic and cook them, stirring occasionally, until the onion is translucent, about 4 minutes. Add the dried plums, tomatoes, chilies, cinnamon, and peppercorns and stir well. Pour in the stock and bring it to a boil. Reduce the heat to medium-low and simmer until the plums are very soft, about 20 minutes. Let the mixture cool completely.

2 Stir the almonds into the plum mixture. In batches, purée the plum mixture in a blender and transfer it to a bowl.

3 Heat the remaining 2 tablespoons oil in a large skillet over medium heat. Add the puréed plum mixture and return it to a boil. Remove it from the heat and stir in the chocolate until it is melted. Season the mole to taste with salt. (The mole can be cooled, covered, and refrigerated for up to 2 days.)

4 **Make the turkey:** Position an oven rack in the center of the oven and preheat it to 350°F (175°C).

5 Brush the turkey skin with oil and season the turkey all over with the salt and pepper. Place the turkey, skin-side up, in a roasting pan. Roast until an instant-read thermometer inserted in the thickest part of the turkey reads 165°F (74°C), about 1¼ hours. Transfer the turkey to a carving board and let it stand for 10 minutes.

6 Pour the turkey drippings into a glass measuring cup. Skim off the clear fat and reserve the juices. Heat the roasting pan over medium heat until it is sizzling. Add the mole and skimmed juices and stir, scraping up the browned bits in the pan with a wooden spoon. Reduce the heat to very low to keep it warm. If the sauce thickens too much, stir in a few tablespoons of stock or water.

7 Using a sharp knife, carve the turkey across the grain, discarding the bones. Transfer the turkey to a serving platter, overlapping the slices. Spoon about half of the mole over the turkey and sprinkle it with the sesame seeds. Serve it hot, with the remaining sauce passed on the side.

FOR THE DRIED-PLUM MOLE:

5 tablespoons canola oil

1 medium yellow onion, chopped

3 garlic cloves, minced

One 7-ounce (200-g) package pitted dried plums, about 1½ cups

One 14.5-ounce (415-g) can chopped fire-roasted tomatoes, drained

2 pasilla chilies, seeded, deribbed, and toasted (see page 23) or ¼ cup (25 g) pure ground ancho chile (do not toast the ground chile)

One 1½-inch (4-cm) piece cinnamon stick

3 black peppercorns

3½ cups (840 ml) chicken stock or reduced-sodium chicken broth

⅓ cup (30 g) sliced natural almonds, toasted

1½ ounces (45 g) unsweetened chocolate, finely chopped

Kosher salt

FOR THE TURKEY:

Two 2½-pound (1.2-kg) bone-in turkey breast halves with skin

Canola oil, for brushing

2 teaspoons kosher salt

1 teaspoon freshly ground black pepper

1 tablespoon sesame seeds

7

RED MEAT

PEPPER-CRUSTED FILET MIGNONS

WITH WILD MUSHROOM & TRUFFLE CHIMICHURRI

Filete mignon empanizado con pimienta y hongos silvestres con chimichurri de trufa

FOR THE WILD MUSHROOM AND TRUFFLE CHIMICHURRI:

2 tablespoons extra-virgin olive oil

1 pound (455 g) assorted mushrooms, such as cremini, oyster, and stemmed shiitake, sliced and coarsely chopped into ½-inch (12-mm) pieces

3 tablespoons minced shallot

2 garlic cloves, minced

1 teaspoon minced fresh thyme

2 tablespoons white truffle oil

2 tablespoons sherry vinegar

1 teaspoon honey

Kosher salt and freshly ground black pepper

FOR THE BEEF:

Four 8-ounce (225-g) filet mignons, cut 1 inch (2.5 cm) thick

2 tablespoons canola oil

1 teaspoon cracked ground black peppercorns

1 teaspoon kosher salt

½ cup (120 ml) hearty red wine

A sizzling steak can be the most satisfying meal in the world. Chimichurri is a tart Argentinian herbed steak sauce, which I've enhanced with mushrooms and truffle oil. I make this with filet mignons because they fit so easily in a large skillet for a party of four at a dinner party. For a larger group, use two skillets, or grill the steaks outside and skip the deglazing.

SERVES 4

1 **Make the chimichurri:** Heat a large skillet over high heat. Add the oil and heat until it is hot but not smoking. Add the mushrooms and cook, stirring occasionally, until the juices have evaporated and the mushrooms are browned and sizzling, about 10 minutes. During the last 2 minutes, add the shallot, garlic, and thyme. Remove the skillet from the heat.

2 In a medium bowl, whisk together the truffle oil, vinegar, and honey. Add the mushroom mixture and mix well. Season it to taste with salt and pepper. Let it cool. (The chimichurri can be covered and refrigerated for up to 1 day. Let it stand at room temperature for 1 hour before serving.)

3 **Make the beef:** Lightly brush the beef with 1 tablespoon of the oil and season it with the peppercorns and salt. Let it stand at room temperature for 30 minutes to 1 hour before cooking.

4 Position a rack in the center of the oven and preheat it to 450°F (230°C).

5 Heat a large ovenproof skillet, preferably cast iron, over high heat. Turn on your stove air vent, as the steaks may smoke. Add the remaining 1 tablespoon oil and tilt the pan to coat the bottom with oil. Add the steaks and cook them, adjusting the heat as needed so the steaks cook steadily without burning, until the undersides are deeply browned, about 2 minutes. Flip the steaks and cook to brown the other sides. Transfer the skillet with the steaks to the oven and roast until the steaks feel only slightly resilient when pressed on top with a fingertip, about 4 minutes for medium-rare meat. Transfer the steaks to a wire cooling rack and let them stand for 3 minutes. (Placing the steaks on a rack instead of a plate helps them retain more of their juices.)

6 Pour out the fat in the skillet. Heat the skillet over medium heat until sizzling. Add the wine and bring it to a boil, scraping up the browned bits in the pan. Remove it from the heat.

7 Transfer each steak to a dinner plate. Spoon the wine mixture over the steaks, and top them with equal amounts of the mushroom chimichurri. Serve them immediately.

These are about as far away from a fast-food taco as you can get. The moist and tender brisket filling is offset by a crisp cabbage slaw and piquant pickled onions. I had never had a taco in a crisp shell until I came to the U.S., so I always serve my tacos in soft tortillas.

SERVES 4

1 **Make the pickled onions:** Toss the onion, sugar, and salt together in a small bowl. Let them stand for 1 hour. Drain but do not rinse the onions. Return them to the bowl. Stir in the vinegar and salsa. Cover and refrigerate the onions for at least 2 hours and up to 1 week.

2 **Make the slaw:** Mix the mayonnaise, lime juice, and chipotle together in a medium bowl. Add the cabbage and mix well. Season the slaw to taste with salt. Cover and refrigerate it for up to 2 hours. (If refrigerated longer, the cabbage will lose its crispness.)

3 Reheat the beef filling in a medium nonstick skillet over medium heat, stirring often, until it is hot, about 3 minutes.

4 Serve the tortillas with the bowls of the beef filling, slaw, pickled onion rings, and avocado. Let each guest make the tacos with the desired ingredients.

BRISKET TACOS

WITH CHIPOTLE SLAW & PICKLED RED ONIONS

Tacos de falda con ensalada de col con chipotle y cebolla morada en escabeche

FOR THE PICKLED RED ONIONS:

1 medium red onion, cut into very thin rounds

2 tablespoons sugar

1 tablespoon kosher salt

1 cup (240 ml) red wine vinegar

½ teaspoon bottled habanero salsa

FOR THE CHIPOTLE SLAW:

⅓ cup (75 ml) mayonnaise

1 tablespoon fresh lime juice

1 canned chipotle chile in adobo, minced

3 cups (195 g) packed shredded green cabbage

2 cups (430 g) Shredded Beef Filling with Tomatoes and Chilies (page 175)

Twelve 6-inch (15-cm) flour tortillas, heated according to package directions

1 large ripe Hass avocado, cut into 12 slices

BEEF & CORN ANTICUCHO

WITH AJÍ AMARILLO SAUCE

Anticucho de carne y maíz con salsa de ají amarillo

FOR THE PERUVIAN MARINADE AND BEEF:

½ cup (130 g) ají panca paste

½ cup (120 ml) canola oil

2 tablespoons soy sauce

2 tablespoons distilled white vinegar

1 tablespoon Sriracha or other hot red pepper sauce

4 garlic cloves, coarsely chopped

½ teaspoon dried oregano

½ teaspoon ground cumin

½ teaspoon kosher salt

½ teaspoon freshly ground black pepper

2 pounds (910 g) beef sirloin, trimmed of excess fat, cut into chunks about 1½ inches (4 cm) square

FOR THE AJÍ AMARILLO SALSA:

1 medium yellow bell pepper, cut into 2-inch (5-cm) chunks

1 teaspoon canola oil

½ cup (120 ml) mayonnaise

2 tablespoons ají amarillo or ají panca paste

1 tablespoon fresh lime juice

Kosher salt

3 ears of corn, husked and cut crosswise into 4 chunks each

SPECIAL EQUIPMENT:

4 long metal grilling skewers

The Peruvian version of beef kebabs is a great introduction to the country's ají chilies, with red ají panca in the marinade and yellow ají amarillo in the sauce. You can always use the substitutes on page 14, but Peruvian ingredients are getting easier and easier to find. Thick and spicy, this is not your average marinade, and you'll be glad that you made it. Inexpensive metal grilling skewers, sold at every supermarket, work best for holding the beef and corn. If you use bamboo skewers, soak them for at least 30 minutes in cold water before using, and wrap exposed handles in aluminum foil to protect them from the heat of the grill. These can also be assembled in smaller portions as appetizers.

SERVES 4

1 Make the marinade: Purée the ají panca, oil, soy sauce, vinegar, Sriracha, garlic, oregano, cumin, salt, and pepper together in a blender. Transfer the marinade to a 1-gallon (3.8-L) zip-top plastic bag. Add the beef. Seal the bag and refrigerate it, turning the bag occasionally, for at least 2 and up to 16 hours.

2 Make the ají salsa: Position a rack in the center of the oven and preheat it to 350ºF (175ºC). Toss the yellow pepper with the oil on a rimmed baking sheet. Bake it, stirring occasionally, until the pepper chunks are very tender but not browned, about 25 minutes. Let them cool completely. Purée the yellow peppers, mayonnaise, ají amarillo paste, and lime juice together in a blender. Season the salsa to taste with salt. (The salsa can be covered and refrigerated for up to 3 days.)

3 Prepare an outdoor grill for direct cooking over high heat. For a charcoal grill, let the coals burn until they are covered with white ash and you can hold your hand about 1 inch (2.5 cm) above the coals for 1 to 2 seconds. For a gas grill, preheat it on high and adjust the heat to 550ºF (285ºC).

4 Remove the beef from the marinade and shake off the excess. Thread 4 chunks of beef and 3 chunks of corn onto each skewer. (Skewer each corn chunk through its center, like a bull's eye.) Brush the grill grates clean. Cook the skewers, turning them once or twice, until the beef is browned, 8 to 10 minutes for medium-rare.

5 Divide the skewers among four dinner plates. Divide the salsa among four ramekins and add a ramekin to each plate. Serve them immediately.

GUAVA-BRAISED BEEF BRISKET

Estofado de falda de res con guayaba

3 tablespoons canola oil

One 3½-pound (1.6-kg) beef brisket, trimmed, with an ⅛-inch (3-mm) layer of fat

Kosher salt and freshly ground black pepper

1 medium white onion, chopped

1 large carrot, chopped

2 large celery ribs, chopped

4 garlic cloves, chopped

4 dried ancho chilies, stemmed and seeded, torn into large pieces, or 3 tablespoons pure ground ancho chile

1 cup (240 ml) thawed frozen guava purée or one 11.3-ounce (335-g) can guava nectar

¼ cup (60 ml) distilled white vinegar

1 tablespoon mesquite liquid smoke (optional)

Chopped fresh cilantro, for serving

Beef brisket is a flavor powerhouse, and slow simmering dissolves its tough parts into succulence. In this recipe, I give it a Latin twist with guava, for an especially tasty sauce. When picking the brisket at the market, choose a thick cut from the wider end—the so-called first cut is sometimes too thin for braising. Serve this with Mashed Potatoes with Oaxaca Cheese (page 145).

SERVES 6

1 Position a rack in the bottom third of the oven and preheat it to 350°F (175 °C).

2 Heat 2 tablespoons of the oil in a Dutch oven over medium-high heat. Season the brisket all over with 2 teaspoons salt and 1 teaspoon pepper. Place it in the Dutch oven and cook, turning it occasionally, until it is nicely browned, 10 to 12 minutes. Transfer it to a plate.

3 Add the remaining 1 tablespoon oil to the Dutch oven. Add the onion, carrot, celery, and garlic and reduce the heat to medium. Cook, stirring the vegetables occasionally, until the onions are very tender and golden brown, about 7 minutes. Stir in the chilies and cook for 1 minute. Pour in the guava, vinegar, and liquid smoke, if using, and bring them to a simmer, scraping up the browned bits in the Dutch oven with a wooden spoon. Return the brisket to the Dutch oven and add enough hot water to come about three-quarters up the sides of the meat. Bring it to a boil.

4 Cover the Dutch oven and transfer it to the oven. Bake until the brisket is fork-tender, about 2½ hours. Transfer the brisket to a carving board and let it stand for 20 minutes.

5 Meanwhile, make the sauce: Strain the cooking liquid through a wire sieve into a large bowl, reserving the solids. Let the liquid stand for 5 minutes. Skim off and discard the clear fat from the top of the liquid. Let the liquid and solids cool for 5 minutes more. In batches, purée the solids and skimmed cooking liquid in a blender and return them to the Dutch oven. (Or return the solids and liquid to the pot and purée them with an immersion blender.) Season the sauce to taste with salt and pepper. Reheat it to simmering.

6 Cut the brisket across the grain into ½-inch (12-mm) slices. Transfer it to a platter and top it with the sauce. Sprinkle it with the cilantro and serve hot.

Spaghetti and meatballs, move over, because this version of noodles and tomato sauce may become your new favorite pasta dish. It's the perfect example of how easy dinner can be when you have Shredded Beef Filling with Tomatoes and Chilies (page 175) in the freezer, ready to use. *Sopa seca* means "dry soup" in Spanish, but it is actually thin noodles (*fideos*) cooked in a spicy tomato sauce until they are tender and have absorbed the sauce. You'll find these skeins of thin pasta strands in the Latin aisle of the supermarket. I like sopa seca best with beef, but you could use Slow-Cooked Mexican Pork Shoulder (page 177) or leftover roast chicken.

"DRY" NOODLE SOUP

WITH BEEF

Sopa seca de fideos con res

█████ ▌ **SERVES 4** ▌ █████

1 Process the tomato purée, chipotle, adobo sauce, and garlic together in a blender until smooth.

2 Heat the oil in a large saucepan over medium heat. Add the unbroken fideo skeins to the oil and cook, turning them once, until they are golden brown on both sides, about 1½ minutes. Transfer them to a plate. Add more oil to the saucepan, if needed. Add the broken fideos (or all of the vermicelli) and cook, stirring them often, until they are golden brown, about 1 minute. Return the skeins to the pot. Immediately pour in the tomato purée mixture and stir well. Stir in the stock and bring it to a simmer. Reduce the heat to medium-low and cook, stirring often, until the fideos are very tender and have absorbed most of the liquid, about 8 minutes. Add more stock or water, if needed, to keep the mixture moist and from sticking to the saucepan bottom. Season the soup to taste with salt.

3 Divide the soup among four deep bowls. Top each with equal portions of the beef, avocado, and cilantro and a dollop of the crema. Serve them hot with the lime wedges.

1⅔ cups (425 g) canned tomato purée

1 canned chipotle chile in adobo, plus 1 teaspoon adobo sauce

2 garlic cloves

⅓ cup (75 ml) canola oil, plus more if needed

One 12-ounce (340-g) package fideos or coarsely broken vermicelli

3½ cups (840 ml) chicken stock or reduced-sodium chicken broth

Kosher salt

2 cups (430 g) Shredded Beef Filling with Tomatoes and Chilies (page 175), heated

1 ripe Hass avocado, cut into ½-inch (12-mm) dice

¼ cup (5 g) finely chopped fresh cilantro

Crema or sour cream, for serving

Lime wedges, for serving

Arepas, thick corn tortillas that are stuffed like sandwiches, have already mainstreamed in Miami, New York, and elsewhere, with restaurants that specialize in this Latin treat from Venezuela and Colombia. Like sandwiches, you can fill them with just about anything (although don't expect to see peanut butter and jelly arepas anytime soon). Similar to English muffins, which are also griddled, they require a special corn flour, readily available at Latin markets.

BEEF & GUACAMOLE AREPAS

Arepas con res y guacamole

SERVES 6

1 Make the arepas: Whisk the corn flour and salt together in a large bowl. Make a well in the center and pour in the oil. Gradually stir in 3 cups (720 ml) lukewarm water to make a smooth dough, working out any lumps with your fingertips. (This is the key to a great arepa.) Let the dough stand for 3 minutes; it should be soft and easy to shape. If necessary, adjust the consistency by working in more corn flour or water as needed with your fingertips.

2 Divide the dough into 6 equal portions. Shape each on a work counter into a thick round about 4 inches (10 cm) in diameter and 1 inch (2.5 cm) thick.

3 Position a rack in the center of the oven and preheat it to 350°F (175°C). Lightly oil a large nonstick skillet or griddle and heat it over medium heat.

4 In batches, add the arepas to the skillet and cook them, turning once, until both sides are splotched golden brown, about 10 minutes. Transfer them directly to the oven rack (without a baking sheet.) Bake until the arepas have formed a taut surface, about 15 minutes. Transfer them to a plate to cool for 5 minutes.

5 Using a serrated knife, split each arepa in half crosswise. Fill each with about ⅓ cup (70 g) of the beef, a generous dollop of guacamole, and about 1 tablespoon crema. Serve immediately, with plenty of napkins.

FOR THE AREPAS:

3 cups (430 g) white corn flour for arepas (see page 15)

2 teaspoons kosher salt

2 tablespoons canola oil, plus more for the skillet

2 cups (430 g) Shredded Beef Filling with Tomatoes and Chilies (page 175)

1 recipe Classic Guacamole (page 44)

Crema or sour cream, for serving

BEEF & POTATO FLAUTAS

Flautas de res y papas

"Flutes" of corn tortillas, filled with creamy potatoes and tender beef and fried until golden and crisp, are one of the tortilla dishes that have made Mexican food beloved around the world. I usually make these with shredded beef brisket filling, but Slow-Cooked Mexican Pork Shoulder (page 177) is a good choice, too. Flautas are like pizza—you can buy them, but nothing beats your sense of accomplishment when you eat a crunchy, fresh-from-the-pot flauta made with your own hands.

SERVES 6; MAKES 12 FLAUTAS

FOR THE POTATO PURÉE:

Kosher salt

12 ounces (340 g) Yukon Gold potatoes, peeled and quartered

2 tablespoons unsalted butter, at room temperature

2 tablespoons heavy cream, heated, as needed

Freshly ground white pepper

FOR THE MAGGI ONIONS:

1 tablespoon canola oil

1 large yellow onion, cut into thin half-moons

½ jalapeño, seeded and finely chopped

1 teaspoon Maggi seasoning or soy sauce, or more to taste

Canola oil, for deep-frying

12 corn tortillas

¼ cup (35 g) all-purpose flour

1 cup (215 g) Shredded Beef Filling with Tomatoes and Chilies (page 175), well shredded

1½ cups (235 g) Tomatillo-Jalapeño Green Salsa (page 179)

12 wooden toothpicks, for securing the flautas

1 **Make the potato purée:** Put the potatoes in a medium saucepan and add enough cold salted water to cover them by 1 inch (2.5 cm). Bring them to a boil over high heat. Reduce the heat to low and simmer until the potatoes are tender, 20 to 25 minutes. Drain the potatoes in a wire sieve. Using a rubber spatula, rub the potatoes through the sieve into a medium bowl. Stir in the butter until it melts. Stir in the cream and season the purée to taste with salt and pepper. Cover and set aside.

2 **Make the Maggi onions:** Heat the oil in a large skillet over medium heat. Add the onions and cover. Cook, stirring occasionally, until the onions are softened, about 5 minutes. Reduce the heat to medium-low. Uncover and cook them, stirring occasionally, until the onions are very tender and deep golden brown, about 20 minutes. During the last few minutes, stir in the jalapeño and Maggi. Let the onions cool. Season them to taste with additional Maggi. (The purée and onions can be covered and refrigerated for up to 1 day. Remove them from the refrigerator 1 hour before using.)

3 **Assemble the flautas:** Place a plate and a rimmed baking sheet near the stove and line them with paper towels. Pour ½ cup (120 ml) oil into a large deep skillet and heat until it is very hot and shimmering. Mix the flour with ¼ cup (60 ml) water in a cup, to use to seal the flautas.

4 Coarsely chop the Maggi onions, transfer them to a bowl, and stir in the beef. For each flauta, using kitchen tongs, dip a tortilla in the oil and cook just until the tortilla is softened and can be folded without breaking, about 10 seconds. Transfer the tortilla to the plate. Spread about 1½ tablespoons of the potato purée on the bottom half of the tortilla. Cover the purée with about 1½ tablespoons of the beef mixture. Starting at the bottom, roll up the flauta. Brush the top of the flauta with a dab of the flour mixture to glue it closed, and secure it shut with a wooden toothpick. Place the flauta on the baking sheet. (The flautas can be covered lightly with plastic wrap and refrigerated for up to 3 hours. Remove them from the refrigerator 1 hour before deep-frying. If making the flautas ahead, turn off the heat from under the oil.)

5 Pour in enough oil to come halfway up the sides of the skillet and heat it over high heat until the oil reaches 350°F (175°C) on a deep-frying thermometer. Position a rack in the center of the oven and preheat it to 200°F (90°C). Place a wire cooling rack over a rimmed baking sheet.

6 In batches, without crowding, add the flautas to the oil and fry them, turning occasionally, until they are crisp and golden, about 2½ minutes. Transfer the flautas to the wire rack and keep them warm in the oven while frying the remaining flautas. Serve them warm, with the salsa for dipping.

TACO FIESTA

Blood Orange Chileda
(PAGE 212)

Revelación (PAGE 211)

Queso Fundido with Wild Mushrooms (PAGE 49)

Solterito of Green Vegetables with Avocado–White Balsamic Dressing & Queso Fresco (PAGE 58)

Tacos with Flank Steak & Portobello Mushrooms (PAGE 128)

Chicken Tinga Tacos (PAGE 105)

Chilean Cabernet Sauvignon

Buttermilk Tres Leches Cake (PAGE 154)

TACOS
WITH
FLANK STEAK
& PORTOBELLO MUSHROOMS

Tacos de alambre

FOR THE MARINATED SKIRT STEAK AND MUSHROOMS:

One 12-ounce (340-g) skirt steak

1 batch orange-chile marinade (see page 104)

1 large portobello mushroom, stem removed

FOR THE ALAMBRE FILLING:

2 tablespoons canola oil

5 ounces (140 g) Spanish-style smoked chorizo, cut into ½-inch (12-mm) dice

1 large red bell pepper, cut into ¼-inch (6-mm) strips

1 large yellow onion, thinly sliced

1 teaspoon Maggi seasoning or soy sauce

In Mexican cuisine, alambre is a kind of hash, with meat, peppers, and whatever other ingredients are at hand to make a mouthwatering mash-up. My favorite recipe has the grilled (or broiled) steak and portobello mushrooms mixed into a sauté of bell peppers, chorizo, and caramelized onions. If you wish, serve the separate components in individual bowls so each diner can personalize his or her taco.

SERVES 4

1 **Make the steak and mushrooms:** Combine the steak and marinade in a 1-gallon (3.8-L) zip-top plastic bag. Refrigerate it for at least 1 and up to 3 hours, no longer. During the last 30 minutes, add the portobello cap and coat it with the marinade.

2 **Meanwhile, make the filling:** Heat 1 tablespoon of the oil in a large skillet over medium heat. Add the chorizo and cook until it is beginning to brown, about 2 minutes. Stir in the bell pepper and cover. Cook, stirring it occasionally, until the pepper is tender, about 5 minutes. Transfer it to a large bowl.

3 Add the remaining 1 tablespoon oil to the skillet over medium heat. Add the onion and cover. Cook, stirring it occasionally, until it is softened, about 5 minutes. Uncover and reduce the heat to medium-low. Cook, stirring it occasionally, until the onion is very tender and golden brown, about 20 minutes. Stir in the Maggi and cook until it is absorbed, about 1 minute. Transfer the onions to the bowl with the chorizo mixture. (The filling can be stored at room temperature for up to 1 hour. Or cool it, cover, and refrigerate it for up to 3 hours.)

4 Prepare an outdoor grill for direct cooking over high heat. For a charcoal grill, let the coals burn until they are covered with white ash and you can hold your hand about 1 inch (2.5 cm) above the cooking grate for only 1 or 2 seconds. For a gas grill, preheat it on high and adjust the heat to at least 550ºF (285ºC). (Or position a broiler rack about 6 inches/15 cm from the source of heat and preheat it on high.)

5 Remove the steak and mushroom from their marinade and shake off the excess marinade. Brush the grill grates clean. Lightly oil the grill grates. Place the steak and mushroom on the grill (or under the broiler). Cook, with the grill covered as much as possible, turning them occasionally, until the steak and mushroom are browned on both sides and the steak feels only slightly resilient when pressed on top in the thickest part, about 6 minutes. The steak should be quite rare. Transfer both to a carving board and let them stand for 3 minutes.

6 Add the tortillas to the grill and cook, turning them occasionally, until they are lightly browned on both sides and heated through, about 1 minute. (Or heat the tortillas in a microwave or standard oven according to the package directions.) Transfer them to a napkin-lined bowl and wrap them in the napkin to keep warm.

7 Return the chorizo mixture to the skillet and reheat it over medium-high heat, stirring often, until it is sizzling. Slice the steak across the grain about ½ inch (12 mm) thick. Cut the sliced steak and mushrooms into bite-size pieces and add them, along with any carving juices, to the chorizo mixture. Transfer everything to a bowl.

8 Serve the tortillas with bowls of the alambre filling, avocado, and pico de gallo, and let each guest make the tacos with the desired amounts of ingredients.

Canola oil, for the grill

Twelve 6-inch (15-cm) flour tortillas

1 ripe Hass avocado, cut into ½-inch (12-mm) dice, or Guacamole (page 44)

1 recipe Pico de Gallo (page 179)

There are many different versions of salpicón, the hearty salad that is a specialty of both Mexican and Colombian cooks. The constants are shredded meat (or poultry or chopped seafood) and a sharp dressing. I like to serve it on grilled tortillas for a smoky crunch that everyone loves. (The tortillas can also be fried in oil, if you wish.)

GRILLED
TOSTADA
WITH BEEF
SALPICÓN

Tostada con salpicón de res

SERVES 6

1 **Make the dressing:** Whisk the vinegar, lime juice, onion, oregano, salt, and pepper together in a medium bowl. Gradually whisk in the oil.

2 **Grill the tortillas:** Prepare an outdoor grill for direct cooking over medium-high heat. For a charcoal grill, let the coals burn until they are covered with white ash and you can hold your hand about 1 inch (2.5 cm) above the cooking grate for about 3 seconds. For a gas grill, preheat it on high, then adjust the heat to 450°F (230°C). Or preheat a stovetop grill pan over medium-high heat.

3 Lightly brush the tortillas on both sides with oil. Place them on the grill and cook, with the lid closed as much as possible, turning them occasionally, until they are crisp and lightly charred, about 2 minutes. Remove them from the grill.

4 **Make the salpicón:** Toss the lettuce, cucumber, tomatoes, radishes, capers, and cilantro with the dressing in a large bowl.

5 Place a tortilla on each of six dinner plates. Divide the lettuce mixture among them, topped by the beef. Top them with the sliced avocado and serve immediately.

FOR THE SALPICÓN DRESSING:

¼ cup (60 ml) distilled white vinegar

3 tablespoons fresh lime juice

3 tablespoons minced red onion

2 teaspoons dried Mexican oregano, crumbled

1 teaspoon kosher salt

½ teaspoon freshly ground black pepper

¾ cup (180 ml) olive oil

FOR THE GRILLED TORTILLAS:

6 corn tortillas

Canola oil, for brushing

FOR THE SALPICÓN:

½ head iceberg lettuce, cored and shredded

½ seedless (English) cucumber, cut into ½-inch (12-mm) dice

2 plum tomatoes, seeded and cut into ½-inch (12-mm) dice

4 radishes, cut into ¼-inch (6-mm) dice

½ cup (90 g) drained nonpareil capers

¼ cup (5 g) coarsely chopped fresh cilantro

3 cups (645 g) Shredded Beef Filling with Tomatoes and Chilies (page 175), at room temperature

2 ripe Hass avocados, thinly sliced

CARNITAS SLIDERS

WITH SRIRACHA MAYONNAISE

Hamburguesitas de carnitas con mayonesa Sriracha

FOR THE SRIRACHA MAYONNAISE:

½ cup (120 ml) mayonnaise, preferably Kewpie

2 teaspoons Sriracha or other Asian hot red pepper sauce

1 teaspoon fresh lime juice

2 garlic cloves, minced

FOR THE LIME-PICKLED ONIONS:

1 small red onion, cut into thin half-moons

½ habanero chile, seeded and minced

1 tablespoon fresh lime juice

2 teaspoons chopped fresh cilantro

1 teaspoon kosher salt

Kosher salt

1 long, narrow orange-fleshed sweet potato, cut into twelve ¼-inch (6-mm) rounds

2 cups Slow-Cooked Mexican Pork Shoulder (page 177)

12 potato dinner rolls or slider buns, split

Here is a globe-trotting mini sandwich with an incredible combination of international ingredients. Starting with the concept of the American slider, it goes to Mexico for pork shoulder and a pickled onion garnish, down to Peru for sweet potatoes, and over to Asia for a spicy mayonnaise.

SERVES 4; MAKES 12 SLIDERS

1 **Make the mayonnaise:** Whisk the mayonnaise, Sriracha, lime juice, and garlic together in a small bowl. Cover and set it aside. (The mayonnaise can be made up to 5 days ahead and kept refrigerated.)

2 **Make the pickled onions:** Combine the onion, habanero, lime juice, cilantro, and salt in a shallow bowl. Cover and let them stand at room temperature for at least 30 minutes and up to 2 hours.

3 Bring a medium saucepan of salted water to a boil over high heat. Add the sweet potatoes and reduce the heat to medium-low. Simmer until they are just tender, 10 to 12 minutes. Drain them carefully, trying to keep the rounds intact. Transfer them to a plate and tent with aluminum foil to keep them warm.

4 Heat a medium nonstick skillet over medium heat. Add the pork and cook, turning it occasionally, until it is heated through, about 3 minutes. Reduce the heat to very low to keep it warm.

5 Drain the onions well. Spread each bun with mayonnaise. Divide the pork among the buns, add a sweet potato round, and then a few onion rings. For each serving, add three sliders to a plate and serve them hot.

Italy is not the only country that makes delicious meatballs, and just about every cuisine has a version. This is a Mexican rendition with ground lamb, which deserves to be used more often in this country. This kind of braised dish is often made in a cazuela, an earthenware cooking casserole that does double-duty as an attractive serving utensil. A heavy skillet (but not a cast-iron one, which could react with the tomatoes) works well, too. Serve it with rice or pasta to soak up the spicy sauce.

LAMB MEATBALLS
WITH ZUCCHINI & GOAT CHEESE

Albóndigas de cordero con calabacitas y queso de cabra

SERVES 4 TO 6

1 Make the meatballs: Using your hands, mix the lamb, garlic, thyme, parsley, mint, salt, paprika, and the black and cayenne peppers together in a large bowl. Do not overmix them. Add the panko and cream and mix again just to incorporate them. Cover and refrigerate the mixture for 15 minutes.

2 Using a heaping tablespoon for each, shape the lamb mixture into meatballs and transfer to a baking sheet. Gradually heat a 12-inch (30.5-cm) cazuela over a 5-minute span from low to medium-high. Add 2 tablespoons of the oil and swirl the cazuela to coat. (Or heat the oil in a large deep skillet over medium-high heat.) Cook the meatballs in two batches, turning them occasionally, until they are browned on all sides, 6 to 8 minutes. Using a slotted spoon, return the meatballs to the baking sheet.

3 Pour off and discard the fat from the cazuela and wipe it out with paper towels. Add the remaining 2 tablespoons oil to the cazuela and reduce the heat to medium. Add the onion and cook, stirring it occasionally, until it is translucent, about 3 minutes. Add the garlic and cook until it is fragrant, about 1 minute. Stir in the puréed tomatoes, olive brine, zucchini, and chilies and bring them to a simmer.

4 Return the meatballs to the pan. Reduce the heat to medium-low. Simmer them, uncovered, occasionally stirring, until the meatballs are cooked through and the sauce has reduced slightly, about 30 minutes. Season the sauce to taste with salt. Sprinkle it with the mint and the cheese and serve the meatballs and sauce hot from the cazuela.

NOTE Some liquor stores and online cocktail ingredient sites sell olive brine without the olives for drinkers who like Dirty Martinis. It's handy for this recipe, too.

FOR THE LAMB MEATBALLS:

2 pounds (910 g) ground lamb

6 garlic cloves, minced

2 teaspoons finely chopped fresh thyme

2 teaspoons finely chopped fresh parsley

2 teaspoons finely chopped fresh mint

2 teaspoons kosher salt

1½ teaspoons smoked sweet paprika

1 teaspoon freshly ground black pepper

¼ teaspoon cayenne pepper

½ cup (35 g) panko

⅓ cup (75 ml) heavy cream

4 tablespoons (60 ml) olive oil

1 medium yellow onion, chopped

6 garlic cloves, thinly sliced

One 28-ounce (800-g) can peeled tomatoes in juice, preferably San Marzano, puréed in a blender

½ cup (120 ml) brine from Spanish green olives (see Note)

2 medium zucchini, diced

2 to 3 chilies de árbol, seeded and stemmed, or 2 tablespoons pure ground ancho chile and ⅛ teaspoon cayenne pepper

Kosher salt

Chopped fresh mint, for serving

1 cup (115 g) crumbled goat cheese

8

VEGETABLES & SIDE DISHES

VENEZUELAN
CORN PANCAKES
WITH SAVORY TOMATO JAM & CHEESE

Cachapas con mermelada de tomate y queso

FOR THE SPICY TOMATO JAM:

One 3-inch (7.5-cm) cinnamon stick

1 star anise

2 pounds (910 g) ripe plum tomatoes, peeled, seeded, and cut into ½-inch (12-mm) dice (see Note)

⅓ cup (75 ml) red wine vinegar

⅓ cup plus 1 tablespoon (85 g) sugar

1 jalapeño, preferably red, cut into thin rounds, seeds removed

2 tablespoons fresh lime juice

2 tablespoons chopped fresh cilantro

2 teaspoons soy sauce

1 teaspoon pure ground chipotle chile

FOR THE CACHAPAS:

2 cups (290 g) fresh corn kernels

½ cup (1 stick; 115 g) unsalted butter, melted and cooled to tepid

½ cup (120 ml) heavy cream

⅓ cup (75 ml) whole milk

1 large egg

¾ cup (105 g) sweet corn flour for arepas (see page 15)

⅓ cup (45 g) all-purpose flour

¼ cup (50 g) sugar

1½ teaspoons kosher salt

Canola oil, for the griddle

1 cup (115 g) shredded Oaxaca or string cheese

I serve these most often as a sweet-and-savory main course with a salad. However, with a side of sausage or pork, they are also a fine brunch dish. One important note: This is a more delicate batter than in American pancakes, so I recommend making a test pancake first to check the cooking time and griddle temperature. The tomato jam will keep for a few weeks in the refrigerator, but it probably won't last that long. You will need sweet corn flour for arepas to make these.

SERVES 4; MAKES ABOUT 12 PANCAKES

1 **Make the jam:** Wrap the cinnamon stick and star anise together in a rinsed piece of cheesecloth and tie them into a packet with kitchen string. Bring the tomatoes, spice packet, vinegar, sugar, and jalapeño to a boil in a medium nonreactive saucepan, stirring often. Reduce the heat to low. Simmer, stirring often and breaking up the tomatoes with the side of the spoon, until the tomatoes are pulpy and the juices are almost completely evaporated, about 1 hour. Transfer the jam to a nonreactive bowl and let it cool. Stir in the lime juice, cilantro, soy sauce, and chipotle. (The jam can be refrigerated in a covered container for up to 3 weeks.)

2 **Make the cachapas:** Purée the corn, butter, cream, milk, and egg together in a blender. Add the arepas flour, all-purpose flour, sugar, and salt and blend until the batter is smooth, stopping the blender to scrape down the sides of the jar as needed.

3 Position a rack in the center of the oven and preheat it to 200°F (90°C). Heat a large griddle or skillet over medium heat.

4 Oil the griddle. Using about ¼ cup (60 ml) for each, pour the batter onto the griddle and cook it until small bubbles form on the surface and the tops of the pancakes look set, about 2 minutes. Turn the pancakes over and sprinkle each with about 1 tablespoon of the cheese. Continue cooking them until the other sides are golden brown and the cheese is slightly melted, about 1½ minutes more. Transfer the pancakes to a large rimmed baking sheet and keep them warm in the oven while cooking the remaining pancakes.

5 Serve the pancakes hot, each topped with a spoonful of tomato jam.

NOTE To peel tomatoes, bring a large saucepan of water to a boil over high heat. A few at a time, drop the tomatoes into the water and boil them just until the skin loosens, about 30 seconds. Using a slotted spoon, transfer the tomatoes to a bowl of ice water. Let them cool briefly, then use a paring knife to peel off the skin.

WILD MUSHROOM & CORN ENCHILADAS

WITH POBLANO SAUCE

Enchiladas de setas silvestres y maíz con salsa Poblana

FOR THE MUSHROOM AND CORN FILLING:

3 tablespoons canola oil

1 medium yellow onion, finely chopped

2 garlic cloves, minced

1 pound (455 g) fresh mushrooms, such as cremini, oyster, and stemmed shiitake, sliced

1 cup (240 ml) whole or part-skim ricotta cheese

1 cup (220 g) roasted corn kernels (see Note, page 59) or thawed frozen

2 tablespoons chopped fresh oregano

Kosher salt and freshly ground black pepper

FOR THE POBLANO SAUCE:

2 tablespoons canola oil

1 small yellow onion, chopped

2 garlic cloves, minced

5 poblano chilies, roasted, seeded, and coarsely chopped

3 cups (720 ml) heavy cream

Kosher salt and freshly ground black pepper

A vegetarian main course like this will make meat-eaters jealous. The mushrooms listed in the ingredients are only suggestions. Experiment with what is available at your grocery or farmers' market. An Asian market is an especially good place to make some discoveries, and I often make this with maitake (or hen-of-the-woods) and king trumpet mushrooms in the mix. Some mushrooms give off more juices than others, so be prepared to adjust the filling cooking time as needed for the juices to evaporate.

SERVES 4

1 **Make the filling:** Heat the oil in a large skillet over medium heat. Add the onion and garlic and cook, stirring them occasionally, until the onion softens, about 3 minutes. In batches, stir in the mushrooms, letting the first addition wilt before adding the next. Increase the heat to medium-high. Cook, stirring them occasionally, until the mushrooms are beginning to brown, about 10 minutes. Transfer them to a bowl and let them cool completely.

2 Stir the ricotta, corn, and oregano into the mushroom mixture. Season it to taste with salt and pepper. (The mushroom filling can be covered and refrigerated for up to 1 day.)

3 **Make the poblano sauce:** Heat the oil in a large saucepan over medium heat. Add the onion and garlic and cook, stirring them occasionally, until the onion is translucent, about 4 minutes. Stir in the chilies and cream and bring them to a boil. Reduce the heat to medium-low and cook the sauce at a steady simmer until the cream has thickened lightly, 12 to 15 minutes. Remove the pan from the heat and let the sauce cool. In batches, purée the poblano mixture in a blender. You should have 4 cups (960 ml) sauce. If necessary, adjust the amount with more cream or reduce the sauce further in the saucepan. Season it to taste with salt and pepper. (The sauce can be cooled, covered, and refrigerated for up to 1 day.)

4 Lightly oil a 10-by-15-inch (25-by-38-cm) baking dish. Spread about ½ cup (120 ml) of the sauce in the baking dish. Heat the oil in a medium skillet over medium heat until the oil is hot but not smoking. Add a tortilla to the hot oil and cook just until it is pliable, about 10 seconds. Using tongs, lift the tortilla from the oil, letting the excess oil drip back into the skillet, and transfer the softened tortilla to a plate. Spoon about 3 tablespoons of the filling into the center of the tortilla, roll it up, and transfer it, seam-side down, to the baking dish. Repeat with the remaining tortillas and filling. Pour the remaining sauce evenly over the enchiladas. (The enchiladas can be covered with plastic wrap and refrigerated for up to 3 hours. Uncover them before baking.)

5 Position a rack in the upper third of the oven and preheat the oven to 350°F (175°C). Sprinkle the cheese over the enchiladas. Bake them until the sauce is bubbling, about 30 minutes (or 40 minutes if the enchiladas have been refrigerated). Let them stand for 5 minutes before serving.

½ cup (120 ml) canola oil, plus more for the baking dish

12 corn tortillas

1 cup (115 g) shredded Oaxaca or string cheese

GORDITAS

WITH SUMMER VEGETABLES

Gorditas con vegetales de verano

FOR THE FILLING:

2 tablespoons olive oil

1 small yellow onion, finely chopped

1 medium zucchini, cut lengthwise into quarters, seeded and cut into ⅛-inch (3-mm) dice

½ cup (110 g) roasted corn kernels (see Note, page 59)

1 plum tomato, seeded and cut into ¼-inch (6-mm) dice

2 garlic cloves, minced

1 tablespoon chopped fresh cilantro

1 tablespoon chopped fresh oregano

1 cup (115 g) shredded Oaxaca or string cheese

Kosher salt and freshly ground black pepper

FOR THE MASA:

2 cups (240 g) masa harina

½ teaspoon kosher salt

Canola oil, for the griddle

1½ cups (350 g) Tomatillo-Jalapeño Green Salsa (page 179)

½ cup (120 ml) crema or sour cream

½ cup (55 g) crumbled cotija cheese

Gorditas ("little fatsos") have an impolite name that calls attention to their plumpness. Usually they are a thick plain tortilla, but I add a vegetable mixture to the dough to make them a satisfying meatless meal. While a tortilla press speeds up the process of making the gorditas, they can also be rolled by hand between plastic sandwich bags.

SERVES 4

1 Make the filling: Heat the oil in a large skillet over medium heat. Add the onion and cook, stirring it occasionally, until it is beginning to soften, about 2 minutes. Add the zucchini and cook, stirring it often, until the zucchini is tender but not browned, about 10 minutes. Add the corn, tomato, and garlic and cook, stirring them often, until the tomato is tender, about 5 minutes. Remove the pan from the heat and stir in the cilantro and oregano. Let the filling cool. Stir in the cheese and season the filling to taste with salt and pepper.

2 Make the masa: Mix the masa harina and salt together in the bowl of a standing heavy-duty electric mixer. Attach the bowl to the mixer and affix the paddle attachment. With the machine on low speed, gradually mix in 1⅓ cups (315 ml) cold water. Mix the dough on medium-low speed until it is smooth, about 1 minute. Remove the bowl from the mixer. Divide the dough into twelve equal pieces (a kitchen scale comes in handy here) and shape them into balls. Loosely cover the balls with plastic wrap.

3 Cut twelve 6-inch (15-cm) square pieces of parchment or waxed paper. For each gordita, put a plastic sandwich bag on the bottom part of a tortilla press. Place a masa ball in the center of the press and top it with a second bag. Close the top to gently press the masa into a round tortilla about 5 inches (12 cm) in diameter. Peel away the plastic bags from the tortilla. (Or roll out each ball between the sandwich bags with a rolling pin.) Place the tortilla in one hand and spoon about 1 tablespoon of the filling into the center. Bring up the edges of the tortilla to cover the filling and pat it into a ball. Don't worry if some of the vegetable mixture peeks through the dough. Place the ball between the plastic bags and press it gently into a thick round about 4½ inches (11 cm) in diameter. (Or roll it out between the sandwich bags.) Transfer the gordita to a plate. As you roll the gorditas, stack them on the plate separated with the parchment paper squares. (The gorditas can be loosely covered with plastic wrap and refrigerated for up to 2 hours.)

4 Position a rack in the center of the oven and preheat it to 200°F (90°C).

5 Heat a seasoned cast-iron skillet over medium heat. Lightly oil the griddle. In batches, add the gorditas and cook, turning them occasionally, until they are lightly browned and heated through, about 2 minutes. Transfer them to a rimmed baking sheet and keep them warm in the oven while cooking the remaining gorditas.

6 Serve the gorditas hot, with the salsa, crema, and cheese passed on the side.

CHIPOTLE
MACARONI
&
CHEESE

*Macarrones en salsa
de queso con chipotle*

Kosher salt

2 cups (225 g) elbow macaroni or small shells

2 tablespoons olive oil

1 small yellow onion, chopped

1 ripe plum tomato, seeded and cut into ½-inch (12-mm) dice

1 poblano chile, roasted, seeded, and cut into ½-inch (12-mm) dice

1 canned chipotle chile in adobo, plus 2 teaspoons adobo sauce

1 cup (240 ml) heavy cream

8 ounces (225 g) pasteurized cheese product, such as Velveeta, cut into large cubes

½ cup (35 g) panko

My basic mac and cheese isn't standard issue, even though I do use pasteurized cheese product (aka Velveeta) in my sauce. (I can't apologize for this, as I have found that other cheeses get gritty from overheating in the oven, which is hard to avoid.) Chipotle gives it zing, and some onion also helps keep it lively.

SERVES 4 TO 6

1 Position a rack in the center of the oven and preheat it to 350°F (175°C). Lightly butter an 8-by-11½-inch (20-by-30-cm) baking dish.

2 Bring a large pot of salted water to a boil over high heat. Add the macaroni and cook it according to the package directions until it is almost tender. (The macaroni will cook further in the oven, so do not overcook it at this point.) Drain it well.

3 Meanwhile, heat 1 tablespoon of the oil in a medium saucepan over medium heat. Add the onion and cook, stirring it occasionally, until it is translucent, about 4 minutes. Add the tomato, poblano, chipotle, and adobo sauce and cook until the tomato is beginning to soften, about 2 minutes more. Add the cream and bring it to a simmer. Reduce the heat to very low. In batches, add the cheese product, stirring until it melts. Stir in the drained macaroni. Transfer the mixture to the baking dish.

4 Mix the panko and remaining 1 tablespoon oil together in a small bowl. Sprinkle them over the macaroni and cheese. Bake until the sauce is bubbling and the topping is browned, about 25 minutes. Let the macaroni stand for 5 minutes, then serve it hot.

So many dishes call out for mashed potatoes to sop up the sauce, but there are mashed potatoes . . . and then there are these. They're made with Yukon Gold potatoes, a variety that has more flavor than standard baking potatoes, and some Oaxaca cheese for an extra boost of richness. I strongly recommend a potato ricer to get the desired fluffy texture, or peel the potatoes after cooking and whip them with a handheld electric mixer.

MASHED POTATOES

WITH OAXACA CHEESE

Puré de papa con queso Oaxaca

2½ pounds (1.2 kg) Yukon Gold potatoes, scrubbed but unpeeled

Kosher salt

⅓ cup (70 g) unsalted butter

3 tablespoons heavy cream

1 cup (115 g) shredded Oaxaca or string cheese

Freshly ground white pepper

SERVES 4 TO 6

1 Put the potatoes in a large saucepan and add enough salted water to cover them by 1 inch (2.5 cm). Cover and bring them to a boil over high heat. Uncover and reduce the heat to medium-low. Simmer until the potatoes are tender when pierced with the tip of a sharp knife, about 20 minutes.

2 Meanwhile, melt the butter with the cream in a small bowl in a microwave on high, or in a small saucepan over low heat; set aside.

3 Drain the potatoes well. Working over the saucepan, put the potatoes through a ricer, discarding the skins as they accumulate in the ricer. Whisk in the butter mixture. Stir in the cheese. Season the potatoes to taste with salt and pepper. Serve them hot.

SHIITAKE & VEGETABLE STIR-FRY

WITH SPICY HOISIN SAUCE

*Salteado de verduras
y setas shiitake con
salsa picante hoisin*

1 ounce (30 g) dried shiitake mushrooms

Boiling water

FOR THE SPICY HOISIN SAUCE:

2 tablespoons hoisin sauce

1 tablespoon reduced-sodium soy sauce

1 tablespoon ají panca paste or
2 teaspoons Sriracha

1 tablespoon balsamic vinegar

Kosher salt

1 pound (455 g) asparagus, woody
stems snapped off, spears cut into
1½-inch (4-cm) lengths

12 ounces (340 g) green beans,
trimmed and cut into 1½-inch
(4-cm) lengths

2 tablespoons canola oil

2 scallions, white and pale green bottom
parts chopped, green tops thinly sliced

1 tablespoon peeled and minced fresh
ginger

3 garlic cloves, minced

8 to 10 cherry tomatoes, halved

3 tablespoons chopped salted
roasted peanuts

Lime wedges, for serving

In traditional Peruvian cuisine, saltado is a meat stir-fry that is usually served with a topping of fried potatoes. The name comes from the Spanish verb *saltar* (to jump) because the ingredients "jump" in the skillet or wok. Here is a vegetarian version that leans heavily on the Asian ancestry of this dish. During the summer, when there is a large selection of string beans in the farmers' market, I make this with green, yellow wax, and flat Romano beans. Feel free to experiment with other vegetables as you wish—some of the more tender ones (such as summer squash) will not need the initial blanching, and can be stir-fried for a minute or two in the usual manner before adding the tomatoes, shiitakes, and sauce.

■ SERVES 4 TO 6 ■

1 In a small bowl, soak the dried shiitakes in enough boiling water to cover until they are softened, about 30 minutes. Strain out the shiitakes and cut them into quarters; set them aside. Strain the soaking liquid through a fine-mesh wire sieve, leaving any grit in the bottom of the bowl.

2 **Make the hoisin sauce:** Measure ¼ cup (60 ml) of the soaking liquid into a bowl. Add the hoisin sauce, soy sauce, ají panca, and vinegar and whisk to dissolve the hoisin sauce.

3 Bring a medium saucepan of salted water to a boil over high heat. Add the asparagus and green beans and cook them (the water does not have to return to a boil) just until they turn a brighter shade of green, about 2 minutes. Drain and rinse them under cold water to stop the cooking. Pat the vegetables dry with paper towels.

4 Heat a wok or large skillet over high heat. Add the oil and swirl the wok to coat the inside with oil. Add the chopped scallion bottoms, ginger, and garlic and stir just until they are fragrant, about 5 seconds. Immediately add the asparagus and green beans and stir-fry them for about 1 minute. Add the tomatoes and mushrooms and stir-fry them until they are heated through, about 1 minute more. Add the sauce mixture and stir-fry the vegetables until they are well coated and the sauce thickens, about 1 minute more. Transfer the stir-fry to a serving dish and sprinkle it with the peanuts and sliced scallion tops. Serve it hot, with the lime wedges.

Corn on the cob prepared this way—slathered with some kind of creamy condiment, then sprinkled with cheese and chili powder—is a popular street food in Mexico City. The ears are usually stuck on sturdy wooden skewers like vegetable pops. These can be deliciously messy to eat, so lacking a skewer, you may want to stick old-fashioned corn holders on the ends.

SERVES 6

1 Bring a large pot of salted water to a boil over high heat. Add the corn and boil until it is tender, about 6 minutes. Drain the corn.

2 Insert a wooden skewer into the stem end of each ear of corn. Spread each ear with 2 tablespoons of the aïoli, followed with 2 tablespoons of the cheese and ½ teaspoon of the chili powder. Serve them immediately, with the lime wedges for squeezing onto them.

NOTE Pointed thick bamboo skewers for food (such as corn dogs and candy apples) are available at craft stores and online at www.amazon.com. These are thicker and sturdier than the common bamboo skewers. You can also poke a slit in the cob end of each ear with a small, sharp knife and insert a flat wooden frozen pop stick.

MEXICO CITY–STYLE CORN ON THE COB

Mazorca de maíz estilo Ciudad de México

Kosher salt

6 ears of corn, husked

¾ cup (180 ml) Chipotle Aïoli (page 182)

¾ cup (105 g) freshly grated Parmesan cheese

1 tablespoon chili powder or pure ground ancho chile

Lime wedges, for serving

SPECIAL EQUIPMENT:
Six ½-inch (5-mm) thick bamboo food skewers (see Note)

9

DESSER

CHOCOLATE DULCE DE LECHE ROULADE

Brazo de Gitano con chocolate y dulce de leche

FOR THE SPONGE CAKE:

Softened butter, for the baking sheet

⅓ cup (45 g) all-purpose flour

2 tablespoons Dutch-processed cocoa powder

Pinch of fine sea salt

6 large eggs, at room temperature, separated

⅓ cup plus 1 tablespoon (75 g) granulated sugar

1¼ teaspoons pure vanilla extract

Confectioners' sugar, for sifting

One 13.4-ounce (380-g) can dulce de leche (see page 15)

FOR THE TOPPING:

1 cup (240 ml) heavy cream

¼ cup (50 g) granulated sugar

½ teaspoon pure vanilla extract

Probably every Latin bakery makes some version of *brazo de gitano*. This translates into "gypsy arm," but none of the stories about how the dessert got its name are particularly pleasant. Maybe that's why, in Chile, it is called *brazo de reina* ("queen's arm"). It is often filled with whipped cream or jam of some kind, but I like it with dulce de leche. If you wish, serve it with chocolate-friendly strawberries and raspberries, sweetened with agave and flavored with a little lime zest.

SERVES 8

1 Position a rack in the center of the oven and preheat it to 350°F (175°C). Lightly butter a 10-by-15-by-1-inch (25-by-38-by-2.5-cm) jelly-roll pan. Line the bottom and sides with parchment or waxed paper, but do not butter the parchment. (To do this easily, cut a piece of paper about 1 inch/2.5 cm larger than the pan on all sides. Using scissors, cut a 2-inch/5-cm slit at each of the four corners. Fit the paper into the pan, folding the paper over at the slits to fit into the corners.)

2 **Make the cake:** Sift the flour, cocoa, and salt together in a small bowl. Beat the egg yolks, granulated sugar, and vanilla in a large bowl with an electric mixer on high speed until the mixture is doubled in volume, thick, and pale yellow, about 3 minutes. Wash and dry the beaters. Whip the egg whites in another large bowl with the mixer on high speed until they form stiff, but not dry, peaks. Scrape the whites onto the yolk mixture. Sift the flour mixture on top and fold everything together with a large rubber spatula until there are no streaks of egg white. Evenly spread the batter into the jelly-roll pan.

3 Bake until the cake has risen and springs back when pressed gently in the center, about 12 minutes. Remove it from the oven. Sift confectioners' sugar over the top of the cake. Place a clean kitchen towel over the cake and top it with another baking sheet or a cutting board. Hold them together and invert the cake onto the towel. Peel off and discard the parchment paper. Starting at a long side, loosely roll up the cake in the towel and let it cool.

4 Unroll the cake. Dollop the dulce de leche all over the cake. Dip an offset spatula into hot water, and evenly spread the dulce de leche. Re-roll the cake. Using a large spatula, transfer the cake, seam-side down, to an oblong serving platter.

5 **Make the topping:** Whip the cream, sugar, and vanilla together in a chilled large bowl with an electric mixer set on high speed just until stiff peaks form. Spread the cream over the roll. Refrigerate it, uncovered, for at least 1 hour and up to 1 day. Run the ends of a fork lengthwise through the topping. Cut it into slices and serve it chilled.

BUTTERMILK
TRES LECHES CAKE

Pastel de tres leches de suero de leche

Creamy and moist, tres leches cake is a favorite cake throughout Mexico and Central America, with a richness that is a siren's call to anyone with a sweet tooth. Canned evaporated and condensed milks are used to moisten the cake, but this version includes tart buttermilk, which balances the sweetness. (Why does the recipe call for canned milks? Because fresh milk was originally hard to come by in the tropics.) This dessert is perfect for entertaining because it must be made ahead and served chilled.

SERVES 8 TO 10

FOR THE CAKE:

Softened butter and flour, for the baking pan

2¼ cups (290 g) all-purpose flour

1 teaspoon baking soda

½ teaspoon salt

½ cup (120 ml) buttermilk

½ cup (1 stick; 115 g) unsalted butter, melted and slightly cooled

1½ teaspoons pure vanilla extract

3 large eggs, at room temperature

2 cups (200 g) sugar

FOR THE SOAKING LIQUID:

One 14-ounce (390-g) can sweetened condensed milk

One 12-ounce (335-g) can evaporated milk

1 cup (240 ml) buttermilk

1 Position a rack in the center of the oven and preheat it to 350°F (175°C). Lightly butter and flour an 8-by-11½-inch (20-by-30 cm) baking pan, tapping out the excess flour.

2 Make the cake: Whisk the flour, baking soda, and salt together in a medium bowl. Whisk the buttermilk, butter, and vanilla together in a small bowl. Whip the eggs and sugar together in a large bowl with an electric mixer fitted with the whisk attachment on high speed until the mixture is very pale and thick, about 3 minutes. Switch to the paddle attachment. With the mixer on low speed, add the flour mixture in three additions, alternating with two additions of the buttermilk mixture, scraping down the sides of the bowl as needed, mixing just until the batter is smooth. Spread it evenly in the baking pan.

3 Bake until the cake is a deep golden brown and a wooden toothpick inserted in the center comes out clean, 35 to 40 minutes. Let the cake cool in the pan on a wire cooling rack for about 30 minutes.

4 Make the soaking liquid: Whisk the condensed milk, evaporated milk, and buttermilk together in a large bowl. Using a chopstick or meat fork, poke the cake well all over. Slowly pour the soaking liquid over the warm cake. Cover it with plastic wrap and refrigerate it until chilled, at least 4 hours or overnight.

5 **Make the compote:** Combine the berries and sugar in a medium heatproof bowl. Place the bowl over a large saucepan of simmering water over low heat. Heat the berries, gently folding the mixture occasionally with a rubber spatula, until the sugar is dissolved and the berries are plumped and giving off some juices, about 10 minutes. Remove the pan from the heat and let the mixture cool. Cover and refrigerate it until chilled, at least 2 hours.

6 **Make the whipped cream:** Whip the cream, sugar, and vanilla together in a chilled large bowl with an electric mixer set on high speed just until stiff peaks form. (If you wish, transfer the whipped cream to a large pastry bag fitted with a ½-inch/12-mm fluted pastry tip.)

7 Spread (or pipe) the whipped cream over the top of the cake. To serve, cut it into eight to ten rectangles and transfer them to dessert plates. Add a spoonful of berry compote and a drizzle of the dulce de leche to each and serve them chilled.

FOR THE MIXED BERRY COMPOTE:

18 ounces (510 g) mixed seasonal berries, such as blueberries, blackberries, boysenberries, and raspberries

¼ cup (50 g) sugar

FOR THE WHIPPED CREAM:

2 cups (480 ml) heavy cream

⅓ cup (65 g) sugar

2 teaspoons pure vanilla extract

½ cup (120 ml) dulce de leche (see page 15), warmed just until pourable

MEXICAN CHOCOLATE & RASPBERRY TART

*Tartaleta de chocolate
Mexicano con frambuesas*

Mexican chocolate has a unique flavor that gives this dessert a Latin flavor. Because it is mainly used for hot chocolate, it is pretty sweet and has a hint of cinnamon, too. This tart has so much going for it—from its almond crust to its silky filling studded with fresh raspberries.

SERVES 8

1 **Make the tart shell:** Stir the all-purpose flour, almond flour, salt, and cinnamon together in a medium bowl. Beat the butter in the bowl of a heavy-duty standing mixer fitted with the paddle attachment on high until it is smooth, about 1 minute. Gradually beat in the sugar, scraping down the bowl as needed, until the mixture is pale, about 1 minute more. Beat in the egg yolk, almond extract, and lemon zest. Reduce the mixer speed to low. Gradually add the flour mixture and beat just until the dough clumps together.

2 Crumble the sticky dough into a 9-inch (23-cm) tart pan with a removable bottom. Using floured fingers, press the dough evenly into the pan, making sure that it is not too thick where the bottom meets the sides. Freeze the pastry-lined pan for 15 to 30 minutes.

3 Position a rack in the center of the oven and preheat it to 375°F (190°C).

4 Line the tart shell with a piece of aluminum foil and fill the foil with pastry weights or dried beans. Place the pan on a rimmed baking sheet. Bake it until the exposed dough is set and beginning to brown, about 15 minutes. Remove the foil with the weights. Pierce the bottom of the crust a few times with a fork. Continue baking it until the dough is lightly browned, about 10 minutes more. Transfer the pan to a wire cooling rack and let the crust cool while making the filling.

FOR THE ALMOND TART SHELL:

⅔ cup (90 g) unbleached all-purpose flour

⅓ cup (35 g) almond flour (also called almond meal)

¼ teaspoon fine salt

⅛ teaspoon ground cinnamon

6 tablespoons (¾ stick; 85 g) cold unsalted butter, cut into ½-inch (12-mm) pieces

2 tablespoons sugar

1 large egg yolk

½ teaspoon pure almond extract

Finely grated zest of ½ lemon

5 **Make the filling:** Reduce the oven temperature to 350°F (175°C). Heat the chocolate, butter, cream, and rum in the top part of a double boiler over barely simmering water, stirring often, until the chocolate is melted and smooth. Whisk the eggs together in a medium bowl. Gradually beat in the chocolate mixture. Scatter the raspberries over the bottom of the cooled pastry shell. Pour in the chocolate mixture (some berries will peek up above the filling). Place the pan on a large rimmed baking sheet.

6 Bake it until the filling is lightly puffed, about 30 minutes. Let it cool completely in the pan.

7 Cover the top with plastic wrap and refrigerate the tart until the filling is chilled, at least 2 hours and up to 1 day.

8 To serve, remove the sides of the pan. Cut the tart into eight wedges and serve them with the whipped cream.

FOR THE CHOCOLATE TART FILLING:

Three 3.15-ounce (88-g) tablets Mexican chocolate, such as Abuelita, finely chopped

½ cup (1 stick; 115 g) unsalted butter, cut into ½-inch (12-mm) pieces, at room temperature

2 tablespoons heavy cream

2 tablespoons dark rum

3 large eggs, at room temperature

6 ounces (170 g) fresh raspberries

Whipped cream (see page 155), for serving

You may have had an American apple pie filling with tart apples and sharp cheese, and this great combination can also be used to stuff Latin empanadas. These turnovers, with a Spanish cheese, can be casually eaten out of hand or served with your favorite ice cream (butter pecan and toasted almond are especially tasty). Granny Smith is a good all-purpose apple, but other tangy green apples from your local farmers are sure to be even better.

SERVES 6

1 Make the filling: Bring the apples, agave, cinnamon stick, lemon juice, and salt to a simmer in a nonreactive saucepan over medium heat. Reduce the heat to medium-low and simmer everything, stirring often, until the apples are tender and have absorbed the agave, about 10 minutes. Discard the cinnamon stick. Pour the filling into a bowl and let it cool completely. Stir in the cheese.

2 Meanwhile, make the empanada dough: Whisk together the flour, sugar, baking powder, and salt in a medium bowl. Add the butter and toss to coat it with the flour. Using a pastry blender or two knives, cut the butter into the flour until the mixture resembles coarse meal with some pea-size pieces. Whisk the cream, ice water, and lemon juice together in a small bowl. Stir enough of the cream mixture into the flour mixture so the dough holds together when pressed. If the dough is too dry, add more ice water, a tablespoon at a time. Gather up the dough and turn it out onto a floured work surface. Shape the dough into a thick disk and wrap it in plastic wrap. Refrigerate it until the dough is lightly chilled, about 30 minutes. (This dough is easiest to work with if it is not chilled until hard.)

3 Have ready 6 pieces of waxed paper to separate the dough disks. Cut the dough into 6 equal pieces and roll them into balls. (A kitchen scale comes in very handy to divide the dough equally.) On a lightly floured work surface, dust a ball with flour and roll it out into a disk about 6 inches (15 cm) in diameter and ⅛ inch (3 mm) thick. Using a 5-inch (12-cm) round pastry cutter or a saucer, cut out a pastry disk, discarding the trimmings. Transfer it to a plate and top it with a piece of waxed paper. Continue with the remaining dough, layering the rounds with waxed paper. Cover them loosely with plastic wrap and refrigerate them again until they are chilled, at least 30 minutes and up to 4 hours.

RECIPE CONTINUES

GREEN APPLE & MANCHEGO EMPANADAS

Empanadas de manzana verde y queso manchego

FOR THE FILLING:

2 green apples, such as Granny Smith, peeled, cored, and cut into ½-inch (12-mm) dice

⅓ cup (75 ml) agave nectar

1½-inch (4-cm) piece cinnamon stick

1 tablespoon fresh lemon juice

Pinch of fine sea salt

½ cup (55 g) shredded Manchego cheese

FOR THE EMPANADA DOUGH:

1 cup (130 g) unbleached all-purpose flour, plus more for rolling out the dough

2 tablespoons sugar

1 teaspoon baking powder

⅛ teaspoon fine sea salt

½ cup (1 stick; 115 g) cold unsalted butter, cut into ½-inch (12-mm) cubes

¼ cup (60 ml) heavy cream

1 tablespoon ice water

2 teaspoons fresh lemon juice

1 large egg yolk beaten with 1 tablespoon heavy cream, for assembly and glazing

2 tablespoons coarsely chopped pecans

Confectioners' sugar, for dusting

SPECIAL EQUIPMENT:
A 5-inch (12-cm) round cookie cutter or saucer for cutting out the dough

4 Line a large rimmed baking sheet with parchment paper. For each empanada, brush the edges of a round with some of the egg yolk mixture. Leaving a ½-inch (12-mm) border, spoon about 2 tablespoons of the cooled filling on the bottom half of the round. Fold it in half and seal the edges closed with the tines of a fork. Transfer the empanada to the baking sheet and cover it loosely with plastic wrap. Repeat with the remaining dough and filling. Refrigerate the empanadas for at least 15 minutes and up to 1 hour. Cover and refrigerate the remaining egg yolk mixture.

5 Lightly brush the tops of the empanadas with the remaining egg yolk mixture and sprinkle them with the pecans.

6 Position a rack in the center of the oven and preheat it to 375°F (190°C). Bake the empanadas until they are golden brown, about 25 minutes. Let them cool on the baking sheet for 10 minutes. Dust them with confectioners' sugar. Serve them warm or let them cool to room temperature.

When sweet summer corn is in season, make this golden yellow dessert, which is more like a pudding than a cake. Accompanied by a caramel sauce that has been flavored and tinted with hibiscus blossoms, this is guaranteed to be a conversation piece with your guests. The recipe uses half a can of condensed milk. If you are wondering what to do with the remainder, use it as Southeast Asians do to sweeten iced coffee or tea.

SERVES 8 TO 10

1 **Make the cake:** Position a rack in the center of the oven and preheat it to 350°F (175°C). Lightly butter and flour an 8-by-11½-inch (20-by-30-cm) baking pan, tapping out the excess flour.

2 Purée the corn, condensed milk, whole milk, butter, flour, eggs, and yolk in a blender until they are relatively smooth. Pour them into the baking pan.

3 Bake until the top is golden brown and the cake feels set when pressed in the center with your fingertips, about 30 minutes. Let it cool completely in the pan on a wire cooling rack. (The cake can be covered with plastic wrap and refrigerated for up to 1 day. Bring it to room temperature before serving.)

4 **Meanwhile, make the caramel sauce:** Bring the cream and hibiscus flowers to a simmer in a small saucepan over medium heat. Remove them from the heat and let them steep for 10 minutes. Strain the cream, pressing hard on the solids. You should have 1 cup (240 ml); add more cream, if necessary.

5 Bring the sugar and ¼ cup (60 ml) water to a boil in a medium saucepan over high heat, stirring constantly. Stop stirring and cook it, occasionally swirling the saucepan by its handle and washing down the sugar crystals that form on the inside of the saucepan with a natural bristle brush dipped in cold water, until the caramel is smoking and the color of an old penny, about 4 minutes. Remove it from the heat. Carefully (the mixture will boil up) stir in the warm cream mixture. Return the pan to low heat and stir until the caramel is completely smooth. Transfer it to a bowl and let it cool. (The caramel sauce can be cooled, covered, and refrigerated for up to 1 day. The sauce will thicken. Reheat it gently over low heat or in a microwave before using, just until the sauce is fluid.)

6 Cut the cake into eight or ten equal rectangles. For each serving, put a piece of the cake on a plate, add a scoop of ice cream, and drizzle it with the sauce. Serve it immediately.

SWEET CORN CAKE

WITH HIBISCUS CARAMEL SAUCE

Pastel de maíz dulce con dulce de leche y Jamaica

FOR THE SWEET CORN CAKE:

Softened butter and flour, for the baking pan

2⅓ cups (340 g) fresh corn kernels, cut from about 3 large ears

½ cup (120 ml) sweetened condensed milk

½ cup (120 ml) whole milk

6 tablespoons (¾ stick; 85 g) unsalted butter, cut into tablespoons, at room temperature

⅓ cup plus 1 tablespoon (50 g) all-purpose flour

2 large eggs plus 1 large egg yolk

FOR THE HIBISCUS CARAMEL SAUCE:

1 cup (240 ml) heavy cream, or more as needed

⅓ cup (15 g) dried hibiscus flowers (*jamaica*)

⅔ cup (130 g) sugar

Vanilla ice cream, for serving

PECAN-RUM TART

WITH LIME CRÈME ANGLAISE

Tartaleta de ron y nueces con crème anglaise de limón

FOR THE CRÈME ANGLAISE:

⅔ cup (165 ml) heavy cream

⅓ cup (75 ml) whole milk

2 large egg yolks

3 tablespoons granulated sugar

1 tablespoon gold or dark rum

Finely grated zest of ½ lime

FOR THE TART DOUGH:

1 cup plus 3 tablespoons (150 g) unbleached all-purpose flour

⅛ teaspoon baking powder

⅛ teaspoon salt

⅓ cup (75 ml) ice water

1 teaspoon cider vinegar

½ cup (1 stick; 115 g) cold unsalted butter, cut into ½-inch (12-mm) cubes

Pecan fossils dating back over eight thousand years have been found in northern Mexico, so to say that the nuts have long been a part of that country's cooking is an understatement. Pecan pie is truly one of the most delicious ways to enjoy pecans, so here I give the American classic a more elegant presentation by making it into a tart and serving it with a lime-flavored cream sauce. I think you'll agree with me that this recipe improves on a time-tested favorite.

SERVES 8

1 **Make the crème anglaise:** Heat the cream and milk together in a medium saucepan over medium heat until they are steaming. Whisk the egg yolks and sugar together in a medium heatproof bowl until they are thick and pale yellow. Gradually beat the hot cream mixture into them. Return the mixture to the saucepan and stir it constantly over medium-low heat, until you can draw a swath with your finger through the custard on the spoon, about 3 minutes. (The custard should read 185°F/85°C on an instant-read thermometer.) Strain it through a wire sieve into a clean bowl. Stir in the rum and lime zest. Place the bowl in a larger bowl of ice water and let it cool, stirring often, until the custard is cold. (The crème anglaise can be stored for up to 2 days, covered and refrigerated.)

2 **Make the dough:** Whisk the flour, baking powder, and salt together in a medium bowl. Mix together the ice water and vinegar. Add the butter to the flour mixture and toss to coat it with the flour. Using a pastry blender or two knives, cut the butter into the flour until the mixture resembles coarse crumbs with some pea-size pieces. Gradually stir enough of the water mixture into the flour mixture until the dough holds together when pressed. If the dough is too dry, add more ice water, a tablespoon at a time. Gather up the dough and shape it into a thick disk.

3 Wrap the dough in plastic wrap. Refrigerate it until it is chilled, at least 2 hours and up to 1 day. (If the dough is cold and hard, let it stand at room temperature for 10 to 15 minutes before rolling it out.)

4 Unwrap the dough. Place it on a lightly floured work surface and sprinkle more flour over the top. Roll it out into a 13-inch (33-cm) round about ⅛ inch (3 mm) thick. Fit it into a 9-inch (23-cm) tart pan with a removable bottom, making sure that the dough fits into the corners of the pan without stretching it. Roll the rolling pin over the pan to trim away the excess dough. Refrigerate the lined tart pan while making the filling.

5 Position a rack in the bottom third of the oven and preheat it to 350°F (175°C).

6 **Make the filling:** Whisk the brown sugar, corn syrup, maple syrup, butter, flour, rum, and salt together in a medium bowl to dissolve the sugar. One at a time, whisk in the eggs, combining them well after each addition. Sprinkle the pecans in the tart pan and pour in the filling (the pecans will float to the top).

7 Place the tart on a baking sheet or half-sheet pan and bake it until the filling is set and evenly puffed, about 45 minutes. Transfer it to a wire cooling rack and let it cool completely.

8 Cut the tart into wedges, transfer them to plates, and pour the crème anglaise around each wedge.

FOR THE FILLING:

½ cup (100 g) packed light brown sugar

⅔ cup (165 ml) dark corn syrup

⅓ cup (75 ml) maple syrup, preferably Grade B

6 tablespoons (¾ stick; 85 g) unsalted butter, melted

4½ teaspoons all-purpose flour

1 tablespoon dark rum

¼ teaspoon salt

3 large eggs, at room temperature

1½ cups (170 g) coarsely chopped pecans

CORN & RAISIN BISCOTTI

Biscotti de maíz y pasas

4 cups (520 g) all-purpose flour

1 cup (130 g) yellow cornmeal, preferably stone-ground

1 tablespoon baking powder

½ teaspoon salt

1 cup (2 sticks; 225 g) unsalted butter, at room temperature

1¼ cups (250 g) sugar

4 large eggs, at room temperature

1½ teaspoons pure vanilla extract

1 cup (130 g) dark seedless raisins

If you are hungry for a cookie that is comfortingly familiar, yet a little out of the ordinary, look no further. These golden biscotti are great for dipping into coffee or tea, but sweet enough for nibbling alone.

MAKES 2 DOZEN BISCOTTI

1 Position racks in the top third and center of the oven and preheat it to 350°F (175°C). Line two large rimmed baking sheets with parchment paper.

2 Whisk the flour, cornmeal, baking powder, and salt together in a large bowl. Beat the butter in the bowl of a heavy-duty standing mixer fitted with the paddle attachment on medium-high speed until the butter turns pale, about 1 minute. Gradually beat in the sugar, scraping down the bowl as needed, until the mixture is pale, about 2 minutes more. One at a time, beat in the eggs, mixing well after each addition, then add the vanilla. With the mixer on low speed, gradually add the flour mixture and mix until the dough is smooth. Mix in the raisins.

3 Turn out the dough onto a lightly floured work surface. Divide it in half and shape it into two rectangles, each about 15 inches (38 cm) long and 2 inches (5 cm) thick. Carefully transfer each piece to a baking sheet.

4 Bake, switching the position of the baking sheets from top to bottom and front to back halfway through baking, until the dough is golden brown and feels firm when pressed with a fingertip, about 35 minutes. Let the logs cool on the pan for about 15 minutes. One at a time, transfer a log to a cutting board. Using a serrated knife, cut it into slices about ¾ inch (2 cm) thick, trimming off the ends. Return the biscotti, cut-sides down, to the pans.

5 Bake them until the biscotti surfaces are beginning to brown. Flip the biscotti over and continue baking until they are lightly browned on the other side, about 10 minutes more. Let the biscotti cool completely on wire cooling racks. (The biscotti can be stored in an airtight container at room temperature for up to 1 week.)

Polverones (sometimes called Mexican wedding cakes) are not just a Mexican recipe, and are a part of every Latin country's cookie culture. Ground pecans, walnuts, and almonds are often used, and here peanut butter gives the cookies an American twist. They are usually rolled in confectioners' sugar, but they can also be dipped to celebrate the winning combination of peanut and chocolate. Cacao is a very important crop in Venezuela and is coming back in Mexico after a disease wiped out many of the plants. The dough must be chilled for a couple of hours before rolling out, so plan ahead.

CHOCOLATE-DIPPED PEANUT COOKIES

Polvorones de mantequilla de maní cubiertas de chocolate

MAKES ABOUT 5 DOZEN COOKIES

1 **Make the dough:** Sift the flour, milk powder, baking powder, baking soda, and salt together into a medium bowl. Beat the butter and peanut butter together in a large bowl with an electric mixer set on high speed until they are smooth, about 1 minute. Gradually beat in the sugar and continue beating until the mixture is light in color and texture, about 2 minutes more. Beat in the egg. With the machine on low speed, gradually mix in the flour mixture to make a soft dough. Transfer the dough to a sheet of plastic wrap and shape it into two thick disks. Wrap them in the plastic and refrigerate them until chilled and firm enough to roll out, at least 2 hours. (The dough can be refrigerated for up to 1 day. If it is very cold and hard, let it stand at room temperature for about 15 minutes to soften slightly before rolling it out.)

2 Position racks in the top third and center of the oven and preheat it to 350°F (175°C). Line two large rimmed baking sheets with parchment paper or silicone baking mats.

3 Working with one disk at a time on a lightly floured surface, dust the top of the dough with flour and roll it out to 1¼ inches (3 cm) thick. Using a 2-inch (5-cm) cookie cutter, cut out rounds of the dough and arrange them about 1 inch (2.5 cm) apart on the baking sheets. Gather up the scraps, press them together, and continue rolling and cutting out the dough until it is used up. If the dough gets too warm and soft, refrigerate it briefly to chill it enough for rolling.

4 Bake the rounds, switching the positions of the baking sheets from top to bottom and front to back halfway through baking, until the cookies are golden brown, about 12 minutes. Let them cool on the baking sheets for 5 minutes.

RECIPE CONTINUES

FOR THE COOKIE DOUGH:

1¾ cups (225 g) all-purpose flour, plus more for rolling the dough

2 tablespoons instant dry milk powder

1 teaspoon baking powder

¼ teaspoon baking soda

¼ teaspoon fine sea salt

½ cup (1 stick; 115 g) unsalted butter, at room temperature

½ cup (130 g) crunchy peanut butter

1 cup (100 g) sugar

1 large egg, at room temperature

FOR THE CHOCOLATE COATING:

12 ounces (340 g) bittersweet chocolate, finely chopped

1 tablespoon non-hydrogenated vegetable shortening

5 **Make the chocolate coating:** Melt the chocolate and shortening together in the top of a double boiler set over a saucepan of barely simmering water over low heat, stirring often. Remove the top pan.

6 Line the baking sheets with fresh parchment paper. Tilt the pan so the chocolate pools in one corner of the pan. One at a time, dip the cookies in the melted chocolate to coat half of the cookie. Drag the bottom of the cookie against the edge of the pan to remove excess chocolate. Transfer the cookie to a baking sheet. Refrigerate the dipped cookies on the baking sheets until the chocolate is set and the cookies release easily from the parchment, about 20 minutes. (The cookies can be stored in an airtight container at room temperature for up to 5 days.)

Americans have a nostalgic place in their hearts for vanilla pudding, and Mexicans (myself included) feel the same way about natilla, a smooth custard. It is usually kids' food, but here I give it a grown-up twist with dark-roast coffee. After all, the agriculture and economy of many Latin American countries (especially Colombia and Mexico) would be very different without coffee, as would their cuisines. If you wish, serve the coffee natillas with the Chocolate-Dipped Peanut Cookies on page 167.

COFFEE NATILLAS

WITH DULCE DE LECHE

Natilla de café con dulce de leche

SERVES 6

1 Make the natillas: Pulse the coffee beans in an electric coffee grinder or food processor a few times until the beans are very coarsely ground. Combine the beans, 3½ cups (840 ml) of the milk, the sugar, and butter in a medium heavy-bottomed saucepan. Bring them to a simmer over medium heat, stirring almost constantly, taking care that the mixture does not boil over. Remove the pan from the heat and let the milk steep for 5 minutes.

2 Rinse and wring out a double-thick piece of cheesecloth and use it to line a wire-mesh sieve set over a medium bowl. Strain the milk mixture through the sieve and press hard on the coffee beans. Discard the cheesecloth with the beans. Rinse out the saucepan.

3 Pour the remaining 1 cup (240 ml) milk into a large bowl. Sprinkle in the cornstarch and whisk to dissolve the cornstarch. Add the egg yolks and whisk to combine. Gradually whisk in the hot milk mixture. Pour this mixture back into the saucepan. Whisking almost constantly, bring the mixture to a boil over medium heat. Reduce the heat to low and let it bubble, whisking often, for 1 minute to be sure that the eggs are thoroughly cooked. Strain the custard through the sieve into a clean bowl to remove any bits of cooked egg white.

4 Spoon the custard into six 1-cup (240-ml) or larger custard cups or ramekins. Cover each with waxed paper or plastic wrap pressed directly onto the surface to keep a skin from forming. Refrigerate them until chilled, at least 2 hours or overnight.

5 Uncover and serve the natillas chilled, topping each with a dollop of whipped cream and a spoonful of the dulce de leche.

FOR THE NATILLAS:

½ cup (40 g) dark-roast coffee beans

4½ cups (1 L) whole milk

¾ cup (150 g) sugar

¼ cup (½ stick; 55 g) unsalted butter, thinly sliced

¼ cup (30 g) cornstarch

6 large egg yolks

½ batch whipped cream (see page 155), for serving

½ cup (140 g) dulce de leche (see page 15), warmed slightly until fluid

PILONCILLO POTS DE CRÈME

2½ cups (600 ml) heavy cream

½ cup (120 ml) whole milk

1 vanilla bean, split lengthwise,
or 1 teaspoon pure vanilla extract

¾ cup (150 g) crushed and packed
piloncillo

9 large egg yolks

Fresh berries, such as raspberries
or blueberries, for serving

The deep, molasses-like flavor of piloncillo gives these custards a similarity to butterscotch pudding. While you can substitute dark brown sugar for the piloncillo, the flavor won't have the same Latin touch. If you want something crunchy to complement the smooth texture of the custards, serve the Corn and Raisin Biscotti on page 164.

SERVES 6

1 Position a rack in the center of the oven and preheat it to 300°F (150°C).

2 Heat the cream, milk, and vanilla bean, if using, in a medium saucepan over medium heat, whisking almost constantly, until bubbles form around the edges of the mixture. Add the piloncillo, reduce the heat to very low, and stir until the piloncillo is melted. Remove the pan from the heat. Remove the vanilla bean halves from the mixture. Using the tip of a knife, scrape the vanilla seeds back into the mixture and discard the empty pods. (If using vanilla extract, stir it in now.)

3 Whisk the egg yolks well in a large bowl until they are pale and thickened. Gradually whisk in the hot cream mixture. Strain the mixture through a wire sieve into a large liquid measuring cup or pitcher. Divide the mixture among six ¾-cup (180-ml) ramekins. Place the ramekins in a large roasting pan. Pour enough hot water to come about one-quarter up the sides of the ramekins. Cover the roasting pan tightly with aluminum foil.

4 Carefully transfer the roasting pan to the oven. Bake until the custards are mostly set with a dime-size unset area in the center, 35 to 40 minutes. Remove the pan from the oven and uncover it. Remove the custards from the water and let them cool until they are tepid.

5 Cover each ramekin with plastic wrap and refrigerate them until they are chilled, at least 4 and up to 24 hours. Top each custard with a few berries and serve them chilled.

After a big meal, a colorful and refreshing fruit salad is often the best choice for dessert. This one starts with the usual suspects (and feel free to use your favorites), but then makes a sharp turn toward the unexpected with a tropical dressing made with passion fruit and orange juice. The frozen passion fruit purée available at Latin markets is one of the great shopping bargains: A packet of frozen purée contains the equivalent of over a dozen fruits for practically the same price as a single fresh one.

SERVES 6

1 Whisk the orange juice, passion fruit purée, and agave together in a large bowl. Add the pineapple, papayas, and green and red grapes and mix everything well. Cover and refrigerate the salad until it is chilled, at least 1 hour and up to 1 day.

2 Serve the salad chilled in soup bowls, with soup spoons to sip the delicious juices.

FRUIT SALPICÓN
WITH PASSION FRUIT DRESSING

Salpicón de frutas con aderezo de maracuyá

¾ cup (180 ml) fresh orange juice

¼ cup plus 2 tablespoons (90 ml) thawed frozen passion fruit purée

3 tablespoons agave syrup

½ ripe pineapple, peeled, flesh cut into bite-size pieces

2 ripe papayas, seeds and skin removed, flesh cut into bite-size pieces

1 cup (175 g) green seedless grapes, halved

1 cup (175 g) red seedless grapes, halved

10
BASICS

THREE MEXICAN FILLINGS

I think that everyone will agree that the most beloved Mexican dishes are based on tortillas. Tacos, enchiladas, tostadas, nachos, and such begin with tortillas that are augmented with fillings or toppings, and finished off with sauce, cheese, and more. Too often, lower-rung Mexican restaurants toss together a filling with ground beef and spices, the kind of thing that has done nothing to advance the reputation of Latin cuisine. My fillings are carefully made and full of delicious flavor.

The three most useful fillings are made with beef brisket, pork shoulder, and chicken breasts. These first two are tough cuts of meat with lots of gelatin that melts during cooking to give them a rich texture and extra flavor. Chicken breasts, in my opinion, are better than the dark meat cuts because the shredded chicken looks more attractive. Often, the fillings are interchangeable, and you can swap them according to taste. Each filling is braised (a method that is another way to help to keep the meat moist) and then cooled and shredded. The actual preparation for the fillings is minimal, even if the cooking times are relatively long.

In the case of the beef and pork fillings, I've scaled them so you have enough meat for at least two recipes. I encourage you to make the entire amount and refrigerate or freeze the leftovers for another meal. Knowing that you have one of these fillings in the freezer, ready to defrost and turn into one of your favorite Mexican dishes, is a huge advantage, whether making a weeknight supper or a dinner for company.

Slowly simmered with tomatoes and jalapeños, this braised brisket is called *ropa vieja* ("old clothes") because the shredded meat looks like raggedy clothes. There will be about a cup or so of the cooking liquid left over—be sure to save it as a sauce for pasta or polenta. You may even want to serve this as a main course with Mashed Potatoes with Oaxaca Cheese (page 145).

SHREDDED BEEF FILLING

WITH TOMATOES & CHILIES

Ropa vieja con tomates y chiles

MAKES ABOUT 4 CUPS (910 G)

1 Position a rack in the bottom third of the oven and preheat it to 350°F (175°C).

2 Heat the oil in a Dutch oven over medium-high heat. Season the brisket all over with 1 teaspoon salt and ½ teaspoon pepper. Place it in the Dutch oven, fat-side down, and cook it, turning after 5 minutes, until it is nicely browned, 10 to 12 minutes. Transfer the brisket to a plate.

3 If needed, add another 1 tablespoon oil to the Dutch oven. Add the onion, jalapeños, and garlic and reduce the heat to medium. Cook, stirring them occasionally, until the onion is softened, about 3 minutes. Stir in the tomatoes and their juices with the oregano and bring them to a boil. Return the brisket to the Dutch oven and add enough hot water to come about three-quarters up the side of the meat. Bring it to a boil over high heat.

4 Cover the Dutch oven and transfer it to the oven. Bake until the brisket is fork-tender, about 2½ hours. Transfer the brisket to a carving board, tent it with aluminum foil, and let it stand for 10 minutes. Set the cooking liquid aside.

5 Using a sharp knife and your fingers, shred the brisket with the grain. Roughly cut the shredded beef across the grain into bite-size pieces. Transfer it to a bowl. Skim off the fat on the surface of the cooking liquid. Stir in about one-third of the cooking liquid to lightly moisten the shredded beef. Add the cilantro, lime juice, and liquid smoke, if using, and mix it again. Season the beef to taste with salt and pepper. (The beef can be cooled, covered, and refrigerated for up to 2 days or frozen for up to 2 months. Reheat it before using.)

2 tablespoons canola oil, plus more as needed

One 2½-pound (1.2-kg) beef brisket, fat trimmed to ⅛ inch (3 mm)

Kosher salt and freshly ground black pepper

1 medium yellow onion, chopped

4 jalapeños, seeded and coarsely chopped

4 garlic cloves, minced

One 28-ounce (785-g) can fire-roasted tomatoes

2 teaspoons dried Mexican oregano

¼ cup (5 g) finely chopped fresh cilantro

2 tablespoons fresh lime juice

1 teaspoon mesquite-flavored liquid smoke (optional)

CHICKEN TINGA FILLING

Tinga de pollo

1 tablespoon canola oil

2 large bone-in chicken breast halves with skin, about 2¼ pounds (1.1 kg)

1 medium onion, sliced into ½-inch (12-mm) half-moons

4 garlic cloves, coarsely chopped

Kosher salt

6 whole black peppercorns

1 recipe Tomato-Chipotle Sauce (page 178)

Freshly ground black pepper

Hailing from Oaxaca, the town in central Mexico famous for its variety of moles, tinga de pollo is spicy shredded chicken and tomato stew that really comes into its own as a filling for tacos and tostadas. Today's supermarket chicken breast halves are huge, but their size allows them to braise without drying out too quickly. Cooling them in the braising liquid will also result in moist and juicy shreds of chicken. You will get a bonus of homemade chicken broth to store for another use.

MAKES 4 CUPS (950 G)

1 Heat the oil in a large saucepan over medium-high heat until it is hot but not smoking. Add the chicken, skin-side down, and cook until the skin is browned, about 5 minutes. Transfer the chicken to a plate. Add the onion and garlic to the hot fat in the saucepan and cook them, stirring often, until the onion is softened, about 2 minutes. Return the chicken to the saucepan and add enough water to cover it, about 2½ quarts (2.5 L). Stir in 2 teaspoons salt and the peppercorns and bring the liquid to a boil. Reduce the heat to medium-low. Simmer the chicken until an instant-read thermometer inserted in the thickest part of the breast reads 160°F (71°F), about 30 minutes. Remove the pot from the heat. Let the chicken cool in the liquid until it is tepid, about 1 hour.

2 Strain the chicken and broth in a colander over a large bowl. Transfer the chicken to a carving board. (The broth can be cooled completely, transferred to covered containers, and refrigerated for up to 3 days or frozen for up to 2 months.)

3 Remove the skin and bones and shred the chicken meat with your fingers or two forks. (The shredded chicken can be covered and refrigerated for up to 2 days.)

4 Heat the sauce in a large skillet over medium heat until it is simmering. Add the chicken and cook, stirring often, until it is heated through. Season the chicken to taste with salt and ground pepper. (The chicken tinga can be cooled, covered, and refrigerated for up to 2 days or frozen for up to 2 months. Reheat it before using.)

There are only three ingredients in my version of carnitas, the classic pork filling for tacos, tortas, enchiladas, and other Mexican favorites. The combination of slow cooking, gelatinous pork shoulder, and lard gives the meat its melting texture and mouthwatering flavor. You don't need anything else because the meat will be mixed with other ingredients when it's used in a recipe.

SLOW-COOKED
MEXICAN PORK SHOULDER

Carnitas

MAKES 4 CUPS (755 G)

1 The day before cooking, season the pork all over with the salt. Wrap it loosely in plastic wrap and refrigerate it for 12 to 18 hours.

2 Position a rack in the bottom third of the oven and preheat it to 300°F (150°C).

3 Rinse the salt off the pork under cold running water and pat it dry with paper towels. Place the pork in a small Dutch oven or deep heatproof casserole just large enough to hold the pieces. Add enough melted lard to barely cover the pork, adding vegetable oil if you run out of lard. Cover it with a lid. Transfer it to the oven and bake until the pork is fork-tender, about 2½ hours. Remove the pork from the oven and let it partially cool in the fat for about 1 hour.

4 Remove the warm pork from the fat and transfer it to a carving board. Transfer about ¼ cup (60 ml) of the warm fat from the pot to a small bowl, cover, and refrigerate it for reheating the pork. Discard the remaining fat. Using two forks or your fingers, shred the pork into bite-size pieces, discarding any excess fat. (The carnitas can be cooled, covered, and refrigerated for up to 2 days or frozen for up to 2 months. Reheat it with the reserved lard before using.)

NOTE You may find refrigerated small-batch lard sold at some Latin supermarkets and specialty butchers. This beige product has much more flavor than the typical supermarket lard, which is stored at room temperature and is white and highly processed. Even so, you can use the white lard in a pinch.

Two 1½-pound (680-g) boneless pork shoulder roasts, cut in half lengthwise to make 4 pieces

1 tablespoon kosher salt

1½ pounds (680 g) store-bought lard (see Note), melted (about 3 cups), as needed

Vegetable oil, if needed

TOMATO-CHIPOTLE SAUCE

Salsa entomatada

1½ pounds (680 g) ripe plum tomatoes

¼ medium white onion

4 garlic cloves, peeled

Olive oil

1 canned chipotle chile in adobo, plus 1 teaspoon adobo sauce

1 tablespoon tomato paste

½ teaspoon dried oregano, preferably Mexican

½ teaspoon cumin seeds

1 cup (240 ml) homemade chicken stock or reduced-sodium chicken broth

Kosher salt

Fresh tomatoes are the backbone of this sauce and give it its name. Broiling the vegetables deepens their flavors. The amount of chipotle can be increased, of course, but this amount is enough to make an impact, yet not so much that kids won't eat it. This is an all-purpose sauce for enchiladas and great for simmering with meat and poultry for a quick meal.

MAKES ABOUT 2 CUPS (480 ML)

1 Position a broiler rack about 6 inches (15 cm) from the source of heat and preheat the broiler on high. Drizzle the tomatoes, onion, and garlic with oil, toss them to coat, and spread them on a broiler rack. Broil until the garlic is browned, about 3 minutes. Transfer the garlic to a bowl. Continue broiling, occasionally turning the tomatoes and onion pieces, until the onion is deeply browned and the tomato skins are charred and blistered, about 3 minutes more. Transfer the tomatoes and onions to the bowl and let the vegetables cool. Peel the tomatoes, cut out the stem ends, and poke out most of the seeds. Return the tomatoes to the bowl.

2 Heat 1 tablespoon oil in a medium saucepan over medium heat. Add the chipotle, adobo sauce, and tomato paste and cook, stirring them occasionally, until the mixture turns dark brown, about 2 minutes. Stir in the oregano and cumin seeds. Stir in the stock and reserved vegetables and bring them to a boil, breaking up the tomatoes with the side of a spoon. Reduce the heat to low and simmer them until the tomato juices have lightly thickened, about 20 minutes. Let the sauce cool.

3 Purée the sauce in a blender. Season it to taste with salt. (The sauce can be covered and refrigerated for up to 3 days or frozen for up to 2 months.)

Tomatillos are unique: They look like green tomatoes, but their papery husk gives away their relationship to gooseberries. In this sauce, their funky tartness is accented with both serrano and jalapeño chilies for an especially delicious salsa verde for enchiladas and tacos, or even as a dip for chips.

TOMATILLO-JALAPEÑO
GREEN SALSA

Salsa verde de tomatillo y jalapeño

MAKES ABOUT 2 CUPS (480 ML)

1 Heat the oil in a large skillet over medium heat. Add the onion, serrano, jalapeño, and garlic and cook just until they soften, about 3 minutes. Stir in the tomatillos. Reduce the heat to low and cover. Cook, stirring the vegetables occasionally, until the tomatillos are very tender and falling apart, 10 to 15 minutes. Stir in the cilantro. Let the vegetables cool.

2 Purée the mixture in a blender and transfer it to a medium bowl. Season it to taste with salt. (The salsa can be covered and refrigerated for up to 1 week or frozen for up to 2 months.)

2 tablespoons olive oil

½ medium yellow onion, chopped

1 serrano chile, seeded and coarsely chopped

½ jalapeño, seeded and coarsely chopped

1 garlic clove, minced

1½ pounds (680 g) tomatillos, husked, rinsed, and quartered

2 tablespoons chopped fresh cilantro

Kosher salt

The name of this chunky fresh salsa translates to "rooster beak," probably because of its sharp flavors of lime and chile. It is used to add a bright splash of color and flavor to many dishes. It is best when freshly made.

PICO DE GALLO

MAKES ABOUT 2 CUPS (480 ML)

Combine all of the ingredients in a medium bowl. Cover them with plastic wrap and refrigerate to chill and blend the flavors, at least 1 and up to 8 hours.

VARIATION **Grilled Corn Pico de Gallo:** Stir 1 cup (220 g) cooked corn kernels, preferably roasted (see page 59), into the salsa.

12 ounces (340 g) large tomatoes, seeded and cut into ½-inch (12-mm) dice

2 tablespoons finely chopped red onion

1 tablespoon finely chopped fresh cilantro

1 tablespoon fresh lime juice

1 serrano chile, seeded and finely chopped

1 teaspoon Maggi seasoning or soy sauce

Kosher salt

MOLE VERDE

Mole verde gets its verdant color from tomatillos, poblano chilies, pumpkin seeds, pistachios, and cilantro, all of which contribute to its complex flavor. While it can be used as a sauce for enchiladas, I also use it as an ingredient in Ahi Tuna Ceviche in Mole Verde Broth (page 74).

MAKES 1 QUART (960 ML)

½ cup (90 g) shelled pistachios

½ cup (90 g) shelled pumpkin seeds (pepitas)

1 tablespoon canola oil

1 medium yellow onion, sliced

3 garlic cloves, minced

3 poblano chilies, roasted, peeled, seeded, and coarsely chopped (see page 23)

3 tomatillos, husked, stem end cored, rinsed, and coarsely chopped

¾ teaspoon ground cumin

¾ teaspoon ground coriander

¾ teaspoon freshly ground black pepper

¾ teaspoon ground allspice

⅛ teaspoon ground cloves

2 cups (480 ml) chicken stock or reduced-sodium chicken broth

1 cup (35 g) packed fresh cilantro

1 tablespoon honey

1 tablespoon distilled white vinegar

1 Heat a medium skillet over medium heat. Add the pistachios and cook, stirring them occasionally, until they are toasted and lightly browned, about 2 minutes. Transfer them to a plate. Repeat with the pumpkin seeds. Add them to the pistachios.

2 Heat the oil in a large saucepan over medium heat. Add the onion and garlic and cook, stirring them often, until the onions are translucent, about 3 minutes. Add the poblanos and tomatillos and cook them until the onions are tender, about 3 minutes more. Add the pistachios and pumpkin seeds, cumin, coriander, pepper, allspice, and cloves and cook until the spices give off their aromas, about 1 minute. Pour in the stock and bring it to a boil. Reduce the heat to medium-low and simmer until the tomatillos are falling apart, about 10 minutes. Stir in the cilantro, honey, and vinegar. Let the mixture cool.

3 In batches, with the blender lid ajar, purée the mole mixture until it is smooth. Transfer it to a bowl and add more vinegar as needed to balance the flavors. Cover and refrigerate it until chilled, at least 2 hours and up to 2 days. (The mole can be frozen for up to 2 months.)

One sure way to improve your cooking is to use homemade ingredients whenever feasible. For example, while you can buy cans of jalapeños en escabeche or jars of nacho slices, it only takes a few minutes to make your own. The color of the rounds is brighter than the store-bought ones, and using unheated vinegar gives them a crisp texture.

PICKLED JALAPEÑOS

Jalapeños en escabeche

MAKES 1 PINT (480 ML)

1 Fill a 1-pint (480-ml) heatproof jar with boiling water and let it stand for 5 minutes.

2 Meanwhile, toss the jalapeños, shallot, sugar, and salt together in a medium bowl. Let them stand for a few minutes until the sugar dissolves. Drain the jar. Pack the jalapeño mixture into the jar. Pour in enough vinegar to come ½ inch (12 mm) from the top of the jar.

3 Warm the oil, oregano, and bay leaf in a small saucepan over low heat until small bubbles begin to appear in the oil. Spoon the oregano and bay leaf into the jar, then pour in enough of the hot oil to almost fill the jar. Let it stand until it has cooled to room temperature. Close the jar and refrigerate it overnight. (The chilies can be refrigerated for up to 2 months. The oil on top will harden when refrigerated, so let the chilies stand at room temperature for about 15 minutes to soften the oil before using.)

4 jalapeños, preferably 2 each red and green, cut into ⅛-inch (3-mm) rounds

½ shallot, thinly sliced

1 tablespoon sugar

2 teaspoons plain table (noniodized) salt

1 cup (240 ml) distilled white vinegar, as needed

¼ cup (60 ml) olive oil

1 teaspoon dried Mexican oregano

1 small bay leaf

PICKLED RED ONIONS

Cebolla morada en escabeche

1 medium red onion, cut into ⅛-inch (3-mm) rings

2 tablespoons kosher salt

1 cup (240 ml) red wine vinegar

¼ cup (50 g) sugar

1 teaspoon habanero hot sauce or Sriracha

I use these sweet, hot, and tangy onion rings to top enchiladas and tacos. I can (almost) make them with my eyes closed, and they keep in the refrigerator for weeks. They really perk up a simple green salad, too.

MAKES ABOUT ¾ CUP (180 G)

1 Toss the onion and salt together in a colander. Let them stand on a plate for 1 hour. Do not rinse the onions.

2 Transfer the onions to a small heatproof bowl. Bring the vinegar and sugar to a boil in a small nonreactive saucepan over high heat, stirring to dissolve the sugar. Pour the liquid over the onions. Let them cool completely. Stir in the hot sauce. The pickled onions can be used immediately or transferred to a covered container and refrigerated for up to 2 months.

CHIPOTLE AÏOLI

Alioli con chile chipotle

1 cup (240 ml) mayonnaise

2 canned chipotle chilies in adobo

This hot and smoky mayonnaise doubles as a very useful condiment and garnish. It's worth making to have on hand for sandwiches and any other dish where you want a spicy spread. I often put it in a plastic squeeze bottle to help apply freeform drizzles on food. Be sure that the chile is very well puréed, because if it is too chunky, it will clog up the bottle nozzle. You may want to trim off the end of the nozzle to make a slightly larger opening to allow for easier passage of the aïoli.

MAKES 1 CUP (240 ML)

Purée the mayonnaise and chipotles well in a blender. Transfer them to a covered container. (The aïoli, if not made with homemade mayonnaise, can be refrigerated for up to 2 months.)

ACHIOTE

When you see Latin food with a reddish orange color, it is very likely that it contains annatto seed. This hard red spice is not used alone, but ground with other aromatic ingredients into achiote. A spoonful of this heady paste adds color and flavor to a dish. You can buy premade achiote, but look for cubes or packets of paste labeled condimento de achiote (which is seasoned), not tubes or jars of the unseasoned pasta de achiote (which is no more than annatto and vegetable shortening). Achiote only takes a few minutes to make in the blender, and should be in the refrigerator of every cook who loves Latin cuisine.

MAKES ABOUT ½ CUP (145 G)

Grind all of the ingredients together in a blender, adding about ⅓ cup (75 ml) water as needed, to make a thick, fairly smooth paste. Transfer it to a covered container and refrigerate it. (The achiote can be refrigerated for up to 2 months.)

¼ cup (40 g) annatto seeds

¼ cup (60 ml) distilled white vinegar

1 tablespoon pure ground ancho chile

1 garlic clove, coarsely chopped

20 black peppercorns

½ teaspoon ground cumin

½ teaspoon kosher salt

3 whole cloves

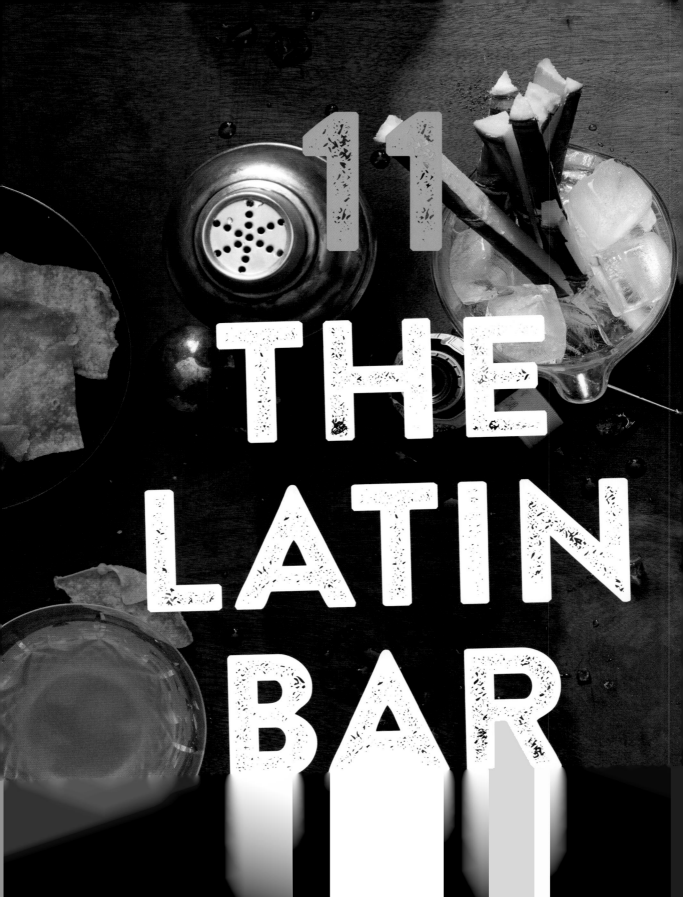

11

THE LATIN BAR

At my parties, the drinks are as carefully considered as the food. For decades, few bartenders took tropical cocktails seriously, and most bars only served a sweet river of slushy margaritas, daiquiris, and piña coladas. Now that there is an ongoing cocktail renaissance, bartenders are making the original versions of these drinks with fresh juices. Caipirinhas and mojitos have joined the previously mentioned libations as favorites, too. And the choice of nonalcoholic drinks has exploded, as well. So I say "Cheers!" (or "¡Salud!") to that.

Every culture has a method of fermenting or distilling local products into alcoholic beverages. Grapes are turned into wine and grains become whiskey or beer. In the Spanish-speaking world, the two most important components for making spirits are the Mexican succulent plants agave and maguey (creating tequila and mezcal) and sugarcane (responsible for rum and cachaça). Grapes in Argentina and Chile are now made into wines that are appreciated around the world, and both Chile and Peru distill grapes into the heady liquor pisco.

The beverages in this chapter are organized by spirit: tequila, mezcal, rum, pisco, and cachaça, as well as beer- and wine-based drinks. Each section includes a brief overview of the category. After all, there have been entire books written on each of these spirits, so I will not come close to being exhaustive. I'll share some of my best cocktail recipes with you so that you can become known as a party-giver whose drinks are as delicious as their food.

SETTING UP THE BAR

To easily prepare a full range of cocktails, you only need a few basic tools. These utensils really make bartending a breeze. I have seen people substitute wooden spoons for a muddler when making mojitos, but the muddler is much more efficient. Conversely, would you use a muddler to stir a pot? I don't think so. Use the right tool for the job. Here are the basic tools you'll need, in order of importance.

THE HOUSE DRINK

Great bartenders have an encyclopedic knowledge of the various formulas for different cocktails. At home, instead of having to make a different drink for each guest, I recommend the "house cocktail," so you just have to make one terrific drink for the party.

You can expand on this by choosing a single spirit with a couple of special ingredients at hand to mix up a tight selection of tasty cocktails. For example, for a Mexican menu, tequila drinks are more than appropriate—some might say they are a necessity! With some grapefruit soda and ginger ale as mixers, I can offer Perfect Palomas or Ginger Fizzes. Watermelon Agua Fresca can be served as is or spiked. Or I could have a Caipirinha selection, muddling various fruits and berries (or even cucumber) into the basic drink for variety.

What makes a great cocktail? If you look closely at the recipes for most famous drinks, especially the Latin ones, it's all about balance. You may begin with a pretty strong spirit, but its strength is mellowed with fruit juice and sweetened with sugar or agave. There might be an accent flavoring in the form of bitters or salt on the rim of the glass. When a drink is served on the rocks or shaken with ice, the slight dilution helps to soften the alcoholic flavor, and this makes a better-tasting drink.

Of course, if someone wants a martini, I'll make one. But more often than not, my guests enjoy a change of pace and like being surprised with what I am offering at a party that might be different from the last get-together. And I always have plenty of booze-free choices.

Jigger: Accurate measuring of ingredients ensures consistent cocktails. Many a well-meaning bartender has ruined a drink through sloppy measuring. Every cocktail has a specific recipe, usually given in fluid ounces. Always measure the ingredients for cocktails with a jigger, which is the name of both the small cup and the measuring increment. One jigger equals 1½ ounces (45 ml), and is sometimes called a shot. A jigger with clearly demarked measurement is the most useful and easiest to use. If you have an unmarked jigger, be sure that you know its volume—there are 1-ounce (30-ml) jigger glasses, not to mention models with two different-size cups.

Cocktail shakers: There is no sound that says "Party!" like the clunk of a shaking mixer. Many of my favorite cocktails (margarita, I'm looking at you . . .) are shaken with ice to combine and chill the ingredients at the same time. Most professional bartenders prefer the **Boston shaker,** consisting of a mixer glass and a metal shaker top, each with a capacity of about 16 ounces (480 ml). The cocktail ingredients are combined with ice in the glass section and capped with the metal shaker. After shaking for about 10 seconds, the cap is removed, and the drink is poured through a cocktail strainer into a glass. (Note that when serving "on the rocks," fresh ice is used in the serving glass, as the ice in the shaker has begun to melt.) The Boston shaker is popular with pros because it is sturdy and easy to wash.

Home bartenders tend to like the **cobbler shaker**, a three-piece unit with a large bottom container, a top with a built-in strainer/spout, and the spout cover. This shaker comes in a variety of attractive styles and materials, mainly glass, metal, or a combination of the two. A third model, the **Parisian shaker**, has a spout sprouting from its side to make it look like a cross between a cobbler shaker and a coffee server.

Cocktail strainers: A Boston shaker is used in conjunction with a cocktail strainer. Position the strainer over the mixer glass, cup your hand over the top of the mixer to hold the two together, and pour the drink through the strainer into the serving glass. There are two styles, which are interchangeable. The **Hawthorne strainer** has a spring around its edge so it fits snugly in the mixer. A **julep strainer** is perforated and slightly concave, and isn't as easy to use as the sturdy Hawthorne, but it does the job well. Some drinks are **double-strained** to remove any bits of fruit or vegetable pulp. In this case, the drink is strained from the mixer through a small wire sieve over the serving glass.

Muddler: This wide stick is used to crush fruit, vegetables, or herbs in the glass so they can release every bit of their flavor into the drink. There are metal, hard plastic, and even polished wood models. A muddler is indispensable for making caipirinhas, not to mention a host of other contemporary and classic cocktails.

Bar spoon: Not all cocktails are shaken. Shaking aerates the drink and gives it a slightly foamy appearance, so if you want a clear cocktail, stirring is better. A long spoon that reaches all the way to the bottom of the glass is ideal, and it is best to have a spoon dedicated for mixing drinks on your bar. The proper length of time to stir a drink is about 8 seconds, which is long enough to chill the liquid and slightly dilute the ice. Contrary to popular belief (disproving the myth that frozen vodka served without ice makes the best martini), the small amount of water from the ice actually improves the drinks as it mellows the harsh alcohol flavor.

Citrus juicers: For a single drink, a wooden citrus reamer works well to extract the juice from citrus. Many bartenders swear by the equally low-tech Mexican metal juicers that work by the lever principle. These come in three sizes and colors for various fruits: orange (large, for oranges and small

BASIC COCKTAIL SYRUPS

These three syrups, easily prepared, are essential ingredients in many cocktails. They can be refrigerated for up to 1 month.

SIMPLE SYRUP: Some cocktails use a light-bodied syrup as a sweetener to ensure that the drink isn't gritty with bits of undissolved sugar. Shake **½ cup (100 g) sugar** and **½ cup (120 ml) hot water** together in a covered container to dissolve the sugar. Let it cool. Makes about ¾ cup (180 ml).

HOMEMADE SWEET & SOUR MIX: Never make margaritas with packaged sweet and sour mix! This blend of sweetened fresh citrus juices is the only way to go. Shake **¼ cup (60 ml) Simple Syrup**, **¼ cup (60 ml) fresh lemon juice**, and **¼ cup (60 ml) fresh lime juice** together in a covered container. Makes ¾ cup (180 ml).

HOMEMADE GRENADINE: Now that pomegranate juice is sold at every supermarket, consider making your own. Bring **1 cup (240 ml) bottled unsweetened pomegranate juice** and **½ cup (100 g) sugar** to a boil in a small saucepan over medium heat, stirring to dissolve the sugar. Reduce the heat to very low and simmer until the liquid is very slightly reduced, about 10 minutes. Let it cool. Transfer to a covered container for storage.

grapefruits), yellow (medium, for lemons), and green (small, for limes). However, when you need to make a lot of juice for a party, an electric citrus juicer cannot be beat.

Channel tool: This metal tool is notched to cut citrus zest into long strips for cocktail garnishes.

Electric blender: The problem with frozen drinks at home is that the noise of grinding ice is . . . well, grating. I have nothing against frozen drinks, as long as they are made with fresh fruit and homemade sour mix, and if they are prepared in a blender that gets the job done quickly with a minimum of noise. The best cocktail blender has a wide-bottomed jar to make a wide surface for crushing ice. This may or may not be the same mixer that you use for cooking.

I only use a blender to make nonalcoholic drinks. Many bartenders stay away from frozen cocktails because of their association with slushy kids' drinks. There is also a connection with frozen drinks and bad margaritas made with cheap *mixto* tequila, and I want to promote the finer things in life—like great tequila.

TEQUILA

Tequila is distilled from the fermented juice of the blue agave plant, a type of succulent with a decidedly blue-gray cast to its spiky leaves.

The production is restricted to an area around Guadalajara. Unless it is labeled as 100 percent blue agave, the tequila is probably a *mixto*, with the spirit diluted or sweetened to reduce the expense of production. Some of the most popular (or, I should say, highly advertised) tequila brands are mixtos. Using a 100 percent blue agave brand will immeasurably improve the quality of your tequila cocktails.

There are four main types of tequila:

Blanco: Also called silver, this clear white tequila is the most common for making cocktails. It is aged for less than sixty days, or sometimes not aged at all, giving it a rougher flavor that can stand up to mixers.

Joven: This mixto tequila has been colored, diluted, and flavored with caramel, giving it a golden color. While the official designation of this unaged tequila is *joven* ("young" in Spanish) it is also called *oro* ("gold"). I don't use this tequila much, but some people like joven tequila precisely because of its sweetness, especially when tossing back a shot . . . or two.

Reposado: Literally meaning "rested," *reposado* tequila is aged in wood casks for at least two and up to nine months. These tequilas have a fuller flavor, and can be used in cocktails where you want a bolder tequila taste. The best ones can be sipped like a fine whiskey.

Añejo: Aged in oak casks (often barrels leftover from American bourbon production) for anywhere from one to three years, *añejo* ("mature") is the Cognac of the tequila world. These tequilas are often served in snifters to fully showcase their earthy aroma and light gold color. Tequilas that have been aged for longer than three years are designated as *Extra-Añejo*.

MARGARITA

4 lime wedges (²/₃ lime)

Kosher salt, for garnish

2½ ounces (75 ml) Homemade Sweet and Sour Mix (page 188)

1½ ounces (45 ml) 100% agave tequila blanco

¾ ounce (25 ml) agave nectar

No one is sure who invented the margarita, although there are many people who claim to have done so. My version improves on the classic with agave to add a more rounded sweetness than from sugar alone.

SERVES 1

1 Lightly rub 1 of the lime wedges around the outside rim of a highball glass to moisten the glass; reserve the lime wedge. Pour a few tablespoons of salt into a saucer. Roll the rim of the glass in the salt and shake off the excess, being sure not to get any salt inside the glass. Save the remaining salt for another use. Fill the glass with ice.

2 Squeeze the remaining 3 lime wedges into a cocktail shaker, discarding the rinds. Add the sweet and sour mix, tequila, and agave. Fill the shaker with ice, cover, and shake it well. Strain the margarita into the glass. Garnish it with the reserved lime wedge.

VARIATION **Jalapeño Margarita:** Add ¼ seeded and thinly sliced jalapeño to the shaker with the tequila, agave, and sweet and sour mix. Crush the jalapeño well with a muddler. Proceed as directed.

STRAWBERRY MARGARITA

4 lime wedges (²/₃ lime)

Kosher salt, for garnish

1½ ounces (45 ml) 100% agave tequila blanco

1½ ounces (45 ml) Homemade Sweet and Sour Mix (page 188)

¾ ounce (25 ml) agave nectar

3 fresh strawberries, hulled

There is no rule that says a fruit margarita has to be a slushy drink, and this strawberry rendition is just as tasty as anything that comes out of a blender.

SERVES 1

1 Lightly rub 1 of the lime wedges around the outside rim of a highball glass to moisten the glass; reserve the lime wedge. Pour a few tablespoons of salt into a saucer. Roll the rim of the glass in the salt and shake off the excess, being sure not to get any salt inside the glass. Save the remaining salt for another use. Fill the glass with ice.

2 Squeeze the remaining 3 lime wedges into a cocktail shaker, discarding the rinds. Add the tequila, sweet and sour mix, agave, and strawberries and crush the strawberries with a muddler. Fill the shaker with ice, cover, and shake it well. Strain the margarita into the prepared glass. Garnish it with the reserved lime wedge.

VARIATION **Mango Margarita:** Substitute ¼ peeled and pitted mango, cut into chunks, for the strawberries.

You'll see big and colorful jars of aguas frescas (fresh fruit juice beverages) for sale at every Mexican outdoor market, and the watermelon flavor is always a favorite. Here it is, jazzed up with tequila.

SPIKED
WATERMELON
AGUA
FRESCA

■■■■■■■■■■ SERVES 1 ■■■■■■■■■■

Fill a cocktail shaker and highball glass with ice. Add the watermelon juice, sweet and sour mix, tequila, and triple sec. Cover the shaker and shake it well. Strain the agua fresca into the highball glass. Garnish it with the lime wedge.

NOTE To make fresh watermelon juice, purée 1 cup (150 g) diced seedless watermelon in a blender. Strain it in a fine-mesh sieve over a bowl. You should have about 2/3 cup (165 ml). The watermelon juice can be refrigerated in a covered container for up to 1 day.

2½ ounces (75 ml) fresh watermelon juice (see Note)

1½ ounces (45 ml) Homemade Sweet and Sour Mix (page 188)

1 ounce (30 ml) 100% agave tequila blanco

1 ounce (30 ml) triple sec

1 lime wedge, for garnish

The Paloma, a refreshing mix of tequila and grapefruit soda, goes down easily on a hot afternoon. It deserves to be much more popular in this country.

PERFECT
PALOMA

■■■■■■■■■■ SERVES 1 ■■■■■■■■■■

Fill a highball glass with ice. Squeeze 3 of the lime wedges into the glass, discarding the rinds. Add the tequila and agave and stir well to combine. Top them off with enough grapefruit soda to fill the glass. Garnish the drink with the remaining lime wedge.

4 lime wedges (2/3 lime)

1½ ounces (45 ml) tequila reposado

½ ounce (15 ml) agave nectar

3 ounces (90 ml) grapefruit soda, as needed

BLOODY MARIA

2 tablespoons kosher salt

½ teaspoon pure ground chipotle chile

2 lime wedges (⅓ lime)

3 ounces (90 ml) Bloody Maria Mix (recipe follows)

1½ ounces (45 ml) 100% agave tequila blanco

1 long celery stick with leaves, for garnish

1 large pimiento-stuffed olive, speared, for garnish

A Bloody Mary with tequila instead of vodka is a no-brainer. But it is the details (a chipotle salt rim, homemade tomato juice mix, and generous garnishes) that make the difference.

SERVES 1

1 Combine the salt and ground chipotle well in a saucer. Rub 1 of the lime wedges around the outside rim of a highball glass to moisten the glass; reserve the lime wedge. Roll the rim of the glass in the salt and shake off the excess, being sure not to get any salt inside the glass. Save the remaining salt for another use. Fill the glass with ice.

2 Squeeze the remaining lime wedge into an ice-filled cocktail shaker, discarding the rind. Add the Bloody Maria mix and tequila and shake them well. Strain the drink into the glass. Garnish it with the celery and olive.

BLOODY MARIA MIX

SERVES 10; MAKES ABOUT 2 CUPS (480 ML)

This homemade tomato juice blend gets a lift from fresh lemon and lime juices. It is much better than any store-bought Bloody Mary mix.

1 cup (240 ml) canned tomato juice

¼ cup (60 ml) fresh lemon juice

¼ cup (60 ml) fresh lime juice

¼ cup (60 g) prepared horseradish

¼ cup (60 ml) Worcestershire sauce

½ teaspoon kosher salt

½ teaspoon freshly ground black pepper

Purée the ingredients in a blender. Strain them through a wire sieve into a pitcher, cover, and refrigerate the mix until chilled, at least 1 hour and up to 2 days.

GINGER FIZZ

This cocktail is simplicity personified, but it sure is good. Ginger beer is less sweet, with a spicier flavor than ginger ale, and like the latter, it is nonalcoholic. The main difference is that ginger ale is usually just ginger-flavored soda water, but ginger beer is actually fermented from scratch with fresh ginger.

SERVES 1

Muddle together 3 of the lime wedges with the mint leaves in a highball glass. Fill the glass with ice. Pour in the tequila and stir well. Top it off with ginger beer to fill the glass. Garnish the drink with the remaining lime wedge.

4 lime wedges ($^2/_3$ lime)

4 fresh mint leaves

1½ ounces (45 ml) 100% agave tequila blanco

3 ounces (90 ml) ginger beer, as needed

TEQUILA SUNRISE

The Tequila Sunrise is as 1970s as a mood ring. It is still worth making with fresh orange juice and a good tequila.

SERVES 1

Pour the orange juice and tequila into an ice-filled highball glass and stir well. Drizzle them with the grenadine. Garnish the drink with the orange slice.

3 ounces (90 ml) fresh orange juice

1½ ounces (45 ml) 100% agave tequila blanco

Splash of grenadine, preferably Homemade Grenadine (page 188)

1 orange slice

TORONHA

Is it a variation of the Paloma, or a twist on the Tequila Sunrise? Who cares? It is a great way to end the work day . . . or start a fun evening.

1½ ounces (45 ml) 100% agave tequila blanco

½ ounce (15 ml) triple sec

2 ounces (60 ml) grapefruit soda, as needed

Splash of grenadine, preferably Homemade Grenadine (page 188)

1 orange slice

SERVES 1

Pour the tequila and triple sec into an ice-filled highball glass. Stir them well to combine. Top them off with grapefruit soda to fill the glass and then the grenadine. Garnish the drink with the orange slice.

BUENAS NOCHES

A dash of chocolate bitters brings out the warm notes in this nightcap.

SERVES 1

2 ounces (60 ml) 100% agave tequila añejo

1 ounce (30 ml) Pedro Ximenez sherry, preferably Alvear 1927 Solera (see Note)

1 dash chocolate bitters, preferably Scrappy's

1 orange twist

Fill a martini glass with ice. Pour the tequila, sherry, and bitters into an ice-filled shaker. Shake them lightly and strain them into the martini glass. Garnish it with the orange twist.

NOTE Pedro Ximenez (nicknamed PX) is a grape variety used to make fine sherry. The producer Alvear makes a Pedro Ximenez Solera 1927 (created from vines planted in 1927) that is really essential to this cocktail. "Solera" refers to a specific barrel-aging process with incremental additions of old wine to young, giving the final bottling a complex flavor. This particular sherry is an affordable indulgence.

Rompope is clearly the Mexican version of eggnog, made with cooked (not raw) egg yolks, and with almonds for additional flavor. Be sure to use aged tequila or rum to cut through the rich creaminess of the base. Here is my family recipe.

ROMPOPE

6 cups (1.4 L) whole milk

½ cup (55 g) blanched almond flour

6 large egg yolks

1 cup (200 g) sugar

½ cup (120 ml) 100% agave tequila añejo or añejo rum

Ground cinnamon, for garnish

■ **SERVES 8** ■

1 Blend 1½ cups (360 ml) of the milk with the almond flour in a blender until the mixture is very smooth. Pour it into a saucepan and add the remaining milk.

2 Heat the milk mixture, whisking often, over medium heat until it comes to a simmer. Remove it from the heat.

3 Whisk the egg yolks and sugar together in a medium bowl. Gradually whisk in about 1 cup (240 ml) of the milk mixture. Whisk the egg yolk mixture back into the saucepan. Cook it over medium-low heat, stirring constantly, until the mixture is lightly thickened and reads 185°F (85°C) on an instant-read thermometer, about 2 minutes. Strain it through a wire-mesh sieve into a heatproof bowl. Let it cool completely. Stir in the tequila.

4 Cover and refrigerate the rompope until it is chilled, at least 2 hours. Pour it into individual cups or glasses, sprinkling each serving with ground cinnamon. Serve it chilled.

PONCHE

½ cup (2.0 g) dried hibiscus flowers (*jamaica*)

One 3-inch (7.5-cm) cinnamon stick

1 cup (200 g) sugar

½ cup (130 g) tamarind pulp, broken into pieces (see Notes)

Two 4-inch (10-cm) pieces fresh or frozen sugarcane, peeled and cut into 12 sticks (see Notes; optional)

24 fresh or drained bottled tejocotes (see Notes)

2 ripe guavas, cut into 12 wedges (see Notes)

One 375-ml bottle (1¾ cups) 100% agave tequila, brandy, or light rum

¼ cup (60 ml) orange-flavored liqueur, such as Grand Marnier

12 pitted dried plums

The Mexican warm fruit punch of the holiday season, ponche is sometimes nothing more than spiced syrup with booze. My family recipe is better, and infused with the tropical flavors of hibiscus and tamarind.

SERVES 10 TO 12

1 Bring 2½ quarts (2.5 L) water to a boil in a large nonreactive saucepan over high heat. Remove it from the heat and add the hibiscus flowers and cinnamon stick. Let them stand for 5 minutes. Add the sugar and tamarind and bring them to a simmer over high heat. Reduce the heat to medium-low and simmer, stirring often to break up the tamarind, for 5 minutes. Strain the liquid into a large heatproof bowl, pressing hard on the solids; discard the solids.

2 Return the liquid to the pot. Add the sugarcane, if using, and bring the liquid to a boil over high heat, stirring to dissolve the sugar. Reduce the heat to medium and cook the liquid at a brisk simmer for 5 minutes. Strain it again to remove any tamarind debris.

3 Return the tea to the pot and add the tejocotes and guavas. Simmer until the guavas are tender, about 5 minutes. Stir in the tequila and liqueur and simmer just until the mixture is hot. Remove it from the heat, add the plums, and let them stand for 5 minutes. (Do not add them earlier or they will get too soft.)

4 To serve, return the pot to very low heat to keep the ponche warm. Ladle the ponche into mugs, adding the fruits to each serving. Serve it hot.

NOTES You can substitute ⅓ cup (75 ml) tamarind concentrate for the tamarind pulp. If neither is available, use ½ cup (120 ml) fresh lemon juice.

Fresh or frozen sugarcane is available at Latin groceries and large supermarkets, and is often sold peeled. If the thick skin needs to be removed, use a large knife to chop the cane into manageable 4-inch (10-cm) lengths. Stand the pieces on end to cut away the peel. Cut the sugarcane lengthwise into thick sticks.

Tejocote is a small round stone fruit (that is, with a large seed in the center). It is sold fresh at Mexican groceries around Christmastime, and in jars year-round. Kumquats or crabapples are good substitutes because they are similar in size to tejocotes. You may want to alert your guests that the tejocote seeds can be spit out.

Pineapple guava, about the size of a large lime, is the most widely available variety around Christmastime. If it is not available, substitute about one-quarter of a pineapple, peeled, cored, and cut into bite-size pieces.

Goya, the leading Latin food product manufacturer, sells a nonalcoholic ponche in a jar with enough tejocotes, sugarcane sticks, and guavas for this recipe. Drain and discard the liquid—you really just want the fruit. Leave the tejocotes intact, but cut the sticks and guavas as needed to yield twelve pieces of each.

SANGRITA

1 cup (240 ml) canned tomato juice

½ cup (120 ml) fresh lime juice

¼ cup (60 ml) fresh orange juice

3 tablespoons fresh grapefruit juice

2 tablespoons ketchup

2 tablespoons chopped red onion

2 tablespoons chopped fresh cilantro

1 tablespoon agave nectar

1 teaspoon red or yellow habanero hot sauce

1 tablespoon pure ground ancho chile

¼ teaspoon kosher salt

¼ teaspoon freshly ground black pepper

Tequila, for serving

Sangrita (meaning "little blood") is not actually a cocktail, but an accompaniment to a shot of tequila—you follow a sip of one with a sip of the other, allowing the flavors to mingle in your mouth. The most popular version is from Mexico City and made with tomato juice, but there are variations that get their red color from grenadine. I prefer this one, with three kinds of fruit juice (or four, if you count the tomato as a fruit . . . which it really is).

SERVES 12; MAKES ABOUT 2 CUPS (480 ML)

1 Purée the sangrita ingredients in a blender. Transfer them to a pitcher, cover, and refrigerate until they are chilled, for at least 1 hour and up to 2 days.

2 Pour a shot of tequila and a shot of the chilled sangrita into separate glasses. Sip the tequila, and follow it immediately with a sip of the sangrita.

MEZCAL

Mezcal is similar to tequila in that it is also made from agave, a plant native to Mexico.

However, tequila production is restricted to the blue agave, whereas there are around thirty other kinds of agave (often called maguey by mezcal producers to differentiate it from the blue variety) that can be distilled into mezcal. The agave is roasted in open pits, giving the final product a smokiness that is often compared to Scotch. Making mezcal is a hands-on, rustic process, so the best ones are quite expensive. Cheap mezcal will sometimes be bottled with a worm, a tradition that supposedly proves that the alcohol content is high enough to preserve the darned thing.

Also like tequila, there are young (*joven*), rested (*reposado*), and mature (*añejo*) types of mezcal. For cocktails, use a moderately priced joven because you will be mixing it with other ingredients. Aged mezcals are best slowly sipped and savored on their own. Espadín is the most commonly used maguey variety to make mezcal, and you will see it listed on the label of many reliable brands.

THE RED & SMOKEY

5 lime wedges (⁵/₆ lime)

1½ ounces (45 ml) brewed hibiscus tea (see Notes)

1½ ounces (45 ml) mezcal joven, preferable arroqueño (see Notes)

½ ounce (15 ml) triple sec

2 ounces (60 ml) club soda, as needed

Consider stirring up a big pitcher of this bright red cocktail for a party. You'll get the best results with the complex flavors of an arroqueño mezcal, which is distilled from a rare type of agave.

SERVES 1

Muddle 4 of the lime wedges and the hibiscus together in a highball glass. Fill the glass with ice, add the mezcal and triple sec, and stir them well. Top off the drink with the club soda. Garnish it with the remaining lime wedge.

NOTES Steep 1 scant tablespoon dried hibiscus blossoms (*jamaica*) with ¼ cup (60 ml) boiling water for 3 minutes. Strain the tea and let it cool completely.

Arroqueño mezcal indicates a mezcal made from *agave americana*, and it has a somewhat bolder flavor profile than other jovens.

This cocktail is a kind of tequila Caipirinha, but the mezcal gives it heft.

━━━━━━━━━━ SERVES 1 ━━━━━━━━━━

Muddle the mint leaves and syrup together in a highball glass. Fill the glass with ice and add the mezcal and tequila. Stir them well. Top off the cocktail with the club soda. Garnish it with the lime wedge.

6 fresh mint leaves

1 ounce (30 ml) Simple Syrup (page 188)

1 ounce (30 ml) mezcal joven

1 ounce (30 ml) 100% agave tequila blanco

2 ounces (60 ml) club soda, as needed

1 lime wedge

Ginger liqueur adds a delicious spiciness to this "up" drink.

━━━━━━━━━━ SERVES 1 ━━━━━━━━━━

Fill a martini glass with ice. Pour the tequila, mezcal, ginger liqueur, agave, and lemon juice into an ice-filled cocktail shaker. Cover and shake them well. Discard the ice from the glass and strain the cocktail into it. Perch the lemon slice on the glass rim.

1 ounce (30 ml) 100% agave tequila añejo

½ ounce (15 ml) mezcal joven

½ ounce (15 ml) ginger liqueur

½ ounce (15 ml) agave nectar

½ ounce (15 ml) fresh lemon juice

1 lemon slice

RUM

Rum, or actually its source—sugarcane—plays an enormous role in Latin American history, especially in the Caribbean.

Fortunes were made and lost in the sugar fields of Cuba, Puerto Rico, and other subtropical countries, where millions of people literally slaved to harvest sugarcane. Rum can be distilled from either molasses (the liquid by-product of sugar production) or directly from sugarcane juice.

In broad terms, three unique styles of rum developed according to the language spoken in the various locales. Rum from the places where Spanish is spoken tends to be light-bodied. British-style rums are more viscous, with a flavor and color that belie their molasses base. The French islands are renowned for their *rhum agricole* (agricultural rum), made artisan style with sugarcane juice. The vast majority of rum sold in the United States is made in large Puerto Rican distilleries, which must be aged in oak for one year before bottling.

Rum evaporates during aging, deepening its flavor and picking up color from the wood. Therefore, older rum is darker and more viscous than young rum. For making cocktails, a lighter rum is often used to marry well with other ingredients without leaving a strong rum flavor. Aficionados of small-batch rums enjoy these spirits as sipping liquors. The main styles of rum are:

Silver: Also called white or light rum, this rum is aged for one year, then filtered to remove the color. While it is not entirely flavorless, its neutral flavor plays well with other ingredients.

Gold: You will also find this kind of rum labeled as "amber" or "pale." Most of these get their golden color from wood aging, but sometimes the hue is acquired by adding caramel.

Dark: A bit darker than gold rum, this rum has been wood-aged for two or more years. **Añjeo** rum has been aged for up to three years.

Black Rum: The wood barrels used to age this molasses-based rum (not to be confused with "dark rum") have been heavily charred, so the end product is very dark and full-flavored.

Other styles of rum include the aforementioned rhum agricole, vintage rum (usually estate bottled), overproof rum, and flavored rum (including spiced rum).

This simple little drink, with muddled mint and lime, has given rum a newfound popularity.

SERVES 1

Muddle together 3 of the lime wedges, the mint, and syrup in a highball glass. Fill the glass with ice and add the rum and sweet and sour mix. Stir them well. Top off the cocktail with the club soda. Garnish it with the remaining lime wedge.

MOJITO

4 lime wedges (²/₃ lime)

6 fresh mint leaves

1 ounce (30 ml) Simple Syrup (page 188)

1½ ounces (45 ml) light (silver) rum

Splash of Homemade Sweet and Sour Mix (page 188)

3 ounces (90 ml) chilled club soda, as needed

Until recently, cucumber was not used as a cocktail ingredient. Now it lends its refreshing flavor to drinks like this one.

SERVES 1

Muddle together 2 of the lime wedges, the mint, and cucumbers in a highball glass. Fill the glass with ice and add the rum, melon liqueur, and sweet and sour mix. Stir them well. Top off the cocktail with the club soda. Garnish it with the remaining lime wedge.

MOJITO CUZCO

3 lime wedges (½ lime)

6 fresh mint leaves

Two ¼-inch (3-mm) slices peeled seedless (English) or standard cucumber

1½ ounces (45 ml) light (silver) rum

1 ounce (30 ml) melon liqueur, such as Midori

Splash of Homemade Sweet and Sour Mix (page 188)

2 ounces (60 ml) chilled club soda, as needed

This libation is a grown-up's piña colada (not that there is anything wrong with a regular colada, but it is a cocktail on its way to becoming a milkshake). I recommend Malibu Red (a combination of rum, tequila, and coconut flavor), which gives the drink a bit more attitude than standard coconut rum.

SERVES 1

Muddle together 3 of the lime wedges, the mint, and sugar in a highball glass. Fill the glass with ice and add the rum and sweet and sour mix. Stir them well, making sure to dissolve the sugar. Top off the cocktail with the club soda. Garnish it with the remaining lime wedge.

MOJITO COCONUT

4 lime wedges (²/₃ lime)

6 fresh mint leaves

1 teaspoon superfine (bartenders') sugar

2 ounces (60 ml) coconut-flavored rum, preferably Malibu Red

1½ ounces (45 ml) Homemade Sweet and Sour Mix (page 188)

2 ounces (60 ml) chilled club soda, as needed

LEFT TO RIGHT: Melocotón; Pisco Sour; Mojito Cuzco; and Perfect Paloma

PISCO

Pisco, a clear grape spirit made from wine, is similar to Italian grappa.

Peru, Chile, and Bolivia all make a version, but aficionados give Peruvian pisco the edge. (Chilean piscos are often oaked, giving them a harsher taste that can conflict with the other ingredients in a cocktail.) Long a part of America's cocktail culture, pisco was originally shipped from Latin America north to the miners of Gold Rush San Francisco. As other liquors became more available, pisco was squeezed out. It is now back in fashion with a vengeance.

Peruvian pisco is bottled at distilled strength, making it a particularly potent libation; Chilean pisco can be cut with water to reduce its alcoholic content—not necessarily a bad thing.

There are four types of Peruvian pisco:

Puro: "Pure" pisco is distilled from one of four nonaromatic black-skinned grapes—Molla, Negra Corriente, Quebranta (the most common), and Ubina. This is the version that you are most likely to find in the average American liquor store, and a good choice for making cocktails.

Aromático: Albilia, Italia, Muscatel, and Torontel (Torrontes) are the four grapes that can be used to make "aromatic" pisco.

Acholado: While pure and aromatic piscos are made from a single grape, acholado can be a blend of one nonaromatic and two or more of the aromatic varieties.

Mosto verde: The other pisco types are distilled from wine, but this variety is created from the fermented "green must" leftover from crushed grapes.

An egg white gives this famous old-school cocktail its distinctive foamy cap. The egg white will mix better with the other ingredients if it is shaken without ice, and then shaken again for chilling. Because the white will be consumed raw, use a pasteurized egg (available at natural food stores and most supermarkets), or at least an organic one. (See photo on page 52.)

PISCO SOUR

SERVES 2

Fill two martini glasses with ice. Pour the pisco, lime juice, syrup, and egg white into a cocktail shaker. Cover and shake them well to fully incorporate the egg white. Add ice, cover, and shake them again. Discard the ice in the glasses and strain the drink into them. Top each drink with 2 to 3 dashes of bitters.

3 ounces (90 ml) puro pisco

3 ounces (90 ml) lime juice

1 ounce (30 ml) Simple Syrup (page 188)

1 large egg white, preferably pasteurized

4 to 6 dashes orange-flavored aromatic bitters

Elderflower liqueur and lychees smooth out pisco's rough edges in this fragrant cocktail. Late spring is the season for domestic lychees. You might find imported lychees in the winter; it's a Chinese fruit that looks like a big, tough raspberry. Out of season, just use canned lychees, available at Asian markets.

PISCO
ELEVATION

SERVES 1

Fill a martini glass with ice. Muddle the lychees in a mixer glass. Add the pisco, elderflower liqueur, and ice. Cover and shake them well. Discard the ice in the glass and strain the drink into it. Garnish it with the orange twist.

3 peeled fresh or canned lychees

1½ ounces (45 ml) puro pisco

1 ounce (30 ml) elderflower liqueur, such as St. Germain

1 orange zest twist

A Negroni is often made with vodka or gin, but pisco matches equally well with the bitter Campari and red vermouth.

PERUVIAN
NEGRONI

SERVES 1

Pour the pisco, Campari, and vermouth into an ice-filled rocks or Old Fashioned glass. Stir them well. Garnish the drink with the orange slice and cherry.

1 ounce (30 ml) puro pisco

1 ounce (30 ml) Campari

1 ounce (30 ml) sweet vermouth

1 orange slice

1 imported cocktail cherry, such as Luxardo brand

CACHAÇA

Cachaça is basically Brazilian silver rum,
but there are major differences.

First, cachaça is always made with fresh sugarcane juice, while rum can be
made with fermented juice or molasses. Rum is aged in wood for at least
one year, but cachaça is usually bottled without aging. This gives it a fiery
flavor that frankly needs to be tempered with ingredients like fruit juice and
sugar. However, fine wood-aged gold and dark styles (which make for darker
and smoother flavors) are showing up in liquor stores, and these should be
drunk straight.

Here it is—the classic Brazilian cocktail that put cachaça on the map.

TRADITIONAL CAIPIRINHA

■■■■■■■■■■ SERVES 1 ■■■■■■■■■■

Muddle together 3 of the lime wedges with the syrup in a highball glass. Fill the glass with ice and add the cachaça. Stir it well. Top it off with the club soda. Garnish the drink with the remaining lime wedge.

4 lime wedges (⅔ lime)

1 ounce (30 ml) Simple Syrup (page 188)

1½ ounces (45 ml) cachaça

3 ounces (90 ml) club soda, as needed

Basil is a member of the mint family, so it is not a stretch at all to add it to strawberries in this summertime cocktail. Try this once and you will be a fan.

STRAWBERRY-BASIL CAIPIRINHA

■■■■■■■■■■ SERVES 1 ■■■■■■■■■■

Muddle together 3 of the lime wedges with the strawberries, basil, and syrup in a highball glass. Fill the glass with ice and add the cachaça. Stir it well. Garnish the drink with the remaining lime wedge.

4 lime wedges (⅔ lime)

2 fresh strawberries, hulled

2 large fresh basil leaves

1 ounce (30 ml) Simple Syrup (page 188)

1½ ounces (45 ml) cachaça

When autumn pears are abundant at the market, make this spice-scented, slightly sweet member of the martini family. Be sure to use very ripe pears.

PEREIRA MARTINI

■■■■■■■■■■ SERVES 1 ■■■■■■■■■■

1 Fill a martini glass with ice. Lightly rub the lemon wedge around the outside rim of the glass to moisten it. Juice the lemon wedge and reserve the juice for the cocktail. Discard the ice and sprinkle the cinnamon around the glass rim, making sure not to get any in the glass.

2 Pour the cachaça, pear purée, and lemon juice into an ice-filled cocktail shaker. Close and shake it well. Strain the drink into the prepared glass. Top it with a few gratings of nutmeg.

NOTE To make the purée, choose a juicy variety of pear, such as Comice or Bartlett. Peel, core, and quarter the pear and purée it in a blender. One ounce of purée equals 2 tablespoons.

1 lemon wedge

Ground cinnamon in a jar with a sprinkle top, for rimming the glass

1½ ounces (45 ml) cachaça

1 ounce (30 ml) fresh pear purée (see Note)

½ ounce (15 ml) fresh lemon juice

Freshly grated nutmeg, for garnish

BEER

Beer is one of the most refreshing beverages you can pour down your throat on a hot day.

In the Spanish-speaking world, steamy weather is a fact of life in many places, so beer is an indispensable thirst-quencher. Also, the grains used to make beer are more easily grown in many locations than temperamental grapes, so in some places, like Mexico, the drinking culture is beer-centric rather than wine-centric. Effervescent and malty, beer can also be a fine mixer for cocktails, as the following drinks show.

A beer variation on the Bloody Mary theme, this is sometimes served in a salt-rimmed glass, but I can do without it.

MICHELADA

SERVES 1

Fill a pint beer mug with ice and let it sit for a few minutes, then discard the ice and quickly dry the mug. Squeeze 3 of the limes into the mug and discard the rinds. Add the Bloody Mary mix and syrup and stir them well. Slowly pour in the beer and stir it gently to combine. Garnish the drink with the remaining lime wedge.

4 lime wedges (²⁄₃ lime)

1 ounce (30 ml) Bloody Maria Mix (page 192)

½ ounce (15 ml) Simple Syrup (page 188)

One 12-ounce (360-ml) bottle chilled lager beer

The "revelation" here is the surprisingly good combination of beer and gin.

REVELACIÓN

SERVES 1

1 Chill a pint beer mug in the freezer or refrigerator. (Or fill the mug with ice, let it sit for a few minutes, then discard the ice and quickly dry the mug.) Lightly rub the lemon wedge around the outside rim of the mug to moisten it; reserve the lemon wedge. Pour a few tablespoons of salt into a saucer. Roll the rim of the glass in the salt and shake off the excess, being sure not to get any inside the glass. Save the remaining salt for another use.

2 Muddle together the lemon wedge, gin, lemon juice, and agave in the mug. Add ice. Top it off with the beer and stir it gently to combine. Garnish the drink with the lemon twist.

NOTE Gin is made in a number of styles. London dry gin is the most popular in America, but other varieties are showing up more often. (Plymouth is another dry British style, and Dutch genever is heavier in body and completely different from United Kingdom brands.) For this drink, an off-dry gin, made according to an old, slightly sweet recipe, is best. Green Hat is a domestic gin from Washington, D.C., and we use it in our restaurants in that city. Otherwise, an Old Tom gin, such as one from Hayman's or Ransom, works well.

1 lemon wedge (⅙ lemon)

Kosher salt, for the glass

1½ ounces (45 ml) off-dry gin, such as Green Hat or Hayman's Old Tom (see Note)

¾ ounce (25 ml) fresh lemon juice

½ ounce (15 ml) agave nectar

One 12-ounce (360-ml) bottle chilled lager beer, as needed

1 lemon zest twist

LEMON LAGER

On a hot day, it will be difficult not to drink this in gulps. Slow down and savor each tangy sip.

SERVES 1

Fill a pint beer mug with ice and let it sit for a few minutes, then discard the ice and quickly dry the mug. Muddle together 2 of the lemon wedges with the syrup and elderflower liqueur in the mug. Slowly pour in the beer and stir it gently to combine. Garnish the drink with the remaining lemon wedge.

3 lemon wedges (½ lemon)

½ ounce (15 ml) Simple Syrup (page 188)

½ ounce (15 ml) elderflower liqueur, such as St. Germain

One 12-ounce (360-ml) bottle chilled lager beer

BLOOD ORANGE CHILEDA

This is another refreshing beer beverage that goes down a little too easily. The blood orange liqueur gives the drink a darker color, but standard orange liqueur will do.

SERVES 1

1 Fill a pint beer mug with ice and let it sit for a few minutes, then discard the ice and quickly dry the mug. Lightly rub the lime around the outside rim of the mug to moisten it; reserve the lime wedge to use as garnish. Pour a few tablespoons of salt into a saucer. Roll the rim of the glass in the salt and shake off the excess, being sure not to get any salt into the glass. Save the remaining salt for another use.

2 Stir the lime juice and blood orange liqueur together in the mug. Add ice and slowly pour in the beer. Stir it gently to combine. Garnish the drink with the reserved lime wedge.

NOTE Solerno Blood Orange Liqueur is made in Sicily with blood oranges, lemon, and a neutral spirit. Most other orange liqueurs have a brandy or Cognac base. You can substitute Cointreau, but Solerno has a deeper, more complex flavor.

1 lime wedge

Kosher salt, for the glass

½ ounce (15 ml) fresh lime juice

¼ ounce (7 ml) orange-flavored liqueur, preferably Solerno Blood Orange Liqueur (see Note)

One 12-ounce (360-ml) bottle chilled lager beer, as needed

NONALCOHOLIC
BEVERAGES

Nonalcoholic beverages, just like cocktails, are having a resurgence, as it has (finally) become obvious that nondrinkers deserve to sip something more interesting than club soda.

At our restaurants, we serve many great fruit-based beverages along the lines of *aguas frescas*, refreshing blends of fruit purée and water that are sold from huge jars at every Mexican *mercado*. The following drinks are great for serving to designated drivers or others who aren't drinking alcoholic beverages—and kids, of course. They are especially thirst-quenching on hot days, and can be spiked—or not—with tequila, rum, pisco, or cachaça. (Mezcal is a bit too strong and smoky for these libations.)

HORCHATA

This milky drink is a popular kids' beverage in Mexico. It may remind you of eggnog without the eggs. It must be refrigerated for at least twelve hours before serving, so plan ahead. Don't be surprised if, like so many Mexican moms, you get in the horchata habit of having a pitcher in the refrigerator at all times. (It is also wonderful as a cocktail with a shot of rum, not unlike a White Russian.)

1 (14-ounce/390-g) can sweetened condensed milk

1 (12-ounce/335-g) can evaporated milk

2 tablespoons raw long-grain rice

2 tablespoons almond flour (also called almond meal)

4 (3-inch/7.5-cm) cinnamon sticks

Ground cinnamon, for garnish

SERVES 4

1 Whisk the condensed milk, evaporated milk, and ²/₃ cup (165 ml) water together in a pitcher, making sure to completely combine the two canned milks. Add the rice and almond flour and whisk again. Add the cinnamon sticks, cover, and refrigerate for at least 12 and up to 24 hours.

2 Strain into a bowl, pressing hard on the solids. Discard the solids. Return the milk mixture to the pitcher. Divide among four tall ice-filled glasses and sprinkle each with ground cinnamon.

FRESCO

Ginger, mint, apple juice, and vanilla combine to make this a pretty perfect thirst quencher.

■■■■■■■■■■■■■ SERVES 1 ■■■■■■■■

5 lime wedges (⅔ lime)

6 fresh mint leaves

Four (⅛-inch/3-mm) slices unpeeled fresh ginger

3 tablespoons apple juice

2 teaspoons vanilla-flavored beverage syrup or 2 teaspoons Simple Syrup (page 188) and ½ teaspoon vanilla extract

1 (12-ounce) can ginger ale, as needed

Fresh mint sprigs, for garnish

Crush the lime wedges, mint leaves, and 3 slices of the ginger in a tall glass with a muddler. Add the apple juice and vanilla syrup and stir. Fill the glass with ice. Add enough ginger ale to fill the glass and stir gently. Garnish with the mint spring and remaining ginger slice and serve.

ROSA COLADA

This is a pink version of a piña colada with both strawberry purée and cranberry juices. You could add an ounce or two of silver rum to the glasses of those who partake of alcohol.

■■■■■■■■■■■■■ SERVES 1 ■■■■■■■■

6 strawberries, hulled and sliced

2 tablespoons cream of coconut (not coconut milk)

1 cup (5 ounces/140 g) ice cubes

½ cup (120 ml) cranberry juice

1 strawberry, for garnish

Purée the sliced strawberries and cream of coconut together in a blender. Add the ice cubes and cranberry juice and process into a slush. Taste, and if the strawberries aren't sweet enough, add the agave and process again. Pour into a tall glass, garnish with the basil sprig, and serve.

Strawberries and basil make a very fragrant beverage, just the thing for summer entertaining when both of them are in season. You'll need a strong blender for crushing the ice.

SERVES 1

Process the strawberries, basil leaves, ¼ cup (60 ml) water, and the ice cubes into a slush. Taste, and if the strawberries aren't sweet enough, add the agave and process again. Pour into a tall glass, garnish with the basil sprig, and serve.

STRAWBERRY & BASIL AGUA FRESCA

7 fresh strawberries, hulled and sliced

2 large basil leaves

1 cup (5 ounces/140 g) ice cubes

2 tablespoons agave nectar (optional)

1 fresh basil sprig, for garnish

SANGRÍA

Wines from Pan-Latin countries, such as Chile and Spain, are finally getting the recognition and respect they deserve. Many of these wines are very fine, and I would never dream of mixing them with fruit and juices.

That being said, sangría is my favorite party drink. Most of us have had red sangría, but only too often, it is tossed together without much thought. The two versions that I recommend (one with red wine, and the other with white) are carefully crafted with just the right amounts of fruit, wine, additional liquor, and sweetener. Both use ginger ale, and I suggest that you buy a top-quality small-batch brand for its superior flavor.

Sangría, fruity but not too sweet, is the ultimate summertime party drink. I make it by the gallon to serve at my backyard barbecues. Start the night before so the fruit has time to flavor the wine.

SANGRÍA
TINTA ROJA

SERVES 8

1 One day before serving, mix the wine, apple, mango, apple juice, mango purée, brandy, vanilla liqueur, and triple sec together in a large nonreactive bowl. Cover and refrigerate them for at least 12 and up to 24 hours.

2 Strain the mixture into a pitcher, reserving the diced apple and mango. For each serving, add a spoonful of the diced apple and mango to a highball glass. Add ice. Pour in ⅔ cup (165 ml) of the wine mixture, and top off the glass with ginger ale. Stir it gently to combine and garnish the glass with an orange slice. Serve it immediately.

One 750-ml bottle Spanish red wine, preferably Tempranillo

1 sweet apple, such as Red Delicious or McIntosh, peeled, cored, and cut into ¾-inch (2-cm) dice

1 ripe mango, pitted, peeled, and cut into ¾-inch (2-cm) dice

⅔ cup (165 ml) apple juice, preferably fresh

⅓ cup (75 ml) fresh or thawed frozen mango purée

⅓ cup (75 ml) brandy

⅓ cup (75 ml) vanilla liqueur, such as Licor 43, or Simple Syrup (page 188) plus 1 teaspoon vanilla extract

⅓ cup (75 ml) triple sec

Ginger ale, for serving

8 orange slices

Here is a peach-flavored sangria made with white wine that is pretty perfect for that sweet time in the summer when local peaches are at their best.

MELOCOTÓN

SERVES 8

1 One day before serving, mix the wine, peaches, orange juice, triple sec, schnapps, simple syrup, lime juice, and two of the cinnamon sticks together in a large nonreactive bowl. Cover and refrigerate them for at least 12 and up to 24 hours.

2 Strain the mixture into a pitcher, reserving the diced peaches. Discard the cinnamon sticks. For each serving, add a spoonful of the diced peaches to a highball glass. Add ice. Pour in about ⅔ cup (165 ml) of the wine mixture, and top off the glass with ginger ale. Stir it gently to combine and garnish the drink with a cinnamon stick. Serve it immediately.

One 750-ml bottle Sauvignon Blanc

2 ripe peaches, cut into ¾-inch (2-cm) dice

⅔ cup (165 ml) fresh orange juice

⅓ cup (75 ml) triple sec

⅓ cup (75 ml) peach schnapps

⅓ cup (75 ml) Simple Syrup (page 188)

⅓ cup (75 ml) fresh lime juice

Ten 3-inch (7.5-cm) cinnamon sticks

Ginger ale, for serving

ACKNOWLEDGMENTS

My name may be on this book as the author, but there were many people who were involved in many different ways to make it a reality.

I must start with my family, because if it weren't for my parents' example, encouragement, and love I would not even be in the hospitality business. First, to my children, GianCarlo and Issa, and my wife, Gabriella, who put up with my treacherous travel schedule and are willing guinea pigs for tasting and criticizing my food. My grandmother, Maruca, trained my palate at a very young age to appreciate good food. My mother has always supported and believed in my dreams, especially at the beginning of my career when I was trying to find my culinary voice. My father instilled an appreciation of the business side of our crazy industry, and without that, I never would be where I am today. My stepfather, Paul Casanova, showed his early support in a very real way—he invested money.

Some of my business associates have been especially helpful to me over the years. Placido Domingo, who needs no introduction, was also an investor to whom I am grateful. Palm Wilby, general manager of Grosvenor House and the Royal Meridien in Dubai, has entrusted me with three restaurants in her hotels and is one of the most passionate professionals with whom I have worked.

Rick Rodgers helped me put my words on paper and, with his assistant, Diane Kniss, cooked every one of these recipes in his home kitchen. Rick would like to thank my longtime friend and corporate pastry chef, Jose Luis Flores, national beverage director Rob Day, chef Forest Hamrick at La Hacienda, and chef Marissa Gerlach at The Commissary in Las Vegas for their help in gathering the recipes. My literary agent, Eleanor Jackson, helped get the book written in countless ways.

It was a pleasure to work with Leslie Stoker and the Stewart, Tabori, and Chang team again. Emily Albarillo shepherded the book through the publishing process. Ann Martin Rolke was our excellent copy editor, and Leda Scheintaub was an eagle-eyed proofreader. Laura Palese gave the book its vibrant design, which truly captures my food's spirit.

My thanks go to the photographer, Penny De Los Santos, and her team, food stylist Lisa Jernow and prop stylist Pamela Duncan Silver. They worked very long, hard hours to give the book its mouthwatering images.

At Richard Sandoval Restaurants, I am blessed to work with a truly great team. Greg Howe, my corporate chef, whose loyalty and dedication I am grateful for, puts up with my crazy ideas and made many contributions to this book. Ivan Iricanin, my national director of operations and a good friend, protects my food's integrity with the chefs at our restaurants around the world. I would also like to thank Bart DeLorenzo, my executive director in charge of new business development, who builds each one of my restaurants, and my publicist, Paulina Naranjo and the RockOrange team.

And last but not least, I need to extend my deep gratitude to every RSR employee—dishwashers, corporate team members, chefs, busboys, and service staff. Without the help of these truly committed, passionate people, I never could have gone on my own personal journey, and RSR would not be the strong company that it is today.

RESOURCES

AMAZON.COM

A remarkably thorough source for just about every ingredient (Latin, Asian, and otherwise) and utensil in this book.

AMIGOFOODS.COM

1829 NW 79th Street
Miami, FL 33126
(800) 627-2544
www.amigofoods.com

Use this site for Latin groceries, especially Peruvian chile pastes.

ASIANFOODGROCER.COM

131 West Harris Avenue
South San Francisco, CA 94080
(800) 482-2742
www.AsianFoodGrocer.com

This is a good place to find Japanese ingredients, from kabayaki sauce to yuzu juice.

THE BOSTON SHAKER

69 Holland Street
Somerville, MA 02144
(617) 718-2999
www.thebostonshaker.com

A brick-and-mortar shop with a well-chosen selection of the very best bartending tools; they also have an excellent online store.

KALUSTYAN'S

123 Lexington Avenue
New York, NY 10016
(212) 685-3451
www.kalustyans.com

This Middle Eastern and international grocer is a Manhattan institution, and their website provides one-stop shopping for spices and condiments.

MEXGROCER.COM, LLC

4060 Morena Boulevard, Suite C
San Diego, CA 92117
(858) 270-0577
www.mexgrocer.com

Check this site for their wide assortment of Mexican ingredients, including chocolate and dried chilies.

MITSUWA

1815 W. 213th Street, Suite 235
Torrance, CA 90501
www.mitsuwa.com

Mitsuwa has brick-and-mortar stores in California and New Jersey, but their website is a reliable place to purchase nonperishables.

PENZEYS SPICES

12001 W. Capitol Drive
Wauwatosa, WI 53222
(800) 741-7787

You'll find an amazing assortment of spices (especially ground chilies) at this website. They have stores across the U.S., too.

INDEX